Suburban Growth

Suburban Growth

Geographical Processes
at the Edge of the Western City

Edited by
JAMES H. JOHNSON
Reader in Geography
University College London

JOHN WILEY & SONS
London · New York · Sydney · Toronto

Copyright © 1974, by John Wiley & Sons, Ltd.

All rights reserved.

Library of Congress Cataloging in Publication Data:

Johnson, James Henry, 1930–
Suburban Growth.

1. Cities and towns—Growth—Addresses, essays, lectures.
2. Suburbs—Addresses, essays, lectures. I. Title.

HT371.J6   301.36′2   73–8195
ISBN 0 471 44390 5

Printed in Great Britain at the Aberdeen University Press, Aberdeen.

Preface

Although urban life stretches back into pre-history, the modern situation, in which a substantial part of the population of many parts of the world has become urban and in which cities increasingly dominate all aspects of life, had its origins in western Europe only two centuries ago. During the nineteenth and twentieth centuries towns and cities have continued to expand swiftly, and the interaction between urban and rural areas has intensified. More loosely-structured megalopolitan areas, with larger total populations than have ever been encountered in cities before, are now becoming established in certain highly-urbanized parts of the world. At the same time urban activities are spilling over into the countryside and an increased number of urban workers are able to seek rural dwellings.

It is with this process of suburban expansion of various kinds that this book is concerned. The interaction between rural and urban is at its maximum at the outer edge of the continuously built-up area, since here is located the undeveloped space into which a town or city expands by circumferential or radial growth. This is the urban fringe; and many of the contributors to this volume of essays concentrate on this particular zone because suburban growth is at its most important here. These essays are also largely concerned with the 'western' city, since it is in the context of western Europe and North America (and in the cities derived from that culture world) that most urban activities are expanding rapidly at the edge of the city.

I am grateful to my contributors for so willingly adjusting their essays to meet the demands of a co-ordinated piece of work and for tolerating the delays inevitable in a project of this kind, particularly when impeded by a complicated residential relocation of the editor within the urban fringe. Most of the maps were drawn or finished by the cartographic unit of the Department of Geography in University College London. As always my wife has helped greatly with the reading of proofs and the preparation of an index.

James H. Johnson

University College London

List of Contributors

MARTIN J. BOWEN, B.Sc. (Econ.) (London) is Leader of the Greater London and South East Sports Council Research Unit. Between 1968 and 1971, based in the Department of Geography at University College London, he prepared material on recreation in London's rural-urban fringe for his doctoral thesis.

HUGH D. CLOUT, B.A., M.Phil. (London) is Lecturer in Geography at University College London. Recent publications include *The Geography of Post-War France: A Social and Economic Approach* (1972) and *Rural Geography: An Introductory Survey* (1972).

JOHN CONNELL, B.A., Ph.D. (London) is a Research Associate at the Council for Pacific Development Studies, Australian National University, Canberra and was formerly Research Officer at the Institute of Development Studies, University of Sussex. He is the editor of *Semnan: Persian City and Region* (1970) and has published other articles on rural development in the Middle East and East Africa, as well as on the urban geography of western cities.

PETER W. DANIELS, B.Sc., Ph.D. (London) is Lecturer in Geography at the University of Liverpool. He is the author of *Offices: an Urban and Regional Study* (forthcoming).

JOHN A. DAWSON, M.Phil. (London), Ph.D. (Nottingham) is Lecturer in Geography at Saint David's University College, Lampeter. He is co-editor of *Evaluating the Human Environment: Essays in Applied Geography* (1973).

JAMES H. JOHNSON, B.A. (Belfast), M.A. (Wisconsin), Ph.D. (London) is Reader in Geography in the University of London, at University College. He is the author of *Urban Geography: an Introductory Analysis* (1967) and co-editor of *Trends in Geography* (1969).

RICHARD J. MUNTON, B.A., Ph.D. (Birmingham) is Lecturer in Geography at University College London. His field of interest concerns economic aspects of agriculture and he is co-author of *Agricultural Geography* (1971).

ALAN J. STRACHAN, M.A. (Edinburgh), M.S. (Wisconsin), Ph.D. (Edinburgh) is Lecturer in Geography at the University of Leicester. His general field of interest is applied social geography.

DAVID THOMAS, M.A. (Wales), Ph.D. (London) is Professor of Geography at Saint David's University College, Lampeter. He was formerly Reader in Geography at University College London and is the author of *London's Green Belt* (1970).

J. W. R. WHITEHAND, B.A., Ph.D. (Reading) is Lecturer in Geography at the University of Birmingham. He was formerly on the staff of the University of Newcastle and of the University of Glasgow and is the author of a number of articles on the physical form of cities.

PETER A WOOD, B.A., Ph.D. (Birmingham) is Lecturer in Geography at University College London. He is vice-chairman of the Regional Studies Association and his special fields of interest include regional planning and industrial location. He is the co-author of *Character of a Conurbation: A Computer Atlas of Birmingham and the Black Country* (1971) and *Employment Location in Regional Economic Planning* (1970).

Acknowledgements

The authors and editor wish to thank the following for permission to redraw illustrations from copyright works: University of North Carolina Press, Figure 2–1; Institute of British Geographers, Figures 3–1 to 3–6, 3–9 and 3–10; Dr M. P. Conzen, Figure 3–7; European Society for Rural Sociology, Figure 6–1; Librairie Armand Colin, Figure 6–3; Hamish Hamilton Ltd., Figure 9–2; London Borough of Croydon, Figure 9–3; Dr F. W. Boal, Figures 10–1 and 10–2.

Contents

List of Figures

List of Tables

CHAPTER 1

Geographical Processes at the Edge of the City

JAMES H. JOHNSON

In the past much work in urban geography has been strongly influenced by the idea of a unicentered city, with various urban land uses and their associated human activities being assessed in terms of distance from the city centre. Interpretations of such features as the density of residential population, the functioning of the urban transportation network, the spatial distribution of manufacturing and the location of retailing have often used the city centre as a point of reference from which locational patterns can be appraised.[1] Current research is tending to move away from this standpoint, since increasingly the expansion of many cities is taking place at a considerable distance from the city centre and often with much less relation to conditions there than was observable in earlier decades. Of course, the growth and decline of individual land uses and human activities occur in all parts of the city but, in absolute terms, change is particularly concentrated in and around the city centre and on the outer periphery of the built-up area.

Changes in land use and population at or close to the city centre have been long-standing geographical features, stimulated by the high value of land and the resulting need for constant readjustments in buildings and land uses, as associated human activities attempt to extract the maximum benefit out of expensive central locations.[2] Changes in city centres have also been encouraged by the growing importance of road transport, which has reduced the relative accessibility to the total urban population provided by a central location.[3] It can be argued, however, that over the years the process of geographical change in the inner parts of cities has received more than its fair share of attention, possibly because change here is more easily noticed, because urban rebuilding often involves the destruction of buildings which are deemed to be architecturally important, and because the redevelopment of residential areas close to the centre poses particularly difficult social problems.[4]

But changes on the edge of the city, although less concentrated and involving less dramatic social issues, are of much greater total importance, since a larger area of land is involved and the day-to-day lives of more people are likely to be affected. In addition, many geographical changes at the urban periphery are associated with the transfer of land from rural to urban purposes, which may be a more fundamental alteration than many other land-use changes which take place in urban areas. Certainly it is accompanied by a much sharper increase in land value than is produced by any other urban land-use change.[5]

The geographical processes operating around the outer edge of large cities are interesting for another reason. Elsewhere in the city urban form is more strongly influenced by past conditions. Although adjustments to modern social and economic demands are always being made, surviving relict features form an inescapable part of the urban pattern, if only because of the relative inflexibility of bricks and mortar. As a result, within the older parts of an urban area it is often difficult to distinguish those features of social and economic geography that directly reflect modern needs from those that are constrained by the legacies of past conditions. In areas where suburban growth is currently taking place, however, life and landscape are in much closer adjustment: the various forms of urban development being built on 'green-field' sites are likely to give a direct expression of the behaviour of contemporary urban society and perhaps provide a more accurate clue to the nature of the future.[6]

This is not to say that suburban growth takes place in a context from which past influences are completely absent. Patterns of landownership have been previously established and are likely to influence the form of the growing city.[7] Lines of communication and associated patterns of accessibility already existed before urban expansion. The land over which suburbs are being extended has previously acquired a particular planning status, possibly with its future use specified in outline form and densities of development indicated, although the vigour with which proposals of this kind are enforced varies from country to country.[8] Even before much residential building occurs, rural areas close to a growing city may have differing levels of social desirability associated with them.[9] Nevertheless, because fresh capital is being invested in many new facilities, the urban pattern at the edge of the city will be closely adjusted to current demands. Hence one particular interest of urban growth at the fringe of the city is that some of the social and economic factors that lie behind it are indicative of forces which will be relevant in other parts of the urban area when redevelopment becomes economically possible.

Some Distinctive Features of the Urban Periphery

Studies of contemporary suburban growth may give an insight into the processes likely to operate in the future elsewhere in the city, but they cannot provide an exact replica, since the edge of the city differs from the rest of the urban area in a number of important ways. In particular, the potential amount of space available for future development is much greater and often there is more choice of sites with basically similar locational attributes available to a developer. As a result, the intrinsic physical characteristics of an individual site take on greater significance than elsewhere in the city.[10] Where planning control is less strict or operates less comprehensively than in Britain, this has encouraged a form of leapfrogging peripheral growth, as sites some distance beyond the existing urban area are chosen for urban development. These particular sites may be attractive for a number of reasons: possibly they are immediately available for purchase, perhaps they are the most suitable size for a particular type of development, maybe they possess some local environmental features which make them more desirable than sites contiguous with the main built-up area.

A second difference at the edge of the city is derived from the fact that here the accessibility of a particular site is often more difficult to assess. Even after allowance is made for the changing patterns of accessibility found in modern cities, a dominant consideration in choosing a city centre location still remains the higher level of access to the whole urban area that it is possible to find there; but at the urban fringe accessibility may mean quite different things to different users of land. For example, attitudes to the length and cost of the journey to work are likely to vary between different socio-economic groups, implying contrasts in the daily pattern of movement undertaken by different types of workers.[11] In the same way catchment areas of varying sizes are produced around nodes of contrasting types of suburban employment.[12] Access to retailing facilities is also more difficult to appraise, partly because of differences in the level of car ownership in different communities. It is also more difficult to assess because of the clearer distinction that has to be made in the outer parts of cities between frequent access to local shops and more occasional access to specialized services in the city centre.[13] Recreational facilities exhibit similar complexities. Immediate access to recreational land of various kinds is an important attraction for many outer urban residents, but the attractiveness varies according to the aptitudes and inclinations of local residents.[14] A golf course, for example, has little attraction for non-golfers. In short, while there tends to be one dominant type of accessibility provided at the city centre, at the edge of the urban area it is appropriate to expect quite varying appraisals of accessibility by different users of land.

This volume concentrates largely, but not exclusively, on the urban fringe – the zone at the edge of the city into which urban growth of various kinds is extending – since it is here that suburban expansion is at its most important, although around the modern city this zone must be defined generously and the precise definition adopted must be varied for different urban activities. There are obvious dangers in selecting a particular segment of an urban area for special attention, even if it appears distinctive and exhibits very clear evidence of change. In the last resort, the transitional area around the outer edge of a city is the result of forces which operate in a variety of ways throughout the whole urban area. To cite but two examples of many, population growth at the fringe is merely a part of the more complex flows involved in intra-urban population movements, and industrial expansion at the edge of the city is only one aspect of the changing pattern of urban employment. Yet, although it would give a false impression to concentrate solely on the fringe as if it were completely unrelated to what is going on elsewhere, the strategy of effective enquiry demands that certain regions of the city should be specially reconnoitred. The urban fringe is one of those key locations and this book presents some tactical assessments of the present position in this critical area.

The Changing Nature of the Urban Fringe

In practice the urban fringe is a part of the city that is very difficult to define.[15] The United States Bureau of the Census, for example, has used the term 'urban fringe' to refer to the portion of a census Urbanized Area that lies outside the central city.[16] In geographical literature the term is used in a more general sense, and usually refers to the area in which suburban growth is taking place and where rural and urban land uses are mixed together to form a transition zone between town and country. It is possible, as Pryor has suggested, to give the term a more precisely-defined means, based on the proportion of the total land area under urban use, and to subdivide the fringe zone into 'rural-urban' and 'urban-rural' components.[17] The selection of suitable percentage limits to do this poses problems in subjective judgement, although not insuperable ones. Too much concern with the problem of subdivision, however, has limited value, since a more critical difficulty is that of producing a generally-acceptable definition of the outer limits of the fringe zone.

This difficulty is largely the result of the fact that the nature of the urban fringe has changed considerably over time. There are good reasons for thinking that the fringes of pre-industrial cities were inhabited by less-advantaged groups, some perhaps employed in the more noxious occupations.[18] In this location they were remote from the city centre, where social influence, political control and economic power were all manipulated. After means of intra-urban travel were greatly improved in the late nineteenth-century industrial city, land at the urban fringe was still used for residential uses, although the rapid conversion of rural land to urban purposes was now a dominant feature of the area. Another contrast lay in the fact that this zone now housed those people who could afford a relatively long journey to work and who had stable places of employment, so that they could accept the fixed daily-journey pattern imposed by mass transport by streetcars, operating along main roads which fingered out from the main built-up area.[19] Some parts of the fringe also provided sites for those space-demanding activities which could not reasonably be located within the main urban area.[20] Thus the fringe was also the location for large establishments of various kinds which did not require immediate access to the whole city population and (in its less attractive areas) the zone provided sites for essential, if noxious, urban uses like waste and sewage disposal.

At this stage the effective urban fringe was still closely associated with the outer limits of the built-up area of a city, although the larger conurbations, formed as clusters of formerly separate towns grew together along main roads, provided more complicated problems in definition. So, too, did large cities with commuter railway services to nearby towns, which in a sense increasingly formed outliers of the central city. Yet, even in these more complicated cases, new suburban development was relatively compact, was constructed at relatively high densities and was clearly associated with particular city centres.

Around many twentieth-century western cities this situation has now been greatly changed, largely as a result of the impact of road transport, particularly the growth of private car ownership. In the absence of strict planning controls, new residential developments are no longer so closely tied to areas already built-up. These new developments are not even necessarily located on main roads leading outwards from a city, but can lie in formerly less accessible areas interdigitated between the main lines of movement. These areas have become available for modern development because the car is an effective method of personal transport along minor roads, providing that they are required to carry a relatively small total traffic. At the same time housing densities tend to be lower. Partly this is because more people aspire to, and can attain, the privacy and more expansive way of life which low-density living allows. It is also because a pattern of more-scattered, lower-density residential areas can only function if personal transport is available. In such an environment normal public-transport facilities cannot be operated economically and, at the same time, the car is at its most effective. As a result, the fringe of the city is now much more difficult to define precisely: it is a zone where more scattered urban expansion is taking place, rather than an easily observable 'tidemark' around the outer edge of a growing city.[21] Also the patterns of daily activity associated with this more scattered development are less clearly directed towards a particular central city. Journeys to the city centre for employment, shopping and recreation still continue, but their relative importance is considerably reduced. Instead new suburban employment, new shopping centres and new foci for recreation have produced more complicated journey patterns on the periphery of cities and have made the city centre only one of many possible destinations.[22] These changing patterns of urban activities have greatly expanded the transition zone between urban and rural land uses during the twentieth century.

New Employment at the Edge of the City

The urban fringe has been broadened further by the dispersal of factories as well as of homes. As a first stage, much manufacturing industry was dispersed from locations close to the city centre to more scattered sites on the fringes of cities, largely as a result of changing methods of production. These changes demanded more space for factory operations and also required less intimate contact between individual producers than was found in the tightly-knit industrial districts closer to city centres. At the edge of the built-up area road transport was again a vital factor since contact could now be maintained between more widely-dispersed factories by lorries, which in any case could operate more effectively in the less densely-developed environs of cities than close to their centres. Such locations for manufacturing were originally made difficult by the problem of assembling a labour force each day, but the rise of private transport of various kinds has eased this problem.[23] In American cities the redistribution of manufacturing may have made employment (or at least the journey to work) more difficult for the disadvantaged populations residing in inner cities; but, at least from the point of view of the industrialist, recruitment of labour has not been a problem, given increased levels of personal mobility.

A parallel influence is the changing relative location of the urban fringe in relation to markets for manufactured goods. The edge of the city has now been converted from being a relatively inaccessible area, to one which often has effective inter-urban links by road. Contact can also be maintained with widely dispersed associated suppliers in the same urban system, particularly if they too have a suburban location.[24] As a result, a second stage in the growth of urban fringe manufacturing has now been reached in some cities, with the fringe itself providing the seedbed for the further growth of manufacturing. Existing firms in the fringe are establishing branch factories nearby, and completely new firms are also being established in fringe locations (instead of employment simply being dispersed from the central city). Underlying this process is the fact that individual firms can now tap the external economies offered by a large city in a much wider zone around its periphery, especially in those satellite locations where a local labour force can be more easily assembled. In particular, those businesses that serve a national rather than a local urban market do not require to be so closely associated with the continuous built-up area of an individual city and can use the cheaper, more extensive sites available within the ambit of a large urban settlement, but not immediately adjoining it.[25]

Some other types of urban employment which have been expanding in the outer suburbs do not enjoy the same freedom of location and remain more firmly tied to the rest of the built-up area. The colonization of 'green-field' sites by large retailing centres is a common feature around many western cities, although in Britain this development has been largely prevented by planning legislation. Retailing outlets are attracted to such sites by ease of access by car and also by the availability of space both for parking and for extensive shop lay-outs.[26] Although these shopping centres vary in size and in their detailed functioning, in the last resort they depend on immediate contact with as large a residential population as possible. As a result, although they may be detached from the main built-up area, they are never far removed from it.

Outlying retail centres often provide a stimulus for further residential growth by improving the day-to-day convenience of their surroundings, as well as providing local employment. Hence one of the reasons why the growth of these centres has been resisted in Britain, rightly or wrongly, is that they increase the pressure for residential expansion in the open country around large cities. It should be recalled that the expansion of retailing has also taken place in established suburbs or in satellite towns, where existing shopping centres have expanded their share of the total market. This feature has been particularly important in Britain because of the discouragement given to the expansion of new retailing centres located outside urban areas; but it is commonly found elsewhere as well.[27] An unresolved problem is the degree to which new large shopping outlets built in the urban fringe will adversely affect existing suburban retail centres which are hemmed in by other urban land uses.

Offices have also been important contributors to recent growth at the outer edge of the city, but their freedom to locate is even more restricted. Some branch offices, for example, require direct access to headquarters in a nearby city centre because they are undertaking the more routine activities that have been decentralized from expensive central sites. Others have no central parent offices, but they still require to be easily accessible to visiting businessmen, who often travel out to them from the centre. In addition many employers find it easier to recruit the female labour, on which they depend heavily, if their offices are located close to an important suburban retailing centre. Many potential women employees living in the suburbs are married; and these married women highly value immediate access to shops at some time during the working day. These women are also often the less well-paid employees who, for reasons both of time and cost, can tolerate only a relatively short journey to work, so that an office location with access to a substantial residential population is also important.[28] As a result, although office developments contribute to suburban spread by the stimulus they give to the expansion of retailing and residential land use, they are unlikely to pioneer urban growth into the countryside. Instead they are more attracted by previously established suburban centres with considerable local accessibility, perhaps with a shopping centre already functioning, and also provided with easy access by road or rail to the city centre.

Residential Land Use in the Urban Fringe

The executives employed in suburban offices and factories can tolerate much longer journeys to work than lower-paid workers, and the expansion of the number of professional jobs available close to the edge of the city has the indirect effect of introducing people of this kind into more distant residential locations. Many professional workers place a high value on a rural setting for their homes; and since they are not involved in a time-consuming journey through the built-up area to the city centre, they can penetrate more deeply into the countryside in their search for a residential location.

Some of these people live in dispersed dwellings, but the exigencies of providing essential services encourage the establishment of detached pieces of low-density suburbia, clustered into 'villages'. In the United States, many of these outlying clusters of professional workers are the creations of estate developers, since true villages are rare in the rural settlement pattern. In western Europe such clusters are often based on pre-existing villages, which provide a more romantic setting for aspiring status-conscious executives.[29] After being drawn into the sphere of influence of a nearby city's labour market, these villages are likely to change their population structure, social background and settlement function. In Britain, commuter villages of this kind have been especially encouraged by restrictions on the expansion of the continuous built-up areas of large cities, with more residential growth than might have been expected being channelled into villages.[30] The results are not always socially desirable, since polarized village communities are created, with the earlier rural inhabitants often living in uneasy juxtaposition with the more recent professional arrivals.[31]

This 'village' development is only one of the forms of residential development associated with the modern urban fringe; but it is an interesting aspect which is explored in detail in Chapter 5. In addition, the residential population of towns close to large cities has also been encouraged to grow in various ways, not only by the establishment of a daily journey to work which binds at least a sector of their population to the larger metropolitan labour market, but also as a result of population growth associated with the development of industrial satellites and the expansion of retailing and service centres. Around many cities the expansion of the continuous built-up area still forms an important feature of suburban growth, except where this is resisted by planning legislation. In some cases, particularly in the United States, the expansion of contiguous suburbs is masked by constricting political boundaries around inner cities, leading to a statistical understatement of the actual growth of the continuous built-up areas of metropolitan centres.[32]

The residential urban fringe does not end with housing built at suburban densities, since around all large modern cities there are dispersed, apparently rural, dwellings, either which have undergone a change of occupancy as a result of urban commuters purchasing country retreats, or whose existing inhabitants have been sucked into a nearby urban labour market. The growth of a dispersed urban residential fringe has reached its most extreme development with the expansion of vacation home ownership in the more distant environs of large cities. This phenomenon has taken place in those societies where increased affluence, greater leisure time and the widespread availability of cars has allowed at least a section of the urban population to own two homes. As a result the urban fringe can be thought of as extending, at least seasonally, for up to a hundred miles from those metropolitan centres that have attractive countryside nearby which is easily accessible by road for a week-end and summer visits.[33]

The people housed in new residential developments at the outer edge of urban expansion are usually thought of as belonging to those more affluent sections of society that are seeking more space for living and can afford the social and economic costs of the journey to work. This observation is often based on conditions in the United States, where it is largely true, although even here some working-class suburbs have been established, associated with the growth of suburban manufacturing employment.[34] The inhabitants of these suburbs, however, are at least creditworthy enough to buy their own houses in the long run.

Elsewhere government involvement in the provision of housing has broadened the social groups found in fringe locations. In Britain the council estate, the new town, the out-county estate and the expanded town are aspects of government-sponsored urban growth which have brought working-class people to the urban fringe.[35] But the inhabitants of these council houses are rarely the poorest in the community. Often they are employed in suburban factories, in semi-skilled or skilled jobs rather than in unskilled occupations. Often, too, they are encouraged to move out from inner residential areas by their desire to provide a better environment for their young families, but even with government subsidy this ambition involves costs which the poorest in the community cannot afford.[36] Nevertheless, they represent a much wider participation in suburban living than is usually the case in North America.

An even more contrasting situation occurs around large cities in the developing world, where a remarkably widespread phenomenon is the growth of shanty 'towns' or squatter settlements, which bring some of the poorest in urban society to the periphery of the city. In their initial stages these shanty settlements consist of temporary buildings, although with the passage of time larger and more permanent buildings are constructed.[37] The people who live in squatter settlements are there because they are occupying land which is not sought after for other uses. Sometimes this is derelict land within the city, but more commonly it is on the urban fringe, beyond the legal limits of the city. These are locations which, in these cities of the developing world, are often distant from employment and are poorly provided with transport and other services. It is possible to debate the essential nature of these squatter settlements. To outsiders they appear to provide squalid homes, but to their inhabitants they may offer the benefits of proximity to a large city, without being controlled by its bureaucracy. They are spared urban taxes, but, as a result, forgo urban services.

Not only are these settlements peripheral within the geographical city, but their inhabitants are also peripheral to urban society. Some view these squatter settlements as being occupied by people who, because of their poverty or their rural background, are unable to enter fully into urban society; others interpret the inhabitants of these fringe settlements as being at a transitional stage on the way to becoming more fully absorbed into urban life.[38] In fact squatter settlements around various cities in the developing world probably exhibit a wide range of social conditions which still require detached systematic study by sociologists, but the basic geographical fact to record here is that these fringe sites are apparently not valued highly for residential purposes by more prosperous urban dwellers in these societies. The squatter settlements thus reflect a different evaluation of urban location from that common in western cities, with access to central facilities still having a strong pull for the leaders of society, leaving residential sites in some parts of the urban periphery disregarded by those with financial power.

Insights to the Future City?

The contributors to this volume of essays have attempted to take up some of the themes introduced in this chapter. They have focused their attention on the 'western' city, since it is in the context of western Europe and North America (and in the cities derived from this culture world) that urban activities are expanding most rapidly at the edge of the built-up area. It is likely, too, that around many western cities these trends towards various forms of suburban growth will continue further in the immediate future.

The authors of the various essays in this book do not reach the extreme position adopted by Martindale, who argued that 'the age of the city seems to be at an end'. He viewed the modern western city as being internally in a state of decay, while 'the new community represented by the nation everywhere grows at its expense'.[39] It is difficult to accept this conclusion at its face value, especially as it appears to depend on a pessimistic assessment of what is happening in the older parts of cities, rather than the situation over the total extent of their functioning areas (including the suburbs). Yet if the somewhat hysterical tone of Martindale's assertion is discounted, there remains some measure of truth, particularly if attention is concentrated on the visible expression of urban morphology, in which suburbs and satellite towns are quite clearly growing at the expense of inner cities.

In the United States, for example, a more loosely-structured style of urban area is becoming more generally prevalent. The classic contemporary example is Los Angeles, where freeways have confirmed what was already a dispersed urban pattern. The system of urban motorways in this conurbation has also inhibited the growth of the central business district to the size and dominance which might have been expected, given the total population of the urban area, since many of the functions of central Los Angeles have been decanted elsewhere in the built-up area to other important business centres which can be reached more easily by car. Dispersed cities of this kind are being duplicated, at least in part, as urban motorways change the internal patterns of accessibility within many other cities. Most American cities now have important suburban shopping centres which have taken some of the functions of the central business district. Usually this process of redistribution has not yet been completed, but many suburban centres are already providing nodes around which other types of employment as well as retailing are clustered. Around them, also, new residential areas, notable for their more tenuous connections with the central city, are rapidly expanding. In other words, even cities originally focused on one dominant centre are becoming multicentered in form. In old-established cities the presence of well-rooted vested interests may prevent this tendency producing the extremes of a Los Angeles. For example central area redevelopment schemes are designed to preserve the attractiveness of many city centres for retailing and other tertiary occupations by providing urban motorways which make it possible to drive to the centre, and parking facilities which allow the potential customer to stop and shop. But where new cities are growing from fresh beginnings it is likely that an extremely dispersed urban form will continue to develop, provided that the population is affluent enough to purchase personal road transport and also that low-density residential development is highly valued by society. In countries where there are rigid planning controls, or where society is inclined to preserve its heritage of older buildings, the pressures towards a dispersed city may be resisted for a while. Yet, in the long run, the growth of dispersed cities is likely, as increased affluence almost everywhere brings a parallel increase in car ownership and encourages a quest for the private space associated with low-density housing.

Flexibility of personal movements will be a feature of the various social and economic activities found in these dispersed cities, provided that road-building within them keeps pace with the increasing number of cars. Other changes besides low-density housing will result from this. For example it will be necessary in the future to produce generalizations about urban structure based on the time required to travel to a number of separate centres rather than on linear distance to the city centre. In the suburbs of modern cities of the future, shopping centres will still draw their customers from distinct zones of influence, in spite of cars and freeways becoming commonplace. Although the zone of influence of a shopping centre may be much larger than commonly found before, the principles involved in its growth and the level of specialization it attains are unlikely to be fundamentally altered. But shops derive positive advantages from clustering together, and it does not follow that this feature will also apply to all other urban land uses. For instance, those types of land use which depend on single, special-purpose trips to allow them to function will have much greater freedom of location, with the one constraint that their increased dependence on road transport to make them accessible will demand parking space and hence a suburban rather than a central location.

The tendency towards specialization may also apply to individual urban settlements. It has been suggested that a situation is likely to arise in which one urban settlement will provide a focus for administration, another will become a trade centre, a third will function as a node in a transportation network and so on.[40] Whether this conclusion is accepted or not depends very much on how an urban area is defined. The incipient links that exist among all urban functions have tended in the past to bring together a large variety of activities within individual cities, particularly the very large one. Even in the future it is hard to imagine a trade centre that is not also involved in transport, or a large administrative centre without any retailing or manufacturing. What becomes increasingly possible, however, is that a large city will consist, not of a continuous built-up area, but of a series of smaller satellite units, either because of planning decisions limiting continuous urban growth or because such an arrangement allows particular features of the local environment to be exploited for specialized purposes. These units may well be geographically distinct from one another, but at the same time they will be joined by close functional ties. In other words, the links which previously existed among specialized areas within a city could in the future operate within a cluster of separate, specialized settlements. Such a dispersed city could be examined in terms of its individual units, but its dispersed character should not be allowed to hide the wider limits of the functioning urban system.

It is quite possible that the activity patterns in such a city will not be very different from those in the large, modernized city of today, particularly if time and cost of travel, rather than the linear distances involved, are considered. At present there are insufficient studies of the actual situation in contemporary, loosely-structured cities. What information there is suggests that, in locating their homes, people still strike a complex balance between what they can afford and accessibility to other valued functional areas concerned with employment, recreation and services. But the morphological results of working out this equation may well be different. This book presents some indication of present trends at the edge of the city in the belief that they will provide some insights into the form of the city of the future

Further Reading

At the end of each chapter in this book some brief suggestions for further reading will be given. These form merely a starting point, although the chapter references form the basis of a much more extensive bibliography.

The most important further reading for this introductory chapter consists of the other contributions to this book.

The authoritative volume on suburban extension in the United States is M. Clawson, *Suburban Land Conversion in the United States: An Economic and Governmental Process* (Baltimore, 1971).

A very readable account of social features in the suburbs is D. C. Thornes. *Suburbia* (London, 1972).

On some aspects of the future city see J. H. Johnson, 'Urbanization and its implications: some general comments', *Geoforum* 3 (1970), 7–16.

References

1. See, for example, on population densities, B. J. L. Berry and F. E. Horton, *Geographic Perspectives on Urban Systems* (Englewood Cliffs, 1970), 276–305; on transportation, J. R. Meyer, J. F. Kain and M. Wohl, *The Urban Transportation Problem* (Cambridge, Mass., 1965) 119–30; on manufacturing, R. E. Murphy, *The American City: an Urban Geography* (New York, 1966), 337–43; on retailing, P. Scott, *Geography and Retailing* (London, 1970), especially Chapter 2, 19–38.
2. R. E. Murphy, *The Central Business District* (Chicago, 1972), provides a recent summary of the literature.

3. A convenient summary of changing transportation and resulting forms of urban growth is contained in J. R. Borchert, 'American metropolitan evolution', *Geog. Review* **57** (1967), 301–23.
4. Some aspects of redevelopment of residential areas in the United States city are examined in J. Wolpert, A. Mumphrey and J. Seley, *Metropolitan Neighbourhoods: Participation and Conflict over Change*, A.A.G. Resource Paper, no. 16 (Washington, 1972); features of the British case are reviewed in R. Mellor, 'Structure and processes in the twilight area', *Town Planning Review* **44** (1973), 54–70.
5. A description of the processes involved in this change is given in M. Clawson, *Suburban Land Conversion in the United States: An Economic and Governmental Process* (Baltimore, 1971), especially 58–140.
6. J. H. Johnson, 'Urbanization and its implications: some general comments', *Geoforum* **3** (1970), especially 14–15.
7. For a nineteenth-century example of this influence see D. Ward, 'The pre-urban cadaster and the urban pattern of Leeds', *Ann. Assoc. Amer. Geogr.* **52** (1962), 150–66.
8. For some contrasts between the situation in Britain and the United States see D. L. Foley, *Controlling Londons Growth: Planning and the Great Wen, 1940–1960* (Berkeley, 1963), 156–8; and a more general analysis of the contrasting attitudes to metropolitan growth is given in P. Hall, *The World Cities* (London, 1966; second edition in preparation).
9. E. Jones, *A Social Geography of Belfast* (London, 1960), 278–9.
10. See, for example, the comments of H. Mayer, 'The pull of land and space', in J. Gottman and R. A. Harper (eds.), *Metropolis on the Move: Geographers Look at Urban Sprawl* (New York, 1967), 30.
11. D. F. Marble, 'A theoretical explanation of individual travel behaviour', in W. L. Garrison & D. F. Marble (eds.) *Quantitative Geography: Economic and Cultural Topics* (Evanston, 1966), 33–54.
12. See, for example, M. Dalton, 'Slough: a study of the journey to work in the Outer Metropolitan area' (Unpublished M.Phil. Thesis, University of London, 1973).
13. See Chapter 8 below, 170–2.
14. See Chapter 11 below, 242–4.
15. R. J. Pryor, 'Defining the rural-urban fringe', *Social Forces* **47** (1968), 202–15; see also the discussion in Chapter 2 below, 18–20.
16. See the use made of this definition in S. A. Queen and D. B. Carpenter, 'The sociological significance of the rural-urban fringe: from the urban point of view', *Rural Sociology* **18** (1953), 102–8.
17. See Chapter 2 below, Fig. 2–1, 19.
18. G. Sjoberg, *The Pre-Industrial City: Past and Present* (New York, 1960), 80–107.
19. This process is best documented in S. B. Warner, *Streetcar Suburbs: The Process of Growth in Boston, 1870-1900* (Cambridge, Mass., 1963).
20. Evidence for an alternation of the importance of large establishments and residential developments in contrasting economic climates is examined in Chapter 3 below, 32–40.
21. R. J. Pryor has attempted to delineate the urban fringe around Melbourne, and has limited his consideration to the area immediately adjoining the continuous built-up area. Even so, the fringe he delineates is over 15 km wide in places. See R. J. Pryor, 'Delineating outer suburbs and the urban fringe', *Geografiska Annaler* **51 B** (1969), 33–8.

22. Studies of the journey to work have tended to neglect this important development, but this theme is now being taken up much more actively. For a pioneer and influential American study see E. J. Taaffe, B. J. Garner and M. H. Yeates, *The Peripheral Journey to Work: a Geographical Consideration* (Evanston, 1963).
23. C. Clark, 'Transport—maker and breaker of cities', *Town Planning Review* **28** (1957–8), 247–9.
24. See Chapter 7 below especially 132–3.
25. For the dispersal of manufacturing from suburban London to a much wider area around the metropolis see D. Keeble, 'Industrial decentralization and the Metropolis: the north-west London case', *Trans. Inst. Br. Geogr.* **44** (1968), 1–54.
26. One summary, among many, of these developments is J. P. Reynolds, 'Suburban shopping in America: notes on shopping developments in the United States and the implications for Britain', *Town Planning Review* **29** 1958–9), 43–59.
27. See Chapter 8 below, 157–8.
28. See Chapter 9 below, 181–3.
29. See Chapter 5 below, 80–3.
30. See Chapter 4 below, 60-2.
31. A pioneer study in Britain of this phenomenon was R. E. Pahl, *Urbs in Rure: The Metropolitan fringe in Hertfordshire* (London, 1965). For a summary of the diversity of suburbs see D. C. Thornes, *Suburbia* (London, 1972), 77–92.
32. The complex problems involved in assessing population change in modern cities are examined in B. J. L. Berry, P. G. Goheen and H. Goldstein, *Metropolitan Area Definition: A Re-evaluation of Concept and Statistical Practice,* U.S. Bureau of the Census Working Paper (Washington, D.C., 1968). See also G. R. J. Linge, *The Delimitation of Urban Boundaries for Statistical Purposes with Special Reference to Australia: a Report to the Commonwealth Statistician* (Australian National University, Research School of Pacific Studies Department of Geography Publications G/2, Canberra, 1965).
33. The United States situation is summarized in R. L. Ragatz, 'Vacation homes in the north eastern United States, seasonality in population distribution', *Ann. Assoc. Amer. Geogr.* **60** (1970), 447–55. For a consideration of the European situation see Chapter 6 below, 104–22.
34. B. M. Berger, *Working Class Suburb: A Study of Auto Works in Suburbia* (Berkeley, 1960); H. J. Gans, *The Levittowners: Ways of Life and Politics in New Suburban Communities* (New York, 1967).
35. See the comment of B. T. Robson on the implications of this trend for classical models of urban structure in his *Urban Analysis: A Study of City Structure with Special Reference to Sunderland* (Cambridge, 1969), 132.
36. See, for example, J. H. Johnson, 'The suburban expansion of housing in London, 1918–1939', in J. T. Coppock and H. C. Prince (eds.). *Greater London* (London, 1964), 161.
37. There is a rapidly growing literature on this topic. See, for example, W. Mangin, 'Latin American squatter settlements: a problem and a solution', *Latin America Research Review* **2** (1967), 65–89; see also an architectural view in J. F. C. Turner, 'Barriers and channels for housing development in modernizing countries', *J. Amer. Inst. Planners* **33** (1967), 167–81.

38. See, for example, G.H. Beyer (ed.), *The Urban Expansion in Latin America; a Continent in Process of Modernization* (Ithica, 1967).
39. D. Martindale, 'Prefactory remarks: the theory of the city', introduction to M. Weber, *The City,* translated and edited by D. Martindale and G. Neuwirth (New York, 1958), 62.
40. See, for example, J. McHale, 'Future city: notes on a typology', *Ekistics* **28** (1969), 86–93.

CHAPTER 2

The Urban Fringe: Approaches and Attitudes

DAVID THOMAS

The urban fringe, like the poor, has always been with us. Leastways, it has been with us since urban civilization first emerged and settlements gradually began to expand at the expense of rural land. In modern times, particularly in the wake of the industrial revolution, towns and cities have expanded swiftly; urban-rural links have increased as greater numbers of urban workers have sought city-fringe or rural dwellings, and as other urban activities have overspilled from towns into the countryside.

Clearly, urban-rural interaction is at its maximum immediately beyond the edges of the continuously built-up areas. Here lies the undeveloped space into which a town or city expands by circumferential or radial growth. It is a zone of mixed land-use elements and characteristics in which rural activities and modes of life are in rapid retreat, and into which not only residential, but also commercial, educational, recreational, public service and other largely extensive uses of land are intruding. In a land-use, and often in an administrative, sense too, the area is only partially assimilated into the growing urban complex. This is the area which has been termed the 'urban fringe', or sometimes the ' rural-urban fringe'.

But here is the enigma. Though urban fringes have existed over so long a period, and though their present characteristics are evident in the plans of towns of the eighteenth and nineteenth centuries and earlier, no geographer or other social scientist paid them other than scant attention until relatively recently. They do not appear to have been identified as distinctive parts of the urban region, with particular characteristics and particular problems, until the early 1940s – the general problems of urban growth were only themselves just beginning to make an impact at that time. Pryor attributes the first use of the term 'urban fringe' to T. L. Smith, who, in a study of the composition and changes of the population of Louisiana in 1937, employed it to signify 'the built-up area just outside the corporate limits of the city'.[1] Within a decade, a host of writers, mainly American, had pronounced upon the subject, and the term had come to acquire more or less the meaning it carries at present. But since the area itself is one characterized by an incoherence of land-use and of social patterns, it is not surprising that problems of definition have always beset studies of the fringe. To some of these difficulties we now turn.

Problems of Definition

The initial problem to emerge from a study of the now vast scholarly literature on the urban fringe is a lack of clarity over what facets of life and landscape are under investigation. Broadly, as Carter has stressed in a recent review of attitudes to the urban fringe,[2] there are two aspects which have attracted most attention. First, there is the notion of the fringe as a distinctive area, primarily designated by characteristic land-use associations. Second, there is the notion that the social characteristics of the population of the fringe are intermediate between those of the town and those of the country – a sparse rural or semi-rural population is interspersed with far larger numbers of ex-urbanites who may live in the country, though socially and economically they are not of the country. But apart from echoing the warning that ideally it is advisable to distinguish clearly between these different attitudes to the urban fringe, in practice this must often remain a council of perfection rather than a prescription for action, since in the literature these two notions are as intermixed as the character of the fringe itself.

Another problem arises simply from the meanings given to the words which denote the features of the fringe. Though many of the written accounts and descriptions of fringe areas are based upon American experience, there is a fair scattering of commentaries from Europe and Australia particularly. The confusion in terminology which results from these various case studies is considerable, and is compounded by the span in time over which the studies were undertaken, the great range in size of the urban centres under investigation, the variations in the degree of control exercised over the fringe area and the differing aims and contexts of the several pieces of research.

This diversity of terminology applies not only to the urban fringe itself, but is characteristic also of many of the related terms and concepts. Kurtz and Eicher have illustrated the problem in their wellknown paper which attempts to differentiate between 'fringe' and 'suburb'.[3] Wissink, in an extensive survey of the fringe areas of American cities, identifies 'fringe', 'suburbs', 'pseudo-suburbs', 'satellites' and 'pseudo-satellites',[4] while many other writers grapple with the complexities of defining different types of 'satellite' and 'suburbs', and of distinguishing between these and other fringe development. Few serious workers have had the courage even to attempt to make comparative assessments of 'rurban' land or of 'slurb' (slopped-over suburb).

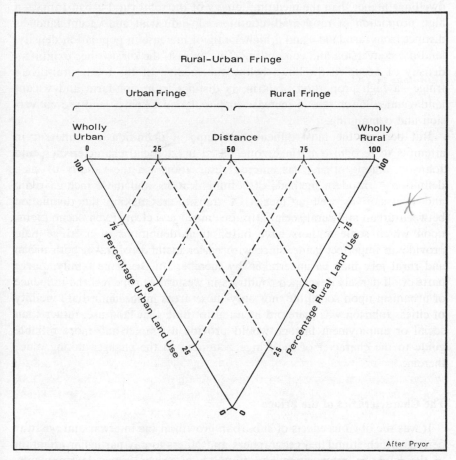

Figure 2–1   Land use in the rural-urban fringe (based on Pryor [1968], 205)

Pryor faced another aspect of this problem when he noted and attempted to resolve the various areal differentiations of the urban fringe which have been proposed.[5] For example, Andrews had distinguished the 'urban fringe' from the 'rural-urban fringe',[6] McKain and Burnight had differentiated the 'limited fringe' from the 'extended fringe',[7] Reinemann had described a 'suburban fringe zone' and an 'outlying adjacent zone',[8]

Wissink had identified ' inner' and 'outer' fringe areas,[9] Duncan and Reiss had postulated 'rural non-farm' and 'rural farm' subdivisions of the fringe,[10] while Myers and Beegle were able to delineate a 'true fringe', a 'partial fringe' and 'adjacent rural townships'.[11] Pryor's solution is summarized in Figure 2–1, in which the rural-urban fringe is shown quantitatively subdivided into an 'urban fringe' and a 'rural fringe' on the basis of its land-use composition. The urban fringe exhibits a density of occupied dwellings higher than the medium density of the total rural-urban fringe – a high proportion of residential, commercial, industrial and vacant land, as distinct from farmland – and a higher rate of increase in population density, land-use conversion and commuting. By contrast, the rural fringe exhibits a density of occupied dwellings below the median of the total rural-urban fringe – a high proportion of farm as distinct from non-farm and vacant land – and a lower rate of increase in population density, land-use conversion and commuting.

But perhaps the most difficult problems of definition are inherent in attempts to recognize a fringe zone based upon social characteristics, and Johnson, among others, has entered reservations on the validity of such definitions.[12] Modern methods of communication, and these include radio and television as well as means of transit, are making the distinction between urban and rural social attitudes much less clear. Even occupations, upon which some authors have based their definitions of a fringe belt, provide an imperfect guide, since with easier methods of travel both urban and rural jobs may be undertaken by members of the same family. Large parts of all densely developed countries in western Europe feel the influence of urbanism upon social life, not only those areas in the immediate vicinity of cities. Johnson was therefore inclined to think that land use, rather than social or employment factors, would provide a simpler and more reliable guide to the character of the fringe zone and to the changes taking place therein.

The Characteristics of the Fringe

It was the obvious effects of suburban growth in the interwar and postwar periods which stimulated geographers and others to pay particular attention to the land-use composition and function of urban fringe developments. Much of our present thinking about the characteristics of the urban fringe stem from the American work in the 1940s and not least from an article published by Wehrwein in 1942, which has now come to be regarded as the early formative paper in this field of study.[13] In his investigation of American cities, and particularly of Indianapolis, the author recognized that railways were among the first decentralizers of urban population and urban land uses, and that their effects were greatly enhanced when the car and hard-surfaced roads provided means of swift unchannelled mass transportation. The structure of simple agricultural zones about a city, such as those postulated by von Thünen, had already been modified by the railways, and was now transformed. Wherever a railway, inter-urban line or highway entered a city, residences, commercial establishments and industrial plants became strung out along their route. Since these means of transportation radiated in all directions whenever physical features allowed, the urban fringe came to consist of rural territory pierced by finger-like projections of urbanized land uses. Between the arms of the star thus produced, agriculture and other non-urban land uses continued, but in more or less modified form.

A closer examination of the urbanized parts of the urban fringe led Wehrwein to identify some of its important characteristics. The first lay in the nature of residential growth. Flexibility of transportation between city edge and city centre encouraged, in the America of the interwar years, a wild expansion of the main urban areas. Land agents and speculators rushed to lay out subdivisions for low-density dwellings, often in excess of the building plots which were demanded. Therefore, in addition to the great areas of built-up land which spread into the rural hinterlands of cities, the over-expansion of residential sites led to vacant, weed-covered land, expensively supplied with streets, water, sewers, gas and electricity, and therefore, for all practical purposes, impossible to return to agriculture or any other rural use. Since such expansions took place in areas which had rural forms of government and lower densities than obtained in cities, the financial burden of unsold, unused and unproductive lots was considerable.

The second characteristic feature of land use stemmed from the recreational demands upon the urban fringe. Wehrwein describes with some gloom a situation on most urban fringes where land suitable for recreation had long been pre-empted for private use. Riparian land along lakes and streams was engulfed by summer cottages, resorts, taverns, dance halls and fun-fairs. Roads leading to such resort areas were lined with established recreation zones and much pressure was exerted upon farmland by hunters in search of game. Nowhere, it seems, were the conflicts between farmers and the remainder of the population greater than in the areas close to cities.

The third characteristic of fringe land uses recognized by Wehrwein was the result of institutional factors. For convenience, and because of their space requirements, many of the public utilities serving cities became located in the urban fringe areas. Recreation land, water supply and radio stations, sewage disposal plants, airports and cemeteries were therefore among the urban necessities found beyond the outer edge of the city. In addition to these uses, there were others, necessary but unwanted in the city, which it had been the practice of cities to force into rural territory by ordinances excluding them from the built-up area as such. Slaughter houses, wholesale oil storage, noxious industries of all sorts, junk yards, caravans and caravan parks, taverns and dance halls, sub-standard dwellings, carnivals and the sale of fireworks had all been subject to restrictive city legislation at one place or another. Such activities escaped urban control by locating in the nearby countryside where rural authorities had neither the powers nor the resolve to take action. In his study of the Indianapolis metropolitan district Wehrwein discovered that within the unincorporated areas which lacked zoning ordinances of their own there were in all forty-three identifiable overspill uses of this kind. Nearly 50 per cent. of these lay within a mile (1·6 km) of the edge of Indianapolis, 66 per cent. lay within two miles (3·2 km), and 85 per cent. lay within four miles (6·4 km) of the city limit.

Wehrwein's pioneering study has been followed by many others focusing upon the land uses of the urban fringe. Many authors (typical is Balk in his work on Worcester, Massachusetts[14]) have provided detailed descriptions of the fringes of particular towns or cities, while some, like Andrews,[15] have attempted to identify the general land-use characteristics of urban fringe zones. Others have paid attention to more limited aspects of the urban fringe. For example Myers and Beegle,[16] Blizzard and Anderson,[17] and Pryor[18] have attempted to define and delimit the urban fringe, Fellman has considered the alterations to the geography of areas close to a city which take place in advance of development,[19] Firey has studied the social and planning implications of rapidly developing zones around cities,[20] Masser and Stroud have written about the influence of commuters upon rural areas,[21] Kurtz and Smith have looked in detail at the social contrasts which arise in urban-dominated rural societies,[22] Roterus and Hughes have described the problems for local government which occur on urban peripheries,[23] Rikkinen has analysed the way in which ownership boundaries affect urban growth and land-use change,[24] Schnore and Klaff have measured the speed of suburbanization over the last decade in the United States, compared with earlier decades,[25] and Whitehand has attempted to recognize the fringe belts of earlier periods in the urban form of present-day cities.[26] The literature is now both copious and diverse, much of it dating from the period 1945–60. Pryor includes 162 papers and books in his bibliography of work on the urban fringe,[27] and after the passage of several years this list is now far from complete. Attention here will be directed to two of the more recent contributions, important not only because they present an up-to-date view of the urban fringe, but also because they consider the dynamics of fringe areas by undertaking studies of processes.

Current Processes within the Fringe

The first of the studies is that by Golledge, who in 1960 published the results of his investigations of Sydney's urban fringe, a study of particular interest since it dealt with a fringe area outside North America and western Europe, hitherto the centres of most attention.[28] The work is also of interest because it spans two periods, the one before land-use controls were introduced, the other following the introduction of a fairly strictly maintained green belt.

Golledge began by setting up a series of propositions or hypotheses describing the features which he expected to develop on the margins of big cities. The urban fringe, in his view, possessed seven major characteristics: it had a constantly changing pattern of land occupance; farms were small; crop production was intensive; the population was mobile and distributed at low or moderate density; residential expansion was rapid; the provision of services and public utilities was incomplete; and speculative subdivision and speculative building were common. He then proceeded to examine each of these characteristics in respect of Sydney's fringe area.

The changing pattern of land was the least difficult feature to demonstrate. As the area of Sydney expanded, so increasing demands were made upon rural land by urban uses. As the edge of the city drew nearer, the more rapid were the changes in land occupance and land use. Farm sizes, he discovered, varied inversely with distance from the centre of the city. On the immediate urban fringe holdings were small, often averaging as little as 5–6 acres (2–2·4 ha) in some areas; at greater distance from the city, for example at 30 to 35 miles (48–56 km) from the centre, the average holding was much more likely to exceed 50 acres (20 ha), and in some areas the average was as high as 250 acres (101 ha). The nature of farming also varied with distance from the city. The small fringe farms were highly specialized upon the production of perishable or semi-perishable market garden crops which gave a high return on invested capital and which helped to cover the higher costs of production associated with proximity to the urban mass. Double cropping and interculture were common. In the outer country areas mixed farming predominated and a much greater emphasis was placed upon the single cropping of grain, hay and fodder crops.

The population of Sydney's fringe area was highly characteristic. While population densities were low, growth rates in the period 1947–54 sometimes exceeded 100 per cent. Most of these sharp increases were contributed by immigrants, whose age structure was heavily overloaded by persons in the age-groups 0–9 and 20–34 years, that is by young married couples and their children. Increases in the number of dwellings matched the growth in population on Sydney's fringe, but the provision of public utilities lagged badly. For example, most parts of Sydney recorded over 80 per cent. of their dwellings fully connected with gas, water and sewage facilities; in the fringe area sometimes as many as three-quarters of the dwellings were supplied with water only. In the better types of development, builder-speculators provided all necessary services, including surfaced roads, and Golledge saw this as beneficial to the area as a whole.

Sydney's green belt, like that of London and other cities, had profound effects upon the processes of change in the urban fringe. Its purpose was to contain the city, to act as a buffer between the city and rural towns, to provide space for recreation and other pursuits which required a rural setting close to the city's edge, to reserve areas for government use and to create a unified area around the city in which desirable standards of agriculture, dwellings, recreation and amenity could be maintained. The belt was first proposed in 1947 and fully implemented in 1951. Its general effect appears to have led to the creation of an artificial urban fringe, less dynamic than that produced by natural growth processes. Dead land, resulting from overdevelopment by speculators, virtually disappeared, land tenure became more stable and a clearer division emerged between urban and rural land. Unsightly urban sprawl was prevented, the residential character of settlements was preserved by restricting industrial growth and, because settlements were more compact than previously, both government and private transport operators were able to provide a better and more economic service. In the long term it appeared inevitable that the green belt would sever the urban-rural continuum, and that it would eventually destroy the fringe by removing many of its salient characteristics, since it tended to remove the interaction between urban and rural land uses.

The second study to throw light on current processes within fringe areas is that undertaken by Pahl.[29] His work focuses largely upon the social character of London's fringe, and whatever the difficulties of defining the urban fringe in social terms or of isolating the particular social identity of the fringe, it does point to the very important urban-influenced social changes which are affecting rural and semi-rural areas, and perhaps more than any other, the urban fringe itself. Pahl recognizes four main processes underway.

The first of these is a tendency towards social and spatial segregation. This stems mainly from the income differences between the middle-class immigrants and the dominantly working-class established population. Income differences create widely differing abilities to compete for new, privately-built housing development, and so it is in the areas of fresh expansion that the newly arrived, fairly affluent, professional population clusters. Any tendency for this immigrant population to become more representative of the city's social structure is deterred by the high cost of new housing on the urban fringe, by the need to compete with the established population for lower-cost housing, and by the costs of commuting. The immigrant middle classes therefore become isolated socially and spatially.

The second process is a tendency towards selective immigration into the urban fringe. Because of the cost deterrent outlined above, fringe areas attract 'mobile, middle-class commuters, who live and work in distinct and separate social and economic worlds from the established populations'.

The impact of this is that they not only represent a rather limited segment of city population, so different in social composition from the rural community, but that they also retain and often enhance these differences by maintaining their patterns of linkages with the city – usually with the city centre. Here the men are employed, the women do their major shopping, and the family engages in social and cultural activities; the urban fringe is the dormitory, and the place for rural recreation and week-end leisure.

The third process is the changing commuting character of the urban fringe. The influx of urban-oriented population having firm city-centre linkages introduces new travel patterns, especially new work journeys. The difference in the numbers undertaking work journeys and also in the length of these journeys is marked when compared with times before the introduction of ex-urban population.

Finally, Pahl points to the tendency towards the collapse of geographical and social hierarchies. With an increasing proportion of the population looking to various parts of the nearby city for its occupations, goods and services, and with a population which, at the same time, is markedly more mobile than average, the service provision within fringe settlements becomes modified, or fails to develop along lines predictable by central place theory. Service centres do not need to carry the array of goods and services commensurate with the populations contained within their tributary areas; they are inclined not to sort themselves into an hierarchical structure, but to assume more limited specialist functions. Pahl suggests that such settlements are better understood as interlocking parts of a dispersed city. That is, they acquire groups of related functions, often quite different from those of neighbouring towns rather than an assortment of different functions, the number being related to the position in a hierarchy of service centres.

While the two studies by Golledge and Pahl illuminate current processes within urban fringe areas, and while the two, explicitly or implicitly, deal with the characteristics both of land use and of socio-economic composition, it is clear that their standpoints are widely different. Golledge, basically, adopts the land-use attitude described earlier. To him the urban fringe is a physical entity with a particular land-use mix brought about by the spread of the city, its functions and its populations into rural areas. Pahl, in contrast, regards the fringe as having distinctness by virtue of the rather special communities which occupy it; that is he adopts the social attitude described earlier. To him the urban fringe is a social entity brought about by the influx of socially-segregated, economically-filtered, urban-oriented, mobile, middle-class families, intermixed, but not intermingled, with a more staid, socially diverse, static, indigenous rural population. But whatever the standpoint of the author there is one very marked common theme which emerges from throughout the scholarly literature, namely that there is virtual unanimity in regarding the urban fringe as a problem area. It provides substantial problems of definition and of analysis. It also presents the perhaps more pressing practical problems which, if unsolved, detract from the quality of the lives of both those who dwell in the fringe, and also those who live in the nearby city. The final section of this chapter turns attention to the salient difficulties of fringe zones.

The Problems of the Fringe

The interpenetration of urban and rural land and of urban and rural society inevitably creates a competitive atmosphere in which conflicts of attitude and of interest appear. These produce problems which, if they do not in themselves provide additional means of characterizing the urban fringe, certainly operate jointly more forcibly in the fringe than elsewhere. Six broad categories of problems emerge.

First, there are those problems which stem from the scattered and piece-meal residential and commercial development that often occurs on un-planned urban fringes. There are a number of dimensions to this set of problems. One aspect is that of amenity (once defined as the right thing in the right place). Whether the sometimes radial, sometimes sporadic, but almost always low-density development on city peripheries is the right way to allow cities to expand, is a long-debated question. Planners, throughout this century, have argued strongly that it is not, though they have not always been quite so united in their prescriptions for the ideal method of growth. Another aspect is the problem of organizing and articulating administratively the small, often straggling, settlements of the fringe. Administrative control is usually in the hands of a rural, rather than an urban, authority whose attitudes to development may be ambivalent, if not positively confused, by its responsibilities to two quite different groups of interests. Yet another aspect of the problem of development stems from the impact of loosely-knit, perhaps formless urban expansion upon nearby rural land uses, uses which are often highly susceptible to interference by man, and his domestic animals.

Second, there is a wide range of problems which, in effect, are an expansion of this last aspect. Great difficulties arise on urban fringes from the intermixture of what are sometimes regarded as non-conforming land uses with the other uses more commonly found in rural areas. Some of the non-conforming activities will have found their way into the fringe zone for purely economic reasons – because their space needs are high, and their competitive positions in respect of urban land are low. For this reason extensive land uses such as water storage, service and government depots, large manufacturing plants, public utility installations and heavy transport parks have not developed and expanded within towns, but upon cheaper land on or beyond the city limit. Yet other non-conforming activities, for example junk yards, slaughter houses, glue factories, oil depots, will have located within the fringe because they have been forced to move or are excluded from urban sites by city regulation, bye-law or planning control (the precise mechanism varies from country to country) on account of their noxious, or in some other way undesirable, natures. Such land uses, if they give offence within towns and cities, are hardly likely to be any more desirable in a rural context. Together these two types of non-conforming activities create conflicts and pressures when juxtaposed with rural and suburban residential land. They present formidable problems to those responsible for maintaining adequate levels of amenity and the efficient economic functioning of urban fringe zones.

Third, there are the problems of reserving land for agriculture and ensuring that it remains economically viable. Agriculture is in a weak competitive position in the urban fringe, and the agricultural area is easily fragmented by urban-based uses. As Wibberley has demonstrated, the processes of change on the peripheries of towns and cities from urban to rural use are far from smooth.[30] Land about to be developed may be 'farmed to quit', that is a farmer may put less into his farm than he removes, causing a sharp decline in fertility, a fall in productivity and a generally run-down farming scene. In other circumstances delays in development may lead to land lying completely idle for a period as abandoned farmland awaits its new use. Problems arise too when urban expansion absorbs only parts of farms. Farms, like any other economic enterprise, are composed of interdependent parts. Remove some of the parts and the whole operates much less effectively or, alternatively, the system has to be changed radically. In either case there is a tendency towards farm decay. Physical proximity to urban land uses also causes difficulties for the farmer: encroachment onto farmland for recreation or other purposes may cause damage to crops and hedges, and disturb stock. Such interference with the farming system is inclined to be greatest where population pressure upon land is high and where towns are expanding and introducing into the countryside an urban population untutored in the ways of the countryside. These are the very conditions which pertain in the urban fringe.

Fourth, a very similar group of problems arises over the reservation of recreation land. In this case it is not a matter of maintaining the *status quo*, but of creating recreation areas to serve the growing demands of the city and also of the expanding population of the fringe. Greatest demands for recreation lands are felt very close to the outer edges of towns and cities: there appears to be a very sharp decline in the number of recreation facilities with distance from centres of urban populations. Competition with residential and commercial land is therefore severe, and without the support of national or local government bodies it has proved to be a very unequal competition.

Fifth, there are a set of problems which stem from the high costs of services to scattered settlements. Costs are not great when compared with truly rural areas; they are simply high in comparison with the figures for the nearby urban mass. High costs also arise from the need to cover the heavy capital charges for the installation of completely new services: water, gas, electricity, public transport and so on. Despite the affluence of the urban fringe zone, high costs often lead to a lower level of service provision than in the nearby urban area, and it is this which really highlights the problem.

Lastly, there are the difficulties which follow from the intermixture of different social groups, some with urban-based and others with rural-based attitudes and ways of life. The work of Pahl, quoted above, has exemplified the major differences and possible areas of conflict. But it is notable that modern means of communication, verbal, visual, literal, as well as physical, have greatly eroded true rural society. Even the indigenous and rurally employed population of the urban fringe is rapidly becoming urban-oriented. This set of problems is the only one of the six which shows any signs of abating.

Of the problems outlined above, it is not surprising that a great deal of attention has been paid both in practice and in the scholarly literature to the controls which may be exercised over land-use development in urban fringe zones. In many countries the urban and regional planning which this implies is a relatively recent innovation. For example in North America, where much of the early work upon the urban fringe was undertaken, the move to organize extra-metropolitan growth on a large scale has come only in the last decade, as for example in Minneapolis–St Paul.[31] In Europe generally there has been a longer tradition of urban planning in which fringe areas have received their fair proportion of attention. In Britain, for example, active consideration from a purely practical standpoint has been given to the control of urban fringe land, particularly that around London, at least since the last decade of the nineteenth century. It was a concern which eventually led to the enactment of the Green Belt Act of 1938, a device to preserve relatively small areas of public open space and unbuilt land suitable for agriculture, woodland and recreation on the fringe of London. In the postwar period it resulted in the establishment of an approved green belt, a broad continuous swath of land approximating to the urban fringe zone where very little new building was allowed, but within which undeveloped countryside was maintained so that recreational and other open space deficiencies of the urban area could be met.[32]

The various planning techniques which have so far been employed to control the urban fringe have achieved varying degrees of success. They have generally had the effect of giving a cleaner edge to town and country, they have reduced the competitive pressures upon certain land uses, like agriculture and recreation, and they have improved the visual attractiveness of limited areas. But on the whole the controls have been preventative rather than stimulative, that is they have been designed principally to restrict the development of undesirable uses rather than to promote a better integrated, smoother-functioning, and aesthetically more satisfying mixture of land-use types. But the mechanisms at work within the urban fringe are so intricate that it is perhaps unrealistic, with the planning tools at present available, to expect more than a modest readjustment of the considerable forces of urban expansion.

Further Reading

The classic account of the urban fringe is given in G. S. Wehrwein, The rural-urban fringe', *Economic Geography* **18** (1942), 217–28.

An extended comparative work on fringe zones is G. A. Wissink, *American Cities in Perspective: With Special Reference to the Development of their Fringe Areas* (Assen, 1962).

A review of attitudes to the urban fringe is provided by H. Carter. *The Study of Urban Geography* (London, 1972).

A useful bibliography of urban fringe studies is contained in R. J. Pryor, 'Defining the rural-urban fringe', *Social Forces* **47** (1968), 202–15.

Two detailed accounts of the urban fringe of a particular city (London) are contained in R. E. Pahl, *Urbs in Rure: the Metropolitan Fringe in Hertfordshire* (London, 1965); and D. Thomas, *London's Green Belt* (London, 1970).

Problems of planning major world cities, including the problems of planning their fringe areas, are discussed by P. Hall, *The World Cities* (London, 1966; second edition in preparation).

References

1. R. J. Pryor, 'Defining the rural-urban fringe', *Social Forces* **47** (1968), 202–15.
2. H. Carter, *The Study of Urban Geography* (London, 1972).
3. H. A. Kurtz and J. B. Eicher, 'Fringe and suburbs: a confusion of concepts', *Social Forces* **37** (1958), 32–7.
4. G. A. Wissink, *American Cities in Perspective: With Special Reference to the Development of their Fringe Areas* (Assen, 1962).
5. Pryor, *op. cit.*
6. R. B. Andrews, 'Elements in the urban fringe pattern', *Journal of Land and Public Utility Economics* **18** (1942), 169–83.
7. W. C. McKain and R. G. Burnight, 'The sociological significance of the rural-urban fringe from the rural point of view', *Rural Sociology* **18** (1953), 109–16.
8. M. W. Reinemann, 'The pattern and distribution of manufacturing in the Chicago area', *Econ. Geog.* **36** (1960), 139–44.
9. Wissink, *op. cit.*
10. O. D. Duncan and A. J. Reiss, 'Suburbs and urban fringe', in *Social Characteristics of Urban and Rural Communities* (New York, 1956).
11. R. B. Myers and J. A. Beegle, 'Delineation and analysis of the rural-urban fringe', *Applied Anthropology* **6** (1947), 14–22.

12. J. H. Johnson, *Urban Geography: an Introductory Analysis* (Oxford, 1967).
13. G. S. Wehrwein, 'The rural-urban fringe', *Econ. Geog.* **18** (1942), 217–28.
14. H. H. Balk, 'The rurbanization of Worcester's environs', *Econ. Geog.* **21** (1945), 104–16.
15. Andrews, *op. cit.*
16. Myers and Beegle, *op. cit.*
17. S. W. Blizzard and W. F. Anderson, *Problems in Rural-Urban Research: Conceptualization and Delineation* (Pennsylvania, 1952).
18. Pryor, *op. cit.*
19. J. D. Fellman, 'Pre-building growth patterns in Chicago', *Ann. Ass. Amer. Geogr.* **47** (1957), 59–82.
20. W. I. Firey, 'Ecological considerations in planning for urban fringes', *Amer. Sociol. Rev.* **11** (1946), 411–23.
21. F. I. Masser and D. C. Stroud, 'The metropolitan village', *Town Planning Review* **36** (1956), 111–24.
22. H. A. Kurtz and J. Smith, ' Social life in the rural-urban fringe', *Rural Sociology* **26** (1961), 24.
23. V. Roterus and I. H. Hughes, 'Governmental problems of fringe areas', *Public Management* **30** (1948), 94–7.
24. K. Rikkinen, 'Boundary changes in a rural-urban fringe area', *Acta Geographica* **26** (1972), 25pp.
25. L. F. Schnore and V. Z. Klaff, 'Suburbanization in the sixties: a preliminary analysis', *Land Econ.* **48** (1972), 23–33.
26. J. W. R. Whitehand, 'Fringe belts: a neglected aspect of urban geography', *Trans. Inst. Br. Geogr.* **41** (1967), 223–33.
27. Pryor, *op. cit.*
28. R. Golledge, 'Sydney's metropolitan fringe: a study in urban-rural relations', *Australian Geographer* **7** (1960), 243-55.
29. R. E. Pahl, *Urbs in Rure: the Metropolitan Fringe in Hertfordshire* (London, 1965).
30. G. P. Wibberley, *Agriculture and Urban Growth* (London, 1959).
31. D. Thomas, 'Twin cities choice: evolution of a regional plan', *Town and Country Planning* **37** (1969), 269–75.
32. D. Thomas, *London's Green Belt* (London, 1970).

CHAPTER 3
The Changing Nature of the Urban Fringe: A Time Perspective

J. W. R. WHITEHAND

The Study of Urban Growth: Some Research Traditions

Studies of the spatial patterns of urban growth may look for inspiration to a variety of methodologies, which to a considerable extent are the product of relatively independent schools of thought. Rather weakly represented in European work, but strongly in American, is the theory of urban rents with its foundations in the work on agricultural rent of J. H. von Thünen. In this genre are the highly theoretical approaches of W. Alonso[1] and R. F. Muth.[2] Often more empirical in content have been studies using stochastic models to simulate urban growth, of which R. L. Morrill's is one of the better known.[3] Another but not unrelated type of American research is that on urban land development, such as has been carried out by the Institute for Research in Social Science at the University of North Carolina.[4]

At the other extreme, and well represented in British work in the traditions of historical scholarship, are the case studies of the historico-geographical development of individual cities and parts of cities, the focus of attention being the description of individual events underlying particular urban developments. H. J. Dyos, the economic historian, and his students have made notable contributions in this direction[5] and M. J. Mortimore's recent study of Bradford is characteristic of the British geographer's contri-bution.[6] Such studies are not unrepresented in the American literature, that of J. D. Fellman being a notable example.[7] Urban and pre-urban ante-cedence take high priority in such an approach. Detailed attention to antecedence is also characteristic of the European morphogenetic tradition exemplified by the work of M. R. G. Conzen,[8] but here the conceptual content tends to be higher, although the essentially inductive approach and

genetic explanations offered are in contrast to the predominantly hypothetico-
deductive approach and functional explanations of American theorists such
as Alonso and Muth.

Studies of growth in a mainly temporal sense represent another research
interest largely independent of the predominantly spatial studies so far
mentioned. Here analyses of various indices of economic and demographic
growth, such as the study of building cycles by J. Parry Lewis,[9] reveal some
of the sequences of events that must in fact underlie the spatial patterns of
physical growth. It is a weakness of studies of the physical character of
urban growth that the spatial consequences of such temporal sequences are
often not deduced.

The present contribution to the study of the spatial patterns of urban
growth focuses on the evolving land-use pattern of the urban fringe and
is to some extent eclectic in that it utilizes the methods and findings of
several of the types of study already mentioned. The chapter falls into three
main parts. First, on the basis of the postulates of urban-rent theory and
of findings on building cycles, a model of an aspect of the development of
the urban fringe over time is deduced and an empirical testing of this model
is described. Second, some aspects of morphogenetic work on the evolution
of urban fringe belts in both Europe and North America are described.
Third, some of the findings of this morphogenetic work are considered in
relation to the model of urban fringe development. As a result of this
consideration some apparent inconsistencies are identified, and these are
then examined in the light of the results of micro-studies of the developmental histories of individual plots in a major British city.

A Model of the Rural-to-Urban Land-Use Conversion Process[10]

The interpretation of land uses in terms of the relative advantage they
accrue from substituting rent for the costs of accessibility is a research
strategy familiar to the American urban-land economists. By assessing the
extent of this advantage each potential land user may be thought of as
arriving at a rent that he is prepared to offer for a particular site (a bid
rent).[11] Confining attention for simplicity to housing and institutions (the
two major types of urban extension in most cities if the latter category is
broadly defined[12]) it seems reasonable to suggest that on average house
builders gain more advantage than institutions from developing sites close
to sources of employment, existing residential areas and services. This is
because the costs of accessibility for the average institution are small
relative to the cost of the large areas of land required. By contrast the costs
of accessibility for the average household are higher relative to the cost
of the comparatively small areas of land a house requires. This situation
will reflect itself in the rents that these two users are prepared to pay for

sites at varying distances from the built-up area. For simplicity these bid rents may be represented as straight lines in Figure 3–1 (A). The house builder (h) is prepared to pay high rents for accessible sites but relatively low rents for sites farther away. On the other hand, institutions (i), for which the decline in accessibility is generally not such a significant disadvantage, have a bid-rent curve with a more gradual slope away from the edge of the built-up area. If these relationships remain fixed the result in the landscape is a zone of residential land surrounded by a zone of institutions.

Thus far one is not diverging significantly from the tenets of urban-rent theory, except in its application to the particular case of institutional land use. However, the findings of research on building cycles would suggest that these bid-rent relationships should not be assumed to remain fixed over time because of the considerable cyclical variations in the overall housing output.[13] It seems probable that institutions are on average more resilient than house builders in the face of the general shortage of capital usually associated with a housing slump, especially if they are backed by government finance. Since land comprises a larger proportion of the initial costs per unit area of establishing an institutional use than of creating a housing estate, a relatively small fall in land prices causes a significant reduction in the overall costs of establishing an average institution on a site. Thus, assuming that the social demand for many types of institutions remains undiminished, the depressed land prices associated with a housing slump provide an opportunity for institutions to acquire sites that might otherwise have fallen to the house builder. In bid-rent terms, during a housing boom the relationships in Figure 3–1 (A) are likely to obtain, but during a housing slump the relationships on Figure 3–1 (B) are more likely. With the onset of a housing slump the housing curve has slid down the rent axis so that, except at the edge of the built-up area, it is entirely below the institutional curve which has slid down the rent axis much less. Since it is assumed that for both uses costs of accessibility remain a constant proportion of total costs, the gradients remain as before.

The bid-rent curves shown in Figure 3–1 are averages in two senses. They are averages of a large number of individually unique curves for each institution and house builder, and they are averages of a large number of detailed shifts within housing booms and slumps. For this reason and others, such as imperfect knowledge of the market and non-economic behaviour, it is realistic to speak, not in deterministic terms, but of the relative probabilities of new institutions and housing locating at various distances from the edge of the built-up area.

It is possible to derive from Figure 3–1 the expected variations in the proportion of new institutional and new housing development with increasing distance from the edge of the built-up area. Figure 3–2 shows these

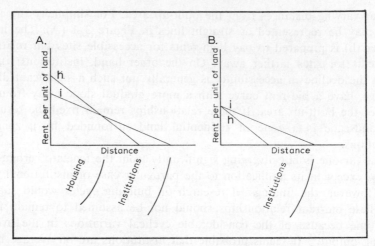

Figure 3-1   Hypothetical bid-rent curves and resultant landscapes
(A) During a housing boom
(B) During a housing slump

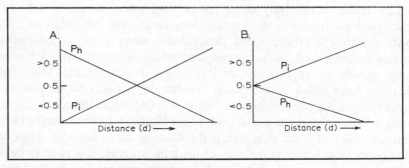

Figure 3-2   Hypothetical variations in the relative proportions of new
institutional and new housing development with distance from the edge of
the built-up area
(A) During a housing boom
(B) During a housing slump

for housing-boom and housing-slump periods respectively. It has been drawn on the assumption that the ratio of new institutional to new housing sitings is related to the differences between the rents or prices that the two uses are prepared to offer for sites. This postulated outcome has significant implications for the land-use composition of extensions to the urban area. Housing-boom periods will be characterized by the acquisition of sites adjacent to the built-up area for new housing construction. Few institutions will be able to compete for these adjacent sites and any new institutional development is likely to occupy more distant sites which are as yet of sub-marginal utility to the house builder. By contrast, housing-slump periods will be characterized by a contraction in the demand for sites by house builders and there will be a much greater probability of development of the more accessible sites by institutions which are now in a position to bid higher prices than the house builders.

Let us now assume that periods of boom and slump conditions are of sufficient length for the postulated proportions of housing and institutions to be reflected in considerable numbers of actual sitings. It has to be appreciated that neither in boom nor in slump periods can the edge of the built-up area be regarded as static. Institutions originally located at some distance from the edge of the built-up area, on what were sub-marginal sites for the house builder, may be surrounded by new residential development by the end of a housing boom. Thus we must envisage a situation in which, by the end of a boom period, a zone of housing will have been added to the built-up area, but scattered beyond it and sometimes lying within it will be the sites of institutions. During a housing slump, while the house builder is largely inactive, institutions will develop the majority of the most accessible sites which, added to what were outlying institutional sites created during the previous housing-boom period, will form a zone with a strongly institutional character. Repeated cycles of booms and slumps are likely to result in a series of alternating zones characterized by different proportions of institutions and housing.

It is extremely difficult to establish whether the actual process of site selection by house builders and by institutions conforms at all to such a model, since it is virtually impossible to establish the rents or prices that potential users are prepared to offer for sites even if land is publicly auctioned. What we can do is see whether the locations of actual institutions and housing areas are such that they could be explained by our postulated mechanism.

A Test of the Model in North-West Glasgow

The data available for Glasgow[14] have made it a suitable area for testing the model in so far as this is possible. Generally in keeping with trends for Britain as a whole, the building output in Glasgow in the past century comprised four approximately 20–30 year cycles, each made up of a boom and a slump period (Figure 3–3). The prime question is whether the location of new institutions and housing in Glasgow in these periods conformed to the postulated patterns in terms of distance from the edge of the built-up area. Attention was confined to the north-west quarter of Glasgow, since outward growth here was known to have been predominantly residential and institutional. The complications afforded by other uses, which in this

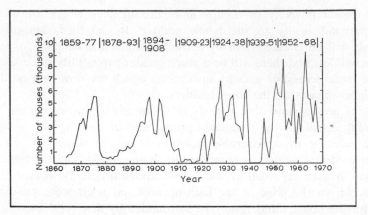

Figure 3–3   Number of houses authorized by the Dean of Guild Court
to be built in Glasgow, 1864–1968

case comprised only 15 per cent of new development at the urban fringe,
were thereby minimized. For the purposes of the test, data were compiled
for two boom periods (1840–58 and 1894–1908) and two slump periods
(1878–93 and 1909–23). Information was also assembled for a fifth period
(1859–77), which comprised both a housing slump and boom. Figure 3–4
shows the actual variations in the proportion of new institutions and new
housing in relation to distance from the edge of the built-up area for the
five periods, compared with schematic curves. If the hypothesis is correct,
the ratio of institutions to housing should increase with distance from the
edge of the built-up area. The schematic curves are in effect regression lines,
any deviation from which may be regarded as unexplained by the
hypothesis.

In general the shape of the ratio curves conformed to the hypothetical
pattern, but much of the value of the comparison is in highlighting the
limitations of such a crude model. For example, during the predominantly
boom period of 1840–58, the ability of institutions to develop sites close to
the built-up area was greater than might have been expected, with marked
positive residuals at approximately 2·5 km. This can partly be explained
by the strong social constraints exercised by the Corporation of Glasgow
in developing as open spaces land which Corporation documents reveal
should on purely economic grounds have been developed for housing. In
1878–93 the housing proportion actually increased slightly at approximately
4·5 km – a trend not explicable in terms of our postulated bid-rent curves.
In other respects the curve conformed to the expected pattern for a slump
period and, except at the immediate edge of the built-up area, institutional
development was predominant.

In Figure 3–5 new development in each period is expressed as a percentage of the land available for development in each distance zone. Here

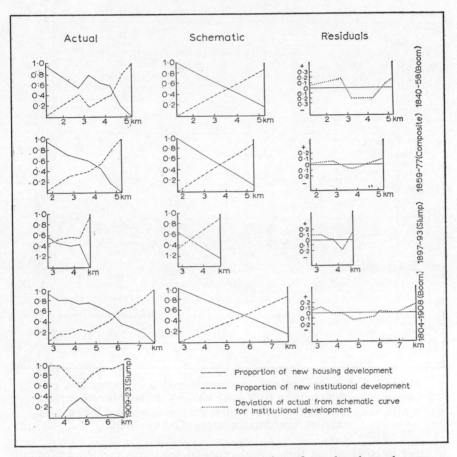

Figure 3–4 Actual and schematic proportion of new housing and new institutional development in north-west Glasgow during five time periods related to distance from the city centre; the actual proportions are the running means of three distance zones of 0·5 km width

the concentration of development on the immediate edge of the built-up area during housing slumps and its more widely-dispersed character during periods in which housing-boom conditions largely prevailed is apparent. The composite character of the 1859–77 period is particularly evident in the intermediate character of its institutional curve. The marked diminution in housing development during slump periods compared with sustained, or even increased institutional development is a pattern consistent with the postulated changes in the relative abilities of the two uses to compete for sites.

In Figure 3–6 the curves of the percentage of available land converted to the two uses during the five periods are superimposed in order to see

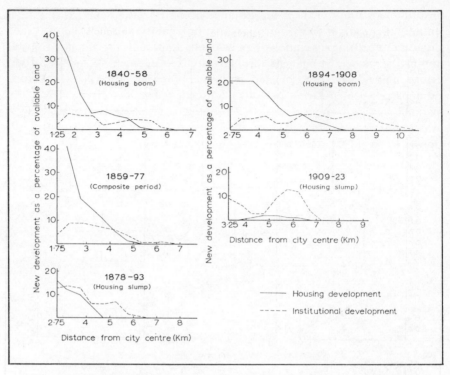

Figure 3–5 New housing and new institutional development, as a percentage of available land, in north-west Glasgow during five time periods related to distance from the city centre, the percentages are the running means of three distance zones of 0·5 km width

whether in combination these developmental sequences created an overall pattern consistent with our model. In general the pattern does suggest that, where outward development was already completed by 1923, the landscape had taken up a form approximating to the one hypothesized and showed signs of doing so in those areas where development was nearing completion. But it is significant that there were three instead of the hypothetical two periods contributing to the inner institutional zone shown in Figure 3–6. Evidently the postulated synchronization between building-cycle phase and land-use development may be considerably distorted in the real world. Furthermore, the deviation of the real-world curves from an expected pattern derived from rent-distance relationships suggests a systematic inadequacy in the model, since some of these deviations were in fixed locations over time and did not move outward as development moved outward. The model assumes that each locational decision is independent of preceding decisions, whereas, in reality, once a particular use has been located, it will tend to attract or repel subsequent bidders for nearby sites. The high occurrence of

institutional sitings at the 3 km distance in the 1909–23 period was almost
entirely the result of new or ancillary institutional development taking place
adjacent to existing institutions – an evidently important process not allowed
for in the model. Permanent residuals at fixed distances from the urban
fringe might also be associated with the presence of physical features,
administrative boundaries and other antecedent features arranged roughly
parallel to the distance zones. Yet, although the actual land-use pattern
was constrained by such factors, the cyclical forces we are postulating do
appear to be of fundamental underlying importance.

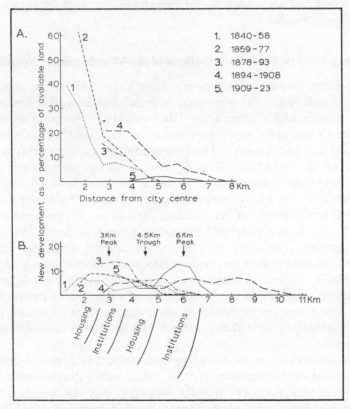

Figure 3–6 New development in north-west Glasgow as a percentage of
available land for five periods superimposed, including approximate
positions of the landscape zones emerging in 1923
(A) Housing development
(B) Institutional development

Many problems concerned with data and with the generality of the
model have been ignored in this brief synopsis, as has the role of other
uses which contribute to the extension of the urban area. In particular, it

should be remembered that the test deals with land-use changes rather than land transactions; measuring by superimposed, geometrical straight-line distance zones that reveal nothing of intra-zonal residuals. Furthermore, for simplicity, the test described was carried out for a predominantly single-nucleus city during periods of relatively compact outward growth. It ignores, too, the appropriateness of the bid-rent/building cycle mechanism for explaining changes that take place once land uses have ceased to be at the urban fringe and have become embedded within the growing built-up area. This last question is of major importance and will be returned to after a consideration of some examples of morphogenetic work on the evolution of past urban fringes.

Past Urban Fringes: Some Contributions of the Morphogenetic Approach

While many urban land economists have laid stress on the importance of new growth, there has also been a good deal of varied research on internal changes within urban areas – the work on the invasion and succession process initiated by sociologists at the University of Chicago is amongst the earliest and best known.[15] The conversion of land from rural to urban use is merely the first of an endless sequence of urban changes which a piece of land experiences. Land colonized by a medieval town fringe may in subsequent centuries have experienced many changes of use, and modifications and replacements of its building structures, in the course of its transformation from a peripheral site to one embedded deeply in a modern urban complex. The study of these changes over time has been an important interest of urban geographers adopting a morphogenetic approach. The emphasis of these developmental studies on urban form rather than on functional organization is undoubtedly partly a matter of the availability of data. The townscape and cartographic evidence from successive periods provide a record of form that is largely lacking in the case of functional organization.

The basic tenet of much morphogenetic work has been the constraint on subsequent developments exerted by initial urban developments. These constitute a 'morphological frame', with reference to which all later developments must take place. Zonal developments, of the kind that characterize the output of the urban-growth model just described, have considerable significance if viewed in this light. Indeed, urban morphological studies have long ago identified the kind of urban-fringe development postulated by our model. In 1936, proceeding on a largely empirical basis, H. Louis recognized, within the urban structure of Berlin, a series of land-use zones related to the institutional zones postulated above and representing former peripheral urban uses encompassed by later accretions to the built-up area and now separating older from younger residential areas.[16] He applied the term '*Stadtrandzone*' to such a zone, later translated by M. R. G. Conzen as 'urban fringe belt'.[17] The land-use composition of such a fringe belt, in addition to including a predominantly institutional component, frequently included country houses and their parks, public utilities, certain types of storage and industry, nurseries and allotment gardens. However, the basically annular form of urban growth is an outcome akin to that postulated by our model.

Work on the evolution of fringe belts provides us with a useful conceptual link between rural-to-urban land-use conversions and internal structural change within the city. Fringe-belt development may be divided into two phases – one of formation and one of modification.[18] The formation phase is essentially one during which rural land is acquired for urban use. The modification phase is that following the inception of the first urban use and the incorporation of that use within the urban area as a whole. An examination of this modification phase thus tells us something of how former fringe uses are changed once they cease to be at the edge of the built-up area.

The conceptual side of such work has been essentially based on inductive inferences from observed patterns of change, rather than from examinations of the underlying decision-making process. It has on these grounds been subjected to criticism by H. Carter[19] and the lack of a sound behavioural basis for inferences is undoubtedly a weakness. On the other hand, the decision-making process is exceedingly time-consuming to study and by its nature only a small fragment of it can ever be unravelled. Under the circumstances, a procedure that infers from morphological change back to underlying causes is often a necessary expedient.

Research on the formation of fringe belts has not been explicit about the roles of building cycles and urban rents, though their importance is implicit in the arguments put forward. The barrier roles of physical and other limitations to urban growth have tended to receive considerable attention and the association of fringe belts with such features is well established. The chronology by which a series of fringe belts has formed around an urban area has been described for several urban areas including the English town of Alnwick, Northumberland[20] and the American city of Madison, Wisconsin.[21] These provide alternative approaches to the one outlined in the first part of this study and merit the careful attention of the student of the morphogenetic approach to urban growth. However, the principal focus of attention here will be the modifications experienced by these fringe belts when they cease to be at the urban fringe – a consideration of the extent to which they survive and continue to exert an influence over the process of internal change experienced by every urban area. This can add a deeper evolutionary dimension to the short time perspective of the rural-to-urban change that has hitherto been our main focus of attention.

The Long-Term Influence of Fringe Belts on the Internal Development of the City

A recurrent view of the evolution of a fringe belt is well expressed by M. R. G. Conzen in his seminal work on Alnwick: 'It is as if such a belt, once established, created its own environment and imposed its own conditions of further development on its area in terms of shape and size of plots, types of land use, and degree of opening-up by streets'.[22] Such perceptions have a charismatic quality that makes them difficult to validate in their present form. One of the current tasks of the urban morphologist is to convert such statements to a testable form and subject them to rigorous testing. In doing so something important in the original will inevitably be lost, but such a procedure does seem necessary in order to provide a sound theoretical basis for future work. There is, however, much to be gained from a review of the qualitative findings of existing work as a basis for assessing the most fruitful lines of future attack in this area of research.

One possible misconception concerning fringe belts that it is necessary to correct is that they simply remain as relics once they become enveloped in the growing urban area. In fact, great changes take place in fringe belts such that within a century of their formation their urban fringe antecedence may only be appreciated by a detailed developmental study. M. R. G. Conzen, in his work on Newcastle upon Tyne,[23] recognized a variety of recurrent developments in the life cycle of the fringe belt that originated on the periphery of the medieval city. These mainly took place after the formation phase, which constituted the periods when many institutions (notably religious houses) and other extensive land uses established and enlarged their sites adjacent to the city wall and eventually constituted an almost continuous low-density zone around the relatively densely built-up residential and commercial core. After this fringe belt had been largely hemmed in by the residential accretions of the first half of the nineteenth century, it experienced changes that were partly contingent upon its changed location. These included the sorting-out of land uses into relatively homogeneous sub-areas, resulting, for example, in the development of an educational/medical complex in its north-western section. In the same complex of sites Conzen identified another recurrent phenomenon, namely that of institutions outgrowing their own sites and expanding into adjacent areas, first converting these from other uses and then later redeveloping them with purpose-built institutional structures. The reverse process – the acquisition of fringe-belt sites for unrelated uses – is particularly associated with increasing commercial land requirements of expanding city centres, and this too has been identified by Conzen on the northern edge of the commercial centre of Newcastle upon Tyne.

M. P. Conzen has recently investigated, for a North American example, the influence of fringe belts on land-use patterns long after they cease to be at the actual fringe of the built-up area.[24] In particular he tested the hypothesis that urban fringe belts are maintained and augmented by their propensity to attract sympathetic land uses despite their loss of fringe location. He suggested that, in the case of Madison, Wisconsin, there was some evidence to support this hypothesis and Figure 3–7 reveals in a generalized manner the extent to which the inner fringe belt of Madison expanded by the addition of new plots and kindred land uses long after it had ceased to be at the edge of the built-up area. Most fringe institutions are, of course, added to peripheral sites (the outer fringe belt in Figure 3–7), but there is also a strong tendency for fringe-belt land within the built-up area to be augmented.

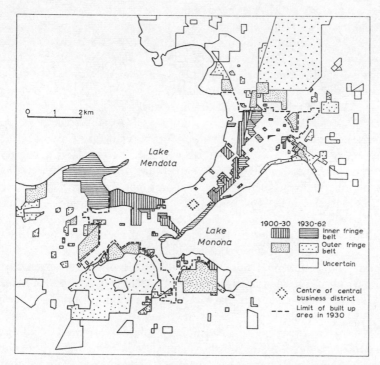

Figure 3–7   The fringe belts of Madison, Wisconsin (after Conzen [1968])

It has been suggested in several studies, including one of the whole Tyneside conurbation,[25] that many of the characteristics of fringe belts are generally recurrent in urban areas. It is necessary, however, to stress that, even if general processes are at work, considerable differences in the outcome inevitably result from variations in the timing of events. For example, major social and economic developments often vary considerably in their timing from one region to another. Such differences are inevitably reflected in the spatial pattern of urban growth and internal development.

In Tyneside, Edwardian fringe belts emerged as a recurrent feature generally distinctive in time and space from medieval fringe belts. In Berlin, Louis recognized a Renaissance fringe belt quite separate from medieval and relatively recent fringe-belt developments, and a Renaissance fringe belt is also present in Copenhagen. A series of relatively distinctive fringe belts is commonplace in the cities of north-west Europe. In southern Europe, major

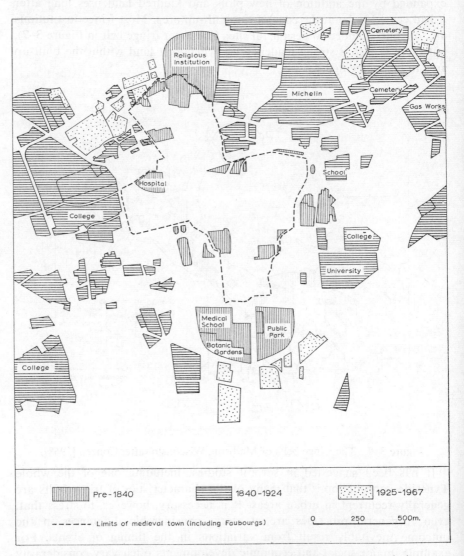

Figure 3–8   The inner fringe belt of Clermont-Ferrand; the uses and plots shown are those in 1967; beyond the medieval limits most of the areas left blank are post-1924 residential accretions

differences of social and economic history, in particular a marked time-lag in the onset of the Industrial Revolution, tend to be associated with a different spatial pattern.

Clermont-Ferrand, in south-central France, experienced none of the large-scale pre-modern phases of residential accretions so characteristic of cities in north-west Europe. In 1920 the population was still almost entirely concentrated within the town's medieval confines. Population growth immediately prior to a late and largely post-1918 Industrial Revolution was mostly accommodated by the multi-occupation of dwellings in the old town.[26] The extensive medieval fringe belt, instead of being encompassed by the rapid nineteenth-century residential accretion so characteristic of north-west Europe, remained open for augmentation by later nineteenth-century institutions and related open spaces, which developed in response to growing economic needs and especially the growing social consciousness of the time. This extensive fringe belt, comprising plots of widely differing ages (Figure 3–8[27]), was not closed off until the interwar period when the build-up of population pressure in the old town exploded into a rash of low-density housing encroaching onto large areas of surrounding countryside. Here is a different outcome from that created by a series of growth pulsations during the same period in most British cities. The basic mechanism would appear to be consistent with that suggested for other regions, but the timing is different and as a result the spatial pattern upon which the process of internal structural change is now working has its own distinctive inheritance. Extensive land uses, including many functioning as open spaces, constitute a higher proportion of land close to the city centre than one would expect in cities of comparable size in Britain. Social pressures for the perpetuation of certain fringe-belt uses are thus not as high in the face of competition from the house builder as they might be in cases where the provision of open areas near the city centre is less generous. It is significant that the present general hospital and Michelin sites shown on Figure 3–8 are both likely to be developed for residential use when relinquished by their present users.[28] Such changes could in a sense be regarded as a readjustment in the land-use pattern towards a more 'normal' distribution.

Building Cycles, Bid Rents and the Modification of Fringe Belts: Some Evidence from Individual Site Chronologies

Having provided examples from several studies of changes experienced by urban fringe belts over time, it is now essential to make an attempt to relate these changes back to our original thesis concerning the underlying importance of the building cycle/bid-rent mechanism. If this mechanism is so fundamental in its impact on the form of outward growth, its significance for the process of internal change is hardly likely to cease abruptly.

Yet the whole idea that fringe belts are perpetuated long after they cease to be at the urban fringe appears contrary to our hypothesis concerning the relative abilities of institutions and house builders to bid for sites.

In order to consider this matter, it is useful to refer to some of the findings of a study of a part of the Glasgow test area used earlier. This sample area of approximately 15 km² includes a hundred fringe-belt plots whose history to date spans several building cycles and for which it has been possible, by recourse to a diversity of sources,[29] to reconstruct the major morphological developments.

The tendency for fringe-belt uses to gain or lose land varies over time. This variation should reflect the changing ability of fringe-belt uses to compete with residential uses for sites. Let us consider for this area the extent to which this variation is related to both the building cycle and the passage of the main wave of house-building activity.

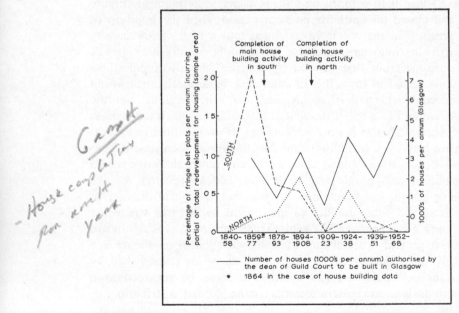

Figure 3–9   The redevelopment of fringe-belt plots for housing as a sample area in north-west Glasgow related to the building cycle, 1840–1968

The southern part of the area experienced the peak of its housing development during the late 1860s and 1870s; the northern part during the late nineteenth and early twentieth centuries. The developments in each area are therefore recorded separately in Figures 3–9 and 3–10.[30] Figure 3–9 shows, for approximately the last hundred years, the percentage of fringe-belt plots per annum experiencing partial or total redevelopment for housing, compared with the number of houses built per annum in Glasgow as a whole during the main housing booms and slumps. As the conversion of rural land to housing reached its peak so did the redevelopment of fringe-belt plots for housing. Thereafter resurgences of decreasing magnitude were associated with succeeding booms until such redevelopments reached a negligible level.

Figure 3–10 shows for the same period the percentage of fringe-belt plots experiencing expansion – that is, enlarging their site areas at the expense of adjacent uses. Preceding the passage of the main house-building activity, expansion was high in the north[31] – almost entirely into land still not in urban use. During, and immediately following, the passage of the main house-building activity, there was little expansion either in the north or in the south, but expansion was renewed within a few decades – this second phase of expansion has, of course, taken place largely at the expense of other urban uses. Any influence of the building cycle on fringe-belt expansion appears to have been subsidiary to these longer term trends relating to the passage of the main house-building activity.

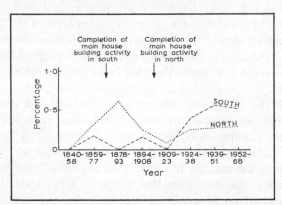

Figure 3–10   Percentage of fringe-belt plots per annum incurring expansion in a sample area in north-west Glasgow, 1840–1968

In general, the study of this small area suggests that some fringe-belt uses, notably country houses and their parks, were vulnerable to the house builder during, and immediately following, the passage of the main phase of building activity. Subsequently there may have been a period of equilibrium during which few fringe-belt sites were acquired by house builders and there was relatively little expansion of fringe-belt uses into adjoining areas. After this, and sometimes without such a period intervening, there was an increasing likelihood of fringe-belt uses actually expanding their site areas at the expense of adjacent housing areas by converting or redeveloping these.

Various explanations may be offered for this important change in the relative abilities of fringe-belt and residential uses to compete for sites. Institutions may be subsidized on social grounds: publicly-owned open spaces, of which there are a number in both parts of the sample area, would appear to come in this category. However, this would not seem to explain the case of various privately-financed institutions, that not only held their ground, but in some cases expanded their sites, by successfully competing in the market for adjacent sites during both the 1939–51 housing slump and the preceding and subsequent booms. It seems reasonable to conclude that many of these institutions were prepared to pay a higher price for their locations and those adjacent to them than were house builders and purchasers for residential use. To understand this one must appreciate that most of these institutions had greatly changed their character since they originally acquired fringe-belt sites. Both capital investment on their sites, and physical movements to and from them, would have greatly increased since they became established there. In turn such changes are likely to have had an effect on the value of adjacent sites for residential use. The ramifications of these changes are in detail complex, but in general terms we can envisage the characteristic well-established and expanding institution on an internal site as having an individual bid-rent curve with a local peak exceeding, for its own and nearby sites only, the generally higher level of the housing curve within the built-up area. This localized deformation in the bid-rent curve may have emerged after a period of equilibrium during which the rent bid by the institution did not markedly differ from the general level for housing at that location.

It is not only the institutions that are long-established on their sites which are able to compete successfully for internal sites. It is not unusual for fringe-belt plots coming on to the market to be acquired by a second or even a third institution. At present it is only possible to offer plausible suggestions as to the reasons for such a succession of similar uses on the same site. Some of the site assets that accrue to a particular land use over time can be passed on to a related use inheriting the site. For example, the buildings will often be more readily adaptable by a related use and the immediate environment is more likely to be compatible with it than with a radically different use. Such factors will tend to increase the prices that related uses are prepared to pay for the site and reduce those that other uses are prepared to pay, creating local deformations in the pattern of bid-rent curves. In addition 'zoning' stipulations in development plans often seek to maintain less densely built-up spaces within the urban area and this may lead, in effect, to the subsidization of non-economic locations out of public funds. The net result of these and other factors is that, in addition to the large majority of institutions that occupy fringe sites during the outward growth process, a small but significant number of institutions do move to internal sites. When this happens the subsequent institutional use tends to be more intensive than its predecessor.

The tendency for there to be sequences of related types of uses on the same site, and for sites near the city centre to become outgrown and increasingly vulnerable to competition from commercial uses, is associated with the gradual displacement of some institutions to sites progressively farther from the city centre. An incomplete record of institutional movements in Glasgow since 1800 reveals several institutions (including the university and botanic gardens) which have occupied three successive fringe belts, each progressively farther from the city centre. More than twenty have made one outward shift. Thus the membership of institutional fringe belts in a large and rapidly growing city is subject to considerable change over time. Furthermore, considerable changes are incurred by the numerous institutions that retain the same site over long periods of time, including the progressive building up of their site areas and, during certain periods, the replacement of some, or even all, of their building stock. In the sample area studied in north-west Glasgow, most fringe-belt sites have experienced major building replacements and some have experienced two complete redevelopments. By way of contrast, the surrounding housing areas, which were developed on average nearly seventy years ago in the north and nearly a hundred years ago in the south, have still to experience any large-scale redevelopment, except where encroached upon by large institutions.

Conclusion: The Need for the Integration of Concepts

This time perspective on the urban fringe has been limited to a relatively few themes. It is not in any sense a comprehensive treatment of developmental approaches to the morphology of the urban fringe. It is not even an adequate summary of work on the fringe-belt concept, which has considerably more facets to it than have been considered here. By severely restricting the aspects considered, it has been possible to elucidate some of the problems of data and method on a limited research front and to indicate in summary form some of the findings and deficiencies of current research. On the other hand, an attempt has been made to take a somewhat broader view than that offered by a single research persuasion and to illustrate the advantages that can accrue from the cross-fertilization of schools of thought.

Empirical work of the type described in this study is some of the most time-consuming in geographical research, since a considerable variety of sources must generally be resorted to in order to compile the requisite data. It is unlikely that satisfactory data will ever be assembled to enable many of the hypotheses considered here to be validated for a range of city types and culture areas. We are never likely to have data for more than a small sample of cities of doubtful representativeness. It is particularly necessary, in a field in which the testing of hypotheses must rest on such a slender empirical base, that wherever possible propositions should be examined to

3

see whether they are logically deducible from higher-order propositions derived from related approaches and fields.

The tension that exists between functional and morphological studies has often been iterated but seldom rationally explored. The two approaches are essentially searching for different types of explanation[32] and this should be explicitly recognized. On the other hand, there is no reason at all why these two important kinds of research should proceed in a mutually exclusive fashion. The limited reconciliation between urban-rent theory and morphogenesis attempted here suggests that a profitable integration can be effected. However, such syntheses would seem to require a more flexible attitude towards research in urban geography than has been prevalent in the last few decades.[33]

Further Reading

The basic concepts and terminology of work on urban fringe belts are discussed in – M. R. G. Conzen, 'Alnwick, Northumberland. a study in town-plan analysis', *Trans. Inst. Br. Geogr.* **27** (1960); M. R. G. Conzen, 'The plan analysis of an English city centre', in K. Norborg (ed.), *Proceedings of the I.G.U. Symposium in Urban Geography, 1960* (Lund, 1962), 383–414; and J. W. R. Whitehand, 'Fringe belts: a neglected aspect of urban geography', *Trans. Inst. Br. Geogr.* **41** (1967) 223–33.

The simplest introduction to bid-rent theory is W. Alonso, 'A theory of the urban land market', *Pap. Reg. Sci. Ass.* **6** (1960), 149–57.

A thorough and clear analysis of building cycles in Britain from a mainly economic perspective is – J. Parry Lewis, *Building Cycles and Britain's Growth* (London, 1965).

Two contrasting studies of the relationship between building cycles and urban form are – J. S. Adams, 'Residential structure of midwestern cities', *Ann. Ass. Amer. Geogr.* **60** (1970), 37–62; and J. W. R. Whitehand, 'Building cycles and the spatial pattern of urban growth', *Trans. Inst. Br. Geogr.* **56** (1972).

References

1. W. Alonso, 'A theory of the urban land market', *Pap. Reg. Sci. Ass.* **6** (1960), 149–57.
2. R. F. Muth, 'Economic change and rural-urban land conversions', *Econometrica* **29** (1961), 1–23.
3. R. L. Morrill, 'Expansion of the urban fringe: a simulation experiment', *Pap. Reg. Sci. Ass.* **15** (1965), 185–99.
4. For example F. S. Chapin and S. F. Weiss, *Factors Influencing Land Development,* An Urban Studies Research Monograph (Institute for Research in Social Science, University of North Carolina and United States Bureau of Public Roads, 1962). For a study laying particular emphasis on the various types of decisions involved in land development, see E. J. Kaiser and S. F. Weiss, 'Public policy and the residential development process', *J. Amer. Inst. Planners* **36** (1970), 30–7.
5. H. J. Dyos, *Victorian Suburb; a Study of the Growth of Camberwell* (Leicester, 1961); R. C. W. Cox, 'Some aspects of the urban development of Croydon, 1870–1940' (Unpublished M.A. thesis, University of Leicester, Leicester, 1966).

6. M. J. Mortimore, 'Landownership and urban growth in Bradford and its environs in the West Riding Conurbation, 1850–1950', *Trans. Inst. Br. Geogr.* **46** (1969), 99–113.
7. J. D. Fellman, 'Pre-building growth patterns of Chicago', *Ann. Ass. Amer. Geogr.* **47** (1957), 59–82.
8. M. R. G. Conzen, 'Alnwick, Northumberland; a study in town-plan analysis', *Trans. Inst. Br. Geogr.* **27** (1960).
9. J. Parry Lewis, *Building Cycles and Britain's Growth* (London, 1965).
10. For a more detailed account of this model the reader is referred to J. W. R. Whitehand, 'Building cycles and the spatial pattern of urban growth', *Trans. Inst. Br. Geogr.* **56** (1972), which forms the basis for the summary presented here.
11. W. Alonso, *Location and Land Use: Toward a General Theory of Land Rent* (Cambridge, Mass., 1964), 16.
12. The main categories of land use defined here as institutional are educational, medical, military, central and local government, research, recreational (including clubs and open spaces) and religious (including burial grounds).
13. Parry Lewis, *op. cit.*
14. These were largely compiled from collections of local histories, maps and plans in Baillie's Institution and the Mitchell Library, Glasgow.
15. See, for example, R. D. McKenzie, 'The ecological approach to the study of the human community', in R. E. Park, E. W. Burgess and R. D. McKenzie (eds.), *The City* (Chicago, 1925), 75.
16. H. Louis, 'Die geographische Gliederung von Gross-Berlin', *Länderkund-Liche Forschung*, Krebs-Festschrift (Stuttgart, 1936), 146–71.
17. M. R. G. Conzen, *op cit.*, 58.
18. J. W. R. Whitehand, 'Fringe belts: a neglected aspect of urban geography', *Trans. Inst. Br. Geogr.* **41** (1967), 230–2.
19. H. Carter, 'A decision-making approach to town plan analysis: a case study of Llandudno', in H. Carter and W. K. D. Davies (eds.), *Urban Essays: Studies in the Geography of Wales* (London, 1970), 66.
20. M. R. G. Conzen, *op. cit.*
21. M. P. Conzen, 'Fringe location land uses: relict patterns in Madison, Wisconsin', unpublished paper presented to the *Association of American Geographers, West Lakes Division, 19th Annual Meeting, Madison, Wisconsin* (18 October 1968).
22. M. R. G. Conzen, *op. cit.* 81.
23. M. R. G. Conzen, 'The plan analysis of an English city centre', in K. Norborg (ed.), *Proceedings of the IGU Symposium in Urban Geography, Lund 1960* (Lund, 1962), 383–414.
24. M. P. Conzen, *op. cit.*
25. J. W. R. Whitehand, *op. cit.* (1967).
26. Ph Arbos, *Étude de Géographie Urbaine: Clermont Ferrand* (Clermont-Ferrand, 1930), 151–2.
27. Based largely on unpublished plans and maps supplied by M. Robert Léon, Town Engineer, Clermont-Ferrand, and a land-use survey of central Clermont-Ferrand undertaken by the Department of Geography, University of Glasgow in 1967. The limits of the medieval town are based on a bird's eye view of Clermont-Ferrand in 1574 by Francoise Fuzier, published in Belle-Forest, *La Cosmographie Universelle, Tout le 'Monde* (Paris, 1575) and reproduced in Ph. Arbos, *op. cit.*, 39.

28. Information provided by the Town Engineer, Clermont-Ferrand.
29. Apart from the histories and records of individual institutions these included Dean of Guild Records, the Register of Sasines, Post Office and Kelly's Directories, Valuation Rolls and Ordnance Survey and other maps and plans.
30. These data and those cited at the end of this section are drawn from a detailed developmental study of part of north-west Glasgow that is currently being carried out by the author. A consideration of this material in a more developed theoretical context is provided in J. W. R. Whitehand, 'Urban-rent theory, time series and morphogenesis: an example of eclecticism in geographical research', *Area* **4** (1972), 213–22.
31. The site chronologies do not start early enough to allow comment for the south.
32. D. Harvey, *Explanation in Geography* (London, 1969), 407–46.
33. A great many individuals and organizations kindly made available source materials and helped in the lengthy task of abstracting the data used in this study. In particular the author is indebted to the following: M. Robert Léon, Ingénieur de la Ville, Clermont-Ferrand; Mr G. Black, Keeper of the Registers of Scotland; Mr J. A. Fisher of the Mitchell Library, Glasgow; Mr H. K. Mackay of Baillie's Institution, Glasgow; Mr I. D. B. Fleming of Montgomerie Fleming, Fyfe, Maclean & Co; Mr John Armour, Master of Works and City Engineer, Corporation of Glasgow; Dr J. B. Caird, Dr A. S. Morris, Mr W. J. Fairweather and Mr A. McCorkindale of the University of Glasgow, Dr M. P. Conzen kindly gave permission for the reproduction of Figure 3–7. The illustrations were drawn by Miss J. G. M. Boulton in the Department of Geography, University of Birmingham.

CHAPTER 4

The Planning Framework for Modern Urban Growth: The Example of Great Britain

ALAN STRACHAN

The Emergence of Town and Country Planning

In most countries the introduction of a policy of planned urban growth has had to await the emergence of a climate of public feeling favourably inclined towards some curtailment of the freedom of the individual. This has usually occurred when a rapidly developing country has experienced greatly accelerated rates of urban growth, which have resulted in an appearance of ill-conceived high-density housing areas adjacent to and intermingled with factories and other features of industrial expansion. The countries in the forefront of the industrial revolution were the ones which displayed the worst features of this process.

Even when the social and health hazards of this form of development were recognized, little was done in most countries to avert the process or to improve the urban environment. Repeated outbreaks of various diseases did, however, result in attempts being made to remedy the situation. In Great Britain these initially took the form of Health Acts, supported later by the introduction of bye-law housing. Although these measures did not radically change things, they constituted the first step towards solving the problem. The next move in this direction was taken in 1909 when the insanitary conditions prevalent in the industrial towns of the Victorian era prompted the government to pass an Act aimed at improving the standard of housing in suburban areas. Although this allowed local authorities for the first time to plan housing schemes on a large scale, and was an important move towards the provision of controls on the standard and form of city expansion, it was not a very comprehensive policy and only a few local authorities – those faced with severe urban development problems – took advantage of the provisions laid down by it.[1]

The First World War brought all house building to a halt. At the same time changes in social and economic standards, including younger marriage, smaller families, higher wages and more flexible forms of public and private transport, had been gathering momentum in Britain since the end of the nineteenth century. Together these changes resulted in a large backlog of demand for houses, each with its own garden. The relatively large amounts of land necessary for this type of development were only available on the outskirts of towns, and consequently residential expansion was rapid in these areas. Such private developments enabled many upper- and middle-class families to move out of the congested urban areas to live in semi-rural surroundings. The more affluent members of the community, however, became increasingly aware that less fortunate families, whose aspirations for better living conditions were similar to their own, could never hope to escape from the squalor of the more central residential districts without help. In response to this growing social conscience and to the immediate need to overcome the housing shortage resulting from the war, the Housing and Town Planning Act of 1919 introduced the principle of state subsidies to help local authorities build houses, and since then council-house estates have played an important role in urban development in Britain. As was the case with private house construction, the large amounts of land required for council housing – especially after the implementation of the Tudor-Walters Report on the standards for working-class housing[2] – necessitated the choice of peripheral locations for these estates and the provision of public transport from them to the town centre, where most of their residents still worked.

Thus municipal estates grew alongside the private suburbs on the periphery of towns. This was a period when the city 'exploded': suburbs were added to the edges of the older built-up areas, ribbon development was strung out along the main roads and small towns and villages near larger urban centres were swallowed up or invaded as dormitory suburbs.

It has been calculated[3] that between 1935 and 1951 the population of Great Britain increased by approximately 3·32 million and the estimated urban area by 0·91 million acres (364,000 ha), whereas between 1951 and 1970 the population increased by 5·27 million and the urban area by only 0·83 million acres (332,000 ha). The urban acreage per thousand people rose from 69·3 (27·7 ha) in 1935 to 90·4 (36·1 ha) in 1970, but only one-third of this increase has taken place since 1951. The annual net loss of agricultural land to urban uses between 1922 and 1970 is given in Table 4–1.

As the pressures encouraging urban expansion increased, several attempts were made to combat them. The Town and Country Planning Act of 1932 broadened the scope of previous legislation to make almost all classes of land subject to planning control, but even this measure was inadequate. Under the 1932 Act it took approximately three years to secure final approval for any one scheme and, in addition, since parliament had to ratify each plan, the entire procedure had to be repeated before any alterations or adjustments could be made to one. Consequently changes were rarely attempted. During the period between the submission and approval of a plan the land under consideration was placed under interim development control, which meant that the local authority could demand the removal of any developments completed during this time if they were not in accordance with the approved scheme.

Table 4–1. Annual average net losses of agricultural land to urban, industrial and recreational uses, Great Britain, 1922–70 ('000 acres)

5–year period	England and Wales	Scotland	Great Britain
1922/3 – 1925/6	22·5	N.A.	N.A.
1926/7 – 1930/1	52·2	N.A.	N.A.
1931/2 – 1935/6	62·0	N.A.	N.A.
Total urban land 1935	2,800·0	360·0	3,160·0
1936/7 – 1940/1	38·2		
1941/2 – 1945/6	25·6		
1945/6 – 1950/1	39·5		
Total urban land 1950/1	3,600·0	470·0	4,070·0
1951/2 – 1955/6	40·8	3·7	44·5
1956/7 – 1960/1	35·1	3·8	38·9
1961/2 – 1965/6	37·9	5·3	43·2
1965/6 – 1969/70	41·5[a]	6·6[a]	48·1[a]
Total urban land 1970	4,330·0[a]	570·0[a]	4,900·0[a]

Source: *A Century of Agricultural Statistics, Great Britain, 1866–1966* (HMSO, London, 1968)

[a] 1970 provisional figures.

This procedure did not have the desired deterrent effect on property developers since the Act did no more than allow the zoning of land for a particular use and, provided that the developer conformed with the land use prescribed for the area, there was little that the local authority could do about the character of buildings erected. Because of the time and effort involved in getting a plan accepted by parliament, local authorities tended to follow trends already apparent within their administrative area and in most cases exaggerated the amount of land required by any particular use. For example in the half of England and Wales that fell within draft planning schemes in 1937, enough land to house 350 million people had been zoned for residential purposes.[4] Another Act which partly failed to achieve its desired effect because of similar technical loopholes was the Restriction of Ribbon Development Act, 1935, by which it was hoped that the sprawl of land uses out along main routeways would be controlled.

The basic underlying reason for the ineffectiveness of planning legislation at this time was the relative newness of the problem and the pace of development. The government, embarking on a radically new approach towards the restrictions that could be imposed on the use of land belonging to private individuals, was unable to cope with the rapidity with which new patterns of development were emerging.

As might be expected, the problems arising from the expansion of urban areas reached their most acute form around London, the largest city. It was therefore not surprising that most of the measures later introduced into planning legislation for the country as a whole had their origin in the numerous committees and reports commissioned during the interwar period to investigate and counter the alarming urban expansion being experienced around the metropolis. The size and complexity of the problems encountered involved a new approach, since in this instance any plans or decisions necessitated the co-operation of several local authorities. Until this time there had been considerable antagonism on the part of local authorities towards any proposals that would take power away from the locally-elected authority – a feeling that had been engendered by the lack of any previous experience of joint action and the fear that the well-being of a district could be adversely effected by decisions taken by a body not directly answerable to the local electorate. Faced with the situation that was rapidly developing around London, however, a committee made up of the representatives of the local authorities within twenty-five miles of the city centre was convened in 1927. This committee had as its technical adviser Raymond Unwin and the two reports submitted, 1929 and 1933,[5] and the two interim reports published in 1931[6] owe much to his guiding influence. In these reports, Unwin highlighted the dangers of the extremely rapid growth taking place around London at that time and went on to outline his proposals to counteract them. These included the expansion of many of the towns located on the periphery of the conurbation and the creation of a 'green girdle' between them and London, which would serve the dual purpose of preserving the separate identities of the settlements in the region and providing much needed recreational facilities and open space for the poorly-endowed urban area. Unfortunately these proposals were made at a time of severe economic crisis and nothing was done to implement them immediately. Nevertheless, they formed the basis for future planning in the region.

Although the economic crisis stopped effective action along the lines suggested by Unwin, it had little effect on the growth of London. As building rates increased, fears that Unwin's prediction of uncontrolled sprawl and engulfment would be realized led London County Council, in 1935, to take the initiative towards the creation of a green belt around the city. They put forward a scheme 'to provide a reserve supply of public open spaces and recreational areas and to establish a green belt or girdle of open space lands, not necessarily continuous, but as readily accessible from the completely urbanized area of London as practicable'.[7] To help ensure the success of the scheme the council undertook to provide grants towards the cost of land purchased or preserved by local authorities for inclusion within the green belt. The response to this appeal was very prompt and within a few months plans had been drawn up to preserve some 18,000 acres (7,200 ha).[8] Doubts about the permanence of agreements between authorities and landowners to preserve land were soon raised, and it was decided to introduce a bill into parliament. When passed in 1938 the Green Belt (London and Home Counties) Act stipulated that no preserved land could be sold or built upon without the consent of the responsible minister and the contributing authorities.

The Barlow Report,[9] published in 1940, was an important policy document in that the commissioners, in answering their brief to investigate the distribution of industrial population, advocated that the distribution of industry should be guided to meet the requirements of the country as a whole and that many of the problems of congestion could be overcome by the development of garden cities and satellite towns around major urban centres. Perhaps the commission's most important recommendation was that there was an urgent need for a central authority to deal with the problems arising from changes in population distribution and that none of the existing governmental departments could be expected to deal with these matters satisfactorily.

The Second World War temporarily solved many of the problems investigated by the commission, but it became increasingly apparent that wartime disruption and devastation was creating an urgent need for some authority to oversee postwar reconstruction. Two committees were set up in 1941 to consider this problem – the Uthwatt Committee on Compensation and Betterment[10] and the Scott Committee on Land Utilization in Rural Areas.[11]

The wide terms of reference given to these commissions reflected a new approach on the part of the government and it was on a wave of newly-acquired confidence that the postwar town and country planning policy was conceived. Gone were the days of local regulatory measures. In the future planning was to be positive and on a regional, if not national, scale.

The Introduction of a Comprehensive Town Planning Policy

The chief aims of planning policy since the war have been to restrict the further growth of the great conurbations, to deal with overspill, to control the location of industry, to guide new developments into the right places, to redevelop areas of obsolete developments, to provide adequate road communications, to protect the character of the countryside and to preserve good agricultural land. These aims were embodied in the Town and

Country Planning Act, 1947, and at the same time all previous planning legislation was repealed. Under the new Act planning power was placed in the hands of the County Councils and County Boroughs, of which there were 147 in England and Wales; in Scotland responsibility was given to County Councils, Large Burgh Councils and certain Small Burgh Councils. Many planners regarded this as a lost opportunity since these administrative units were not necessarily amenable to regional planning, but when it is remembered that they replaced nearly 2,000 district councils it must be regarded as a major step forward. The 1947 Act did much to reduce the variations in the standard of planning that are inevitable when there is a great disparity in both the size and spending power of local authorities, and it helped to overcome the possible undesirable effects of petty jealousies and rivalries. The Act, however, did require the County Councils to meet with the smaller district councils to discuss planning proposals, so that they could benefit from local knowledge, before submitting their plans to the Ministry.

Under the Act local planning authorities were required to carry out surveys of their areas and to prepare Development Plans which were to be submitted to the appropriate ministers (Minister of Housing and Local Government in England and Wales, Secretary of State for Scotland in Scotland) for approval or amendment after consideration of all relevant objections. Approval was dependent on the Development Plan fitting in with those for adjacent areas and with desired planning objectives. A Development Plan showed and programmed the local authority's proposals for the use and future development of the land in its area, and explained its policies. It consisted of two volumes, one of maps and the other a written statement.

Development Plans provided the broad basis for the exercise of planning control, and planning permission was usually only given when the proposed development accorded with the Plan. Important cases in which the local planning authority wished to give a permission at variance with the Plan were notified to the minister. Development Plans were reviewed every five years and could be varied in the meanwhile with the minister's agreement. The Plan was, therefore, a relatively flexible instrument which took account of changing circumstances.

The interwar period of urban expansion had created extensive tentacles of urban development along the roads reaching out into the surrounding countryside, leaving between them wedges of agricultural land, which were subjected to all the problems and pressures associated with city expansion. This led, in many instances, to the inefficient use of the nation's land resource – a limited resource – with both urban and agricultural areas on the fringes of cities being unable to function as effective units. The Development Plan stated the use to which every parcel of land, no matter how large or small, was to be put, and was therefore a suitable instrument for rationalizing this problem. Further building out along the main roads was felt to be undesirable and a policy of containment was the preferred alternative. Through the medium of the Development Plan the future growth of the urban area was guided into the wedges of agricultural land left between existing built-up areas, a process which was greatly facilitated by the very rapid increase in every kind of road transport. As a result, cities were given a much more cohesive form, which would allow utilities and services to be provided more economically than previously. Advantage was also taken of the opportunity to provide industrial estates and much needed recreational facilities. The ability to specify the use to which a very small plot of land could be put contrasted very markedly with the ponderous and broad zoning policies of the prewar period. A similar streamlining was achieved in the creation of what were in effect green belts, although formal approval had not been given for the creation of such areas, except around London. Under the 1947 Act a local planning authority no longer needed to buy land or come to uncertain agreements with landowners in order to preserve open space; permission could simply be refused for development. In this way very tight controls were placed on the areal expansion of cities and, in the case of any strong representation by landowners about loss of value of their property, compensation could be claimed from the government. Equally, if the land appreciated in value as a result of the planning process 40 per cent of the development value could be claimed on behalf of the nation through the betterment levy.[12] Compensation and betterment provisions have always proven difficult to administer.

The powers given to the local planning authority did not cease with the compilation of the Development Plan, since this was merely designed to act as a guide to potential land developers. Each developer still had to submit detailed plans of his proposal, specifying building character and layout. It was then the planning authority's responsibility to decide whether or not these accorded with their desired objectives for the area, before final permission for development was given. For detailed planning of this kind to be successful it had to be enforceable; this had been one of the major defects of the interwar legislation. Under the 1947 Act, development undertaken without permission was not an offence in itself, but ignoring an 'Enforcement Notice' issued by a planning authority was. These were issued against an individual who had carried out a development without permission, or in breach of conditions laid down when permission had been granted, and stated the grounds on which the local authority had decided that the development was not in the interests of good planning. There was, however, some protection for a developer who was served with an Enforcement Notice. This involved a full investigation of the circumstances and, in the last resort, appeals to the minister ultimately responsible and to the courts. The outcome of such investigations resulted in financial penalties being imposed on the unsuccessful party.

Green Belts and Urban Growth

The most difficult postwar planning problem in Britain has been to accommodate the rapidly increasing urban population while preventing the continued outward growth of existing cities or the haphazard spread of development over the countryside. The policy adopted to stop uncontrolled growth has been to define green belts of open country around the great cities and to locate new developments in compact areas beyond them. Under the 1947 Act, a metropolitan green belt had been defined around London in the various County Development Plans. In 1955, the Ministry of Housing issued a circular which advocated an even stronger policy towards the creation of green belts. This has been one of the most controversial decisions adopted since the introduction of planning legislation.

The circular stated that the only really effective way to control urban expansion was through the formal designation of clearly-defined green belts, and that local authorities should consider the need for these in the areas under their control.[13] It was recommended that green belts be created in order to check the growth of large built-up areas such as London and Birmingham, to prevent neighbouring towns from merging into one another as was happening with Nottingham and Derby, and to preserve the special character of a town as in the case of Oxford and Cambridge. It was recommended that, wherever possible, a green belt should be wide enough to preserve an appreciable rural zone around the built-up area concerned. As with the original green belt around London, except under very special circumstances approval was not to be given for new buildings (or changes in the use of buildings) except for appropriate uses like agriculture, sport, cemeteries and institutions standing in extensive grounds. In addition, only a limited amount of 'infilling' or 'rounding-off' was to be allowed in towns and villages located within the green belt, and no land uses were to be permitted if they were likely to increase local demand for labour, and consequently housing. Close co-operation between adjacent authorities was also advocated.

A second circular, issued in 1957,[14] set out in detail the procedure that was to be followed in arriving at the boundaries of a green belt and of any settlements included within it. The form of the sketch plan to be submitted to the minister for his approval was also specified. This document introduced amenity as another feature which should be taken into account in the delimitation of the area and, with reference to rural areas in general, it stressed that the implementation of strict controls close to urban areas should not lead to permission being given for development elsewhere, if this would

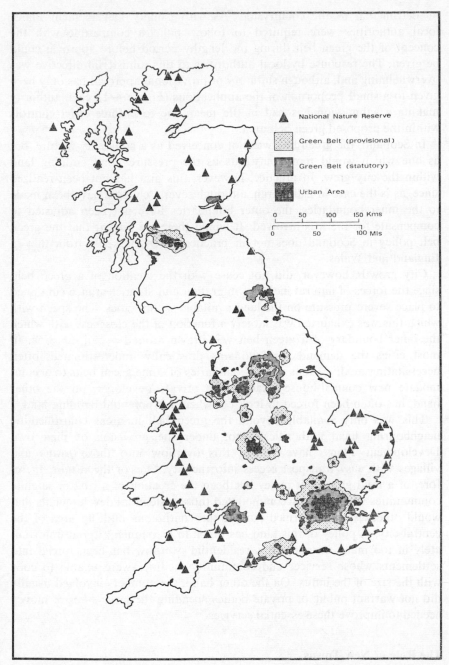

Figure 4-1   Green belts and national nature reserves, Great Britain, 1972

be detrimental to the countryside. As with County Development Plans, local authorities were required to follow policies compatible with the concept of the green belt during the lengthy period before approval could be given. The response by local authorities to this ministerial directive was overwhelming and, although statutory or provisional approval has only been given to a small proportion of the applications (Figure 4–1), each authority making a submission has had in the meantime to enforce strict controls within the proposed green belt area.

In Scotland, the green belt was not conceived as a stationary feature, but as one which would move outwards as the pressure upon building land within the city grew. In practice, however, this aim has not been realized since, as is the case in Edinburgh, although several changes have been made to the inner boundaries, the outer boundaries have not been adjusted to compensate for the loss involved. It would therefore appear that the green belt policy in Scotland does not in practice differ markedly from that in England and Wales.

City growth, however, did not cease with the creation of a green belt, since the forces of natural increase, migration and slum clearance continued to place severe pressure on the land available within cities. The speed with which this was exhausted was largely a function of the closeness with which the inner boundary of a green belt was drawn around a built-up area. In most cities the demand for land was drastically underestimated, often necessitating modifications of the boundaries of some green belts to accommodate new council-house estates. The private developer, on the other hand, has often been forced to look elsewhere for potential building land.[15]

This was only available beyond the green belt in areas controlled by neighbouring local authorities, who, under the provision of their own Development Plans, have guided this overflow into those towns and villages with easy transport access into the city. One of the results, therefore, of a rigid green-belt policy has been the creation of a ring of satellite communities which have accommodated those residential developments that would otherwise have formed part of the continuous built-up area of the central city. A policy of this kind has much to recommend it, but unfortunately in too many instances this residential overflow has been forced into settlements whose services and community facilities were unable to cope with the size of the influx. On the other hand, the numbers involved usually did not warrant public or private bodies spending the large sums of money needed to improve these essential services.

The Role of New Towns

The rapid expansion of London during the twentieth century prompted far-sighted individuals to adopt Ebenezer Howard's concept of the garden city as the best solution to the problems facing the metropolis and the region around it. Suggestions for the creation of new towns were put forward by several planners during the early twentieth century, but it was not until Raymond Unwin, in 1933,[16] and later Patrick Abercrombie, in his 1944 Greater London Plan,[17] had indicated the seriousness of the situation that it was officially recognized that dramatic action was essential if irreparable damage was not to be done to the London Region. The government showed its determination to deal with the problem by introducing the New Towns Act in 1946, and through this agency a further method of controlling the haphazard outward spread of existing cities was established.

It was only natural that London should receive immediate attention, and in the course of four years eight new towns were designated in the region to accommodate more than 400,000 people from London. The new towns procedure was also used where housing for large numbers of workers in particular industries was urgently required but could not be provided quickly enough under existing local arrangements. Accordingly the new town of Peterlee (1948) was designated mainly in connection with coal mining, Corby (1950) with steel production, and Newton Aycliffe (1947) and Cwmbran (1949) with diverse light industries. In Scotland, East Kilbride (1947) was designated to take population from overcrowded areas in Glasgow and northern Lanarkshire, while Cumbernauld (1955) will ultimately receive at least 80 per cent. of its population from Glasgow. Originally Glenrothes (1947) was intended to cater for miners moving into an expanding coalfield, but the town is now playing an increasingly important part in the accommodation of Glasgow's overspill population.

Between 1961 and 1966 a second phase of new town designation was undertaken, aimed at fostering regional development while drawing off surplus population from large urban complexes. Eight new towns were designated during this period, two for Merseyside, two for the West Midlands, one for Tyneside, two for central Scotland and one for central Wales. In the most recent phase new towns have been conceived as 'partnership towns' with the development being undertaken by a development corporation and the local authority working in consort. To date Peterborough, Northampton and Warrington are of this type.

The amounts of development planned for the new towns and the cities from which the majority of their populations was expected to be drawn are given on Table 4–2. From this it can be seen that the concept of a new town has changed over the years, with the more recent designations being major regional developments based on well-established, though not necessarily thriving, old towns, not on almost virgin sites as was the case with most of the earlier designations.

The policy behind the establishment of new towns was not to create extensive dormitory suburbs within reach of major employment foci, but

Table 4–2. Progress of the first twenty-seven new towns, Great Britain, 1971

Name of town	Date of designa- tion	Associated urban area (distance from new town in km)	Population		
			Original	1971 total (based on preliminary report of Census)	Ultimate total[a]
Phase 1					
Basildon	1949	London (48)	25,000	77,154	103,600
Bracknell	1949	London (45)	9,100	70,465	155,000
Crawley	1947	London (48)	5,140	33,953	60,000
Harlow	1947	London (40)	4,500	57,791	90,000
Hatfield	1948	London (33)	8,500	25,211	25,000
Hemel Hempstead	1947	London (47)	21,000	69,966	65,000
Stevenage	1946	London (50)	6,700	66,975	80,000
Welwyn Garden City	1948	London (35)	18,500	40,369	42,000
Aycliffe	1947	No one centre	60	20,190	40,000
Peterlee	1948	No one centre	200	21,836	28,000
Corby	1950	No one centre	15,700	47,713	65,000
Cwmbran	1949	Cardiff (29)	12,000	40,999	50,000
East Kilbride	1947	Glasgow (14)	2,400	63,943	82,500
Cumbernauld	1955	Glasgow (24)	3,000	31,728	70,000
Glenrothes	1948	No one centre	1,100	27,573	55,000
Phase II					
Milton-Keynes	1967	London (80)	44,000	46,473	200,000
Redditch	1964	Birmingham (22)	32,000	37,648	70,000
Runcorn	1964	Liverpool (22)	30,000	35,646	73,500
Skelmersdale	1961	Liverpool (21)	10,000	26,681	75,800
Telford	1963	Birmingham (48)	70,000	75,579	225,000
Washington	1964	Newcastle (9)	20,000	25,269	65,000
Newton	1967	No one centre	5,700	5,621	11,000
Livingston	1962	No one centre	2,000	13,636	70,000
Irvine	1966	Glasgow (42)	34,600	42,256	100,000
Phase III					
Northampton	1968	London (106)	131,120	133,594	230,000
Peterborough	1967	London (133)	82,910	87,493	187,890
Warrington	1968	Manchester	116,740	119,534	202,000

Source: *Town and Country Planning* (1971), 46–7; *Census 1971, Preliminary Report* (London, 1971)
[a] Population size at which planned migration will stop.

to build balanced communities which would provide the majority of their residents with employment, services, community facilities and recreation areas. Attempts, not always successful, have been made to match the rate of development of residential areas with the availability of industrial employment. The new town corporations are permitted to build factories for renting as well as to lease sites on which firms can build their own premises. Firms moving to new towns can also benefit from considerable tax concessions to facilitate the move and to cushion the settling-in period. Having given them these powers to attract industries, it was also essential to ensure that the new town authorities were able to provide homes for the labour force. The development corporations have built 83 per cent and private builders 7 per cent of the housing, with increasing emphasis now being placed on owner-occupancy in an attempt to give the community structure a better balance and to lower the housing bill of the development corporations. A characteristic of the new towns, which adds emphasis to the dilemma that would otherwise have confronted the older urban areas, is the overwhelming demand for homes with gardens. This has resulted in most new towns being developed at a relatively low density, although there are exceptions, such as Cumbernauld. Attempts have been made, however, by the development corporations to provide a wide variety of house types and densities to meet all possible tastes and to create an urban structure which is as varied and as interesting to live in as possible.

The selection of sites for new towns is based on an investigation undertaken by government officers in order to assess the pressures caused by urban development in a particular area. If it is found that these are severe and their relief is in the national interest, the most suitable location for a new town will be chosen. Once this has been done a public enquiry will be held to allow any dissenting opinions to be voiced and any reasons for alterations brought to the attention of the government minister responsible. Once a town has been designated, a development corporation is given the task of planning it and of acquiring the necessary land, either by voluntary agreement or compulsory purchase. This body has very wide powers to hold, manage and dispose of land and provide the services and facilities required by the incoming population. The development corporations do not, however, constitute local authorities: education, local health services, sewage disposal and the supply of electricity, water and gas are the responsibility of the various local statutory authorities within whose areas the new town is located. This situation may lead to a certain amount of conflict, especially, over the allocation of capital expenditure, but through consultation a considerable measure of flexibility and co-operation has been brought about. The very large amount of capital required to build a new town has necessitated the implementation of special arrangements. The development corporations are wholly financed by the central government, from whom sums of money can be borrowed over a sixty-year period at the current rate of interest. How the new 'partnership' towns will be financed is not yet apparent. As the new towns in England and Wales near completion their assets are handed over to the Commission for New Towns, set up in 1959 as a national holding and management agency. The commission does not extend to Scotland. So far Crawley, Hemel Hempstead, Hatfield and Welwyn Garden City have been transferred to this agency.

The fact that there is still considerable concern about the expansion around major urban areas in Great Britain, despite the designation of twenty-eight new towns, is ample proof of the immensity of the problem. The contribution of the new towns is difficult to assess since what would have happened had they not been authorized is not known. However, around London alone they had absorbed a total of 372,390 people by 1970 and over the country as a whole this figure was 708,958. If each of these towns achieves its projected population total they will have housed some 1,777,760 people.

There can be little doubt that of all the planning measures introduced since the last war the New Towns Act is the most spectacular, and, of even greater significance, it has been one of the most successful. Many questions have been raised about the building priorities of the various development corporations in the provision of service facilities, but their role as 'relief valves' for congested urban areas has been of crucial importance. In addition they have provided planners and architects with an unparalleled opportunity to design cities almost from scratch, enabling them to employ concepts in keeping with the requirements of modern society, without having to face the insuperable problems associated with an established and outdated urban fabric.

The Policy of Expanded Towns

Another form of overspill policy was introduced to England and Wales in the Town Development Act, 1952, and to Scotland in the Housing and Town Development (Scotland) Act, 1957. These acts had the expressed aim of encouraging the expansion of existing towns in country districts and in this way helping to relieve some of the pressures of urban congestion. It was felt that there were many small towns which could be considerably 'expanded' without serious loss to themselves and sometimes with tangible gains in viability. The basic concept was that two local authorities would mutually agree to transfer population from one to another, the exchange being largely implemented by the provision of houses for families on the sending authority's waiting list. This policy was slow to come into operation because of financial and organizational difficulties in making satisfactory agreements, but by 1970 more than twenty towns were being expanded under agreements to receive overspill from London, Birmingham and other West-Midland towns, Manchester, Merseyside and Bristol (see Table 4-3 on p. 68).

To facilitate these exchanges the government undertook to provide a 50 per cent. grant towards the cost of the main sewerage, sewage works and waterworks required by the proposed development, while the local authority from which the people were moving was required to make some contribution to the receiving authority for each family involved. The families selected to take part in this scheme were either from those waiting to be housed by the sending city authority or the family of any person able to find employment; this formed the major stumbling block to the widespread acceptance of this scheme, since no local authority would be willing to contemplate an influx of people if there was no work available for them, especially county authorities where the expansion of employment tended to be limited. Consequently it has become increasingly common for overspill schemes to have as their cornerstone the movement of industries along with people. Only on this basis were most county authorities prepared to entertain the idea of accepting city families, and it was with this possibility in mind that many of them contacted urban authorities with a view to entering agreements. For example the city of Birmingham has attempted to negotiate with more than a hundred authorities all over the country. There was, however, no way in which a city could force industries to move out, apart from pointing out the advantages of a new factory. In fact, experience has shown that very few firms were willing to leave familiar surroundings for some remote town. Even after agreements were reached and employment provided, many problems have emerged. In particular the change in the way of life required by city families moving into a new social environment is often too great, resulting in a high turnover of population as families return to the city. The problem has been quite considerable in Scotland, where overspill families from Glasgow have been unable to adjust to small town life, leaving the city council with the task of finding new families willing to move out. Experience in England has been much more favourable, but, as can be seen in Table 4-3, the policy has not been an unqualified success.

The government has sought to relieve the congestion of urban areas by the movement of population and industry to completely separate new settlements, and to extensions of new towns. Since 1949, when work began on Stevenage, some 247,000 dwellings[18] have been built as a result of these policies. During the same period, some six million dwellings[19] were built in Great Britain and thus the contribution of new and expanding towns represents only a very small proportion (4 per cent) of total house construction. It is, however, a measure of the extent of direct government influence in urban control. The magnitude of

Table 4–3. Town development schemes, England and Wales, 1970

Overspill Authority	Number of schemes	Dwellings built as part of these schemes		Number of firms relocated 1970
		Total to be built	completed 1970	
London	31	89,453	41,445	623
Newcastle upon Tyne	2	10,517	1,513	44
Liverpool	4	18,526	4,970	54
Manchester	4	8,514	1,361	21
Salford	1	4,518	4,518	—
Birmingham	15	21,222	7,458	142
Wolverhampton	4	4,527	4,327	11
Bristol	4	2,278	2,278	—
Wasall	2	444	444	—
Total	67	159,999	68,341	895

Source: *Town and Country Planning,* **39** (1971), 48–51

the problem of urban congestion which the new town and the expanded town policies were designed to relieve is far from static, due to such factors as the high birth rates in the conurbations, the continued growth of manufacturing and service industries in major centres, rates of slum clearance and changing residential density standards in redevelopment areas. The replacement of obsolescent buildings and the displacement of population from existing urban areas is likely to continue in the foreseeable future, which means that there will be a need for planned developments, either of the type already in existence or in some modified form.[20]

The Preservation of the Countryside

The planning measures already outlined have had a direct bearing on urban expansion around all urban areas in Great Britain, but there are several other land-use controls which in specific instances have been of great importance for urban growth. These had as their basis the growing awareness of the importance of areas of great natural beauty and of historical or scientific value, and the need to preserve them from destruction or disruption. This prompted the government in 1949 to pass The National Parks and Access to the Countryside Act. This established a National Parks Commission, now the Countryside Commission, an advisory body whose role was to advise both the minister and local authorities on questions affecting the beauty of the countryside. Its main executive function was to carry out studies of the entire country and then to select, after consultation with the relevant local authorities, those areas most suited to being designated National Parks (Figure 4–2). Within the boundaries of these parks ordinary rural life, rural industry and afforestation were to continue normally. All executive functions were to be the responsibility of local authorities, and the Act provided that where a park was in the area of more than one authority a joint planning board or a joint advisory committee should be established. In this way it was hoped that the natural beauty of the area would not be damaged unnecessarily. Urban development in these areas was strictly prohibited. The policy effectively removed some 19,890 square kilometres from possible urban development (Table 4–4).

Table 4–4. Major restraints on development, England and Wales (figures compiled for dates between 1966 and 1970, '000 acres)

	England and Wales	Scotland	Great Britain
I Urban area 1970	4,330	565	4,895
II Policy restraints – conservation areas			
1. National Parks	3,366	1,530	4,896
2. Forest Parks	167	262	429
3. National Nature Reserves	77	147	224
4. Areas of Outstanding Natural Beauty	2,746	—	2,746
5. Green belts – statutory	1,211	333	3,989
– non statutory	2,445		
6. Areas of high landscape value	5,974	5,160	11,134
7. Deduction for overlap of the areas included in section II	–583	N.A.	N.A.
Total conservation areas	15,403	7,432	23,418

Source: Department of the Environment, *Long Term Population Distribution in Great Britain – A Study* (HMSO, London, 1971), Table 4.7, 55

In general the National Parks and urban areas are well separated. Only the Peak District Park is contiguous with an urban area, that of the city of Sheffield, forming a massive barrier to its expansion in a southerly and westerly direction. This park is also co-terminous with the green belts of Halifax, Stoke-on-Trent and Manchester.

The 1949 Act also gave the National Parks Commission the power to designate Areas of Outstanding Natural Beauty. These areas are subject to the same restrictions as those imposed on the National Parks, but in this

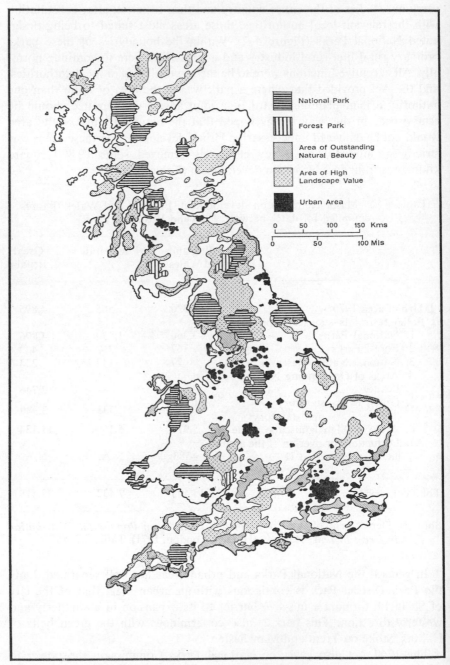

Figure 4–2   Areas designated to preserve the rural landscape,
Great Britain, 1972

instance they are the sole responsibility of the local planning authority. Once designated they are eligible for the same improvement grants as the National Parks, but, despite this, local authorities have been disappointingly slow to take advantage of the scheme. This is mainly due to a short-sighted attitude towards the recreational needs of both local people and holiday-makers, and to the fact that a certain amount of additional finance must be forthcoming from the local authority itself. At the present time some twenty-five Areas of Outstanding Natural Beauty have been designated, many of which have an important influence on urban expansion. Probably the most significant of these are the Chilterns, the Surrey Hills and the Kent Downs, which together form an area of 2,080 square kilometres of protected land around London (see Figure 4–2 p. 70). Some of this land lies within the designated green belt, but for the most part it constitutes an additional barrier to urban expansion over the district beyond the belt. In other parts of the country Areas of Outstanding Natural Beauty impose restraints on the growth of smaller towns and villages in, for example, Devon, Cornwall and the Isle of Wight.

In some parts of the country land has been designated as having high or great landscape value (see Table 4–4 and Figure 4–2, pp. 69 and 70). These are areas which have been set aside because of their local scenic importance; within them development control is strictly applied, permission usually being granted only for activities and building-types which will blend in with the landscape. Although not subject to such stringent controls as Areas of Outstanding Natural Beauty, they do cover a far greater area of the country and have been significant positive contributions to urban planning in such areas as northern Lancashire, the Malvern Hills and Salisbury Plain.

Restrictions can also be imposed in several other ways, but in most instances these do not constitute extensive barriers, since the amount of land involved is not necessarily great. The Nature Conservancy is important in this respect through nature reserves owned or managed by it, as is the case on the western outskirts of Nottingham, and through the preservation of sites of special scientific interest. A similar role is fulfilled by the National Trust under whose auspices places of historical importance are acquired and maintained for the benefit of the general public, a scheme that involves anything from a single house to extensive estates. This body has recently become involved in a project which has brought quite large amounts of land under its control. This is 'Enterprise Neptune', which is aimed at extending the protection of the National Trust over as much of the remaining unspoiled coastline of the country as is possible. At the present time it has acquired nearly 10 per cent. of the 4,800 kilometre coastline of England and Wales, and in doing so have curtailed the possibility of the coastwise expansion of numerous small towns. In most instances, however, the coastline adjacent to the larger urban areas has been so extensively despoiled that the National Trust does not consider it worth purchasing, leaving the local authorities to deal with it under Development Plan proposals or as part of green belts.

Ministry of Defence property covers some 2,700 square kilometres, or 2 per cent of the land area of England and Wales. Partial access to some of this land for recreational purposes has been allowed, mainly the 96 hectares of 'Defence Land' located within the National Parks and Areas of Outstanding Natural Beauty, but in general this land is 'sterilized' as far as urban development is concerned, as for example in the Aldershot area west of London.

The New Approach to Planning

The Town and Country Planning Act, 1947, has been amended on several occasions in an attempt to eradicate the shortcomings that were encountered in its operation and to improve and extend its influence. It has become increasingly apparent, however, that the Development Plan, the core of this legislation, offered too inflexible an instrument to deal with conditions of continual change. It had become essentially a map of land allocation, and as such lacked the necessary framework to enable transport (a factor of ever-increasing importance) and land-use planning to be integrated in a realistic way, and the social and economic implications of the proposals to be readily established. In an attempt to overcome these problems the 1968 Town and Country Planning Act was introduced. In this new legislation the Development Plan is not the very precise land-use document required under the earlier acts. The 1968 Act requires local authorities to submit a Structure Plan to the minister for his approval. This document is to be a written statement of broad strategy, with the effects of that strategy discussed in relation to various alternatives. It must contain a consideration of the local authority's proposals in relation to those made by neighbouring areas and of any other matters that the minister may have asked to be studied. The basic idea behind the new concept is that the Structure Plan should not only consider the economic planning and development of the authority's area as a whole in the light of current national policies, but should also take into account the resources available for its implementation. Attention is to be focused on major trends and objectives, and the mass of detail which was previously included within the Development Plan is no longer requested, since it is now felt that the inclusion of information of this type is a hindrance to continual reassessment of the plans. The Structure Plan will make special note of areas where major changes are proposed. The 'Action Areas' thus defined will also be considered on a broad scale, and their nature indicated but not identified exactly. This will allow the previous inflexible situation, with local planning authorities specifying rigidly detailed proposals in the Development Plan, to be avoided in the future.

After the approval of a Structure Plan the provisions of the Act make the details of design and implementation the responsibility of the local authorities; 'local plans', not requiring ministerial approval, are to be the instruments through which this will be achieved. Another innovation is that detailed plans must be included only for developments undertaken by the local authority itself, whereas private developments need only be broadly outlined. The main reason for this differentiation is that those people likely to be affected by the large local authority schemes should know precisely what is planned.

The 1947 Act required a local authority to carry out a survey as part of its Development Plan submission, thereby placing the entire onus for the work on its own staff. The type of survey envisaged in the 1968 Act, however, will necessitate the use of highly-skilled personnel, and many local authorities are not in a position to recruit this type of staff. In order that the standard of expertise needed will be available, the new Act states only that a local authority has a duty to institute a survey of the appropriate type, thereby allowing outside consultants to be brought in to carry out some of the more complex aspects of producing a Structure Plan. Authorities have also been grouped together, such as Leicester City and Leicester County, to form much larger units for which planning proposals can be made.

It will be some time before the 1968 Act becomes fully operational and only then can its effectiveness be assessed, but in its attempt to reserve local decisions for the relevant local authority, with the central government being responsible for the broader regional pattern, it would appear to be a significant improvement on previous legislation.

Conclusion

The effects of planning legislation briefly outlined on the previous pages can be clearly seen in the study of any city in Great Britain. The clear break between urban and rural areas, the absence of highway blight, the preservation of the agricultural area from indiscriminate house construction, the multiplicity of peripheral parks and recreational facilities and the importance placed on the conservation of amenity, places of interest and the landscape can all be directly attributed to the willingness of the British people to forgo the rights of the individual and give both local and national government the power to plan the future uses of the country's land resources.

The containment of urban sprawl is a problem which has been faced with varying degrees of success in most developed countries, but the political philosophy prevailing in a particular state has played an important part in influencing the policies and procedures used to achieve an improvement in the quality of the environment.

In the Soviet Union[21] and some Eastern European countries, for example, physical and economic planning are closely integrated and directly under central government control; the redistribution of population, inherent in attempts to control urban sprawl and redevelop central areas, has therefore been relatively easy to achieve. On the other hand, in the United States[22] the central government's role in planning is much weaker and responsibility is mainly in the hands of a multiplicity of incorporated districts. The ability of these areas to implement planning control is largely dependent on their size, and their effectiveness in doing so is dependent on co-operation with adjacent authorities. The latter rarely occurs, because of the competition between them to acquire development which will increase their tax revenue. This system has not proved to be an effective means of controlling the form and character of urban expansion. Highway blight, residential sprawl and the wasteful use of land around cities are commonplace features in the United States. Only comprehensive planning controls will remove these and bring about an overall improvement in the environment. Experience in the Netherlands[23] has shown that such a system can be operated in a democracy. Here the comprehensiveness of the planning machinery is unrivalled, a reflection of the pressing need, in the face of increasing population and urbanization, to maximize the use made of limited land area.

Many other countries will shortly have to consider the implementation of more stringent planning controls as the problems of urban growth make themselves manifest. At present urbanization is proceeding at an ever-increasing rate in most countries of the world. In Great Britain this process has been operating for longer than most. For this reason the evolving experience of this country may prove a useful guide – or perhaps a warning – to those nations that are not yet totally committed to any particular strategy for land-use allocation in the context of large-scale suburban growth.

Further Reading

The Genesis of Modern British Town Planning (London, 1954).
The Genesis of Modern British Town Planning (London, 1954).
    Some current policies are examined in J. B. Cullingworth, *Town and Country Planning in England and Wales* (London, 1970).
    The origins of London's green belt and recent developments in this area are analysed in D. Thomas, *London's Green Belt* (London, 1970).

References

1. W. Thomson, 'The Ruislip-Northwood and Ruislip Manor joint town planning scheme', *Town Planning Review* **4** (1914–15), 133–44.
2. *Report of the Committee on Question of Building Construction in Connection with the Provision of Dwellings for the Working Classes* (HMSO, London, 1918).
3. Department of the Environment, *Long Term Population Distribution in Great Britain: A Study* (HMSO, London, 1971).
4. J. B. Cullingworth, *Town and Country Planning in England and Wales* (London, 1970).
5. Greater London Regional Planning Committee, *First Report* (London, 1929); *Second Report* (London, 1933).
6. Greater London Regional Planning Committee, *Interim Report on Open Spaces* (London 1931); *Interim Report on Decentralisation* (London, 1931).
7. Mrs. H. Dalton, 'The Green Belt around London', *Journal of the London Society* **225** (1939), 70.
8. Ministry of Housing and Local Government, *The Green Belts* (HMSO, London, 1962), and D. Thomas, *London's Green Belt* (London, 1970).
9. *Report of the Royal Commission on the Distribution of the Industrial Population* (HMSO, London, 1940).
10. Ministry of Works and Planning, *Expert Committee on Compensation and Betterment Final Report* (HMSO, London, 1942).
11. Ministry of Works and Planning, *Committee on Land Utilization in Rural Areas, Report* (HMSO, London, 1942).
12. Central Office of Information, *Town and Country Planning in Britain* (HMSO, London, 1968), and P. Hall, *Land Values* (London, 1965).
13. Ministry of Housing and Local Government, *Green Belts,* Circular No. 42/55 (HMSO, London, 1955).
14. Ministry of Housing and Local Government, *Green Belts,* Circular No. 50/57 (HMSO, London, 1957).
15. W. Lean, *Economics and Land Use Policy, Urban and Regional* (London, 1969), 151.
16. Greater London Regional Planning Committee, *Second Report* (London, 1933).
17. P. Abercrombie, *Greater London Plann 1944* (HMSO, London, 1945).
18. Department of the Environment, *Long Term Population Distribution in Great Britain: A Study* (HMSO, London, 1971).
19. *Ibid.,* 67.
20. For example, as envisaged in *Tayside: Potential for Development* (HMSO, Edinburgh, 1970).
21. A. Zhuravlyev and M. B. Fyedorov, 'The micro-district and new living conditions', *Soviet Review* **2**, No. 4 (1961), 37–40.
22. A. B. Gallion and S. Eisner, *The Urban Pattern* (New York, 1963).
23. Netherlands Government Physical Planning Service, *Annual Reports (Jaarverslag)* (The Hague).

CHAPTER 5

The Metropolitan Village: Spatial and Social Processes in Discontinuous Suburbs

JOHN CONNELL

An unequivocal definition of the residential suburb has never been formulated, yet two elements are clear: first, a measure of separation from the central city and, second, a degree of dependence upon it.

Separation is partly physical. Scharer, too formalistically, recognized an area as suburban only if open spaces completely surround the clusters of houses.[1] In his view suburbs are areas of relatively low housing density; many were formerly parts of rural areas engulfed by residential expansion. In North America these suburban residential areas also tend to remain politically distinct, and there this political distinctness provides a useful additional criterion for a suburb; there, too, the reconstruction of city boundaries lags behind functional change.

Dependence is less obviously spatial. Primarily residential suburbs have no major sources of employment; indeed, their social status may be a measure of their lack of local employment. They are therefore dependent on the central city for this[2] and also for certain services, especially transport and public utilities, shopping, entertainment and some administration. Thus a high outgoing journey to work is recorded. A measure of dependence on the central city is the percentage of the workforce travelling to it.

There is also a third, more elusive element: the overall concept or *ethos* of the suburb. Suburbs evoke many emotions, not least in planners and academics. Suburbs are often seen as soulless places where people are bored, lonely and dull; where individuals lack roots and have no sense of belonging to a community, and where relationships are 'window to window' rather than 'face to face'.[3] Yet this view is no longer generally maintained; Berger has shown how there are varieties of American suburb[4] and the emergence of suburban council estates in England has complicated the suburban residential pattern. For those who still retained the view that the social life of the suburb was homogeneous, restricted and narrow, Gans[5] and Donaldson[6] have effectively demonstrated the variety and complexity. Bell adds British fuel to this particular pyre.[7]

Because of the elusive nature of these partial attempts at definition, quantification and comparison are scarcely possible. Physical separation is rarely clear. The earliest suburbs may no longer be thought of as suburban; the inner edge of suburbia has no simple boundary line.[8] Dependence is certainly measurable, but what measures are important? Definitions of suburbs according to the percentage working in the central city produce curious patterns[9] as does a definition according to density of development.[10] Outdated concepts of suburbia are of no use.

A certain minimum size, however, is a useful criterion and one which would allow comparison. Waugh suggests that a community of 6,000 is the minimum size needed to constitute a suburban area, since at that size there will be sufficient local services to justify recognition as a separate entity.[11] The suburb is seen therefore as a particular kind of central place, yet its service function is unimportant and for some areas of less than 6,000 local services exist. In outer metropolitan areas suburban growth has been superimposed on a pre-existing hierarchy of central places, already separate entities and with their own services. Because of the high level of car ownership of the newcomers to these areas, further development of the local services has often been unnecessary.

Especially since the Second World War the growth and development of new and old suburbs have been increasingly constrained by the proliferation of town planning legislation,[12] and the physical expansion of suburbs has been restricted by a series of acts following from the Restriction of Ribbon Development Act of 1935. Subsequently the green belt policy, that so effectively prevented London's further expansion since the war, has been adopted around all major cities to provide a real barrier to growth.[13] Yet in the postwar period, because of the expansion of employment within London, pressure on residential land around the metropolis was maintained, and indeed increased, with two significant results. The first was the rapid rise in urban land values which made redevelopment and infilling worthwhile, thus steadily increasing the residential densities of all city suburbs.[14] The second was the leapfrogging of large-scale development beyond the city boundary to towns and villages beyond, and occasionally within, the green belt, epitomized in the metropolitan region in the rapid expansion of towns such as Guildford and Saffron Walden. The same kind of expansion is visible at Harrogate, north of Leeds; indeed it is found in many small towns round all large cities. In addition, there has been an organized decentralization of residential development from several cities. Again the epitome of this is London, where there are out-county estates beyond the fringes of the conurbation,[15] constructed largely to solve the immediate postwar housing problem. There are also expanded towns, some over 160 km from London, which receive overspill under the 1952 Town Development Act. Finally there is also the ring of eight new towns, up to 50 km from London (Figure 5–1). Elsewhere the problems of residential reconstruction have not necessitated the first two solutions, but the West Yorkshire conurbation is now the only one that has not yet built a new town to ease central housing difficulties. Meanwhile the scale of development has increased as new towns become new cities.[16]

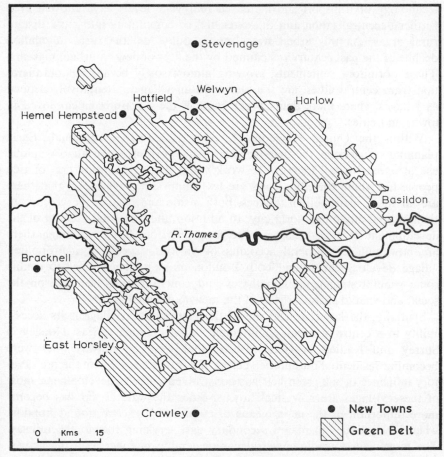

Figure 5–1   Location of East Horsley in relation to London's green belt and new towns

The Metropolitan Village

At a more informal level, but much more ubiquitously, individual households have decentralized from the central cities to the villages within commuting distance, itself increasing, from the centre. Some decentralization
of city centre employment to suburban locations has further encouraged
this process, since more distant villages have become more accessible to
suitable employment. Within the micro-planning framework some villages
have expanded rapidly, others have been allowed infilling only, whilst in
exceptional circumstances and contrary to legislative trends, new villages
have been constructed (of which the only important example is New Ash
Green in Kent),[17] all to cater for a massive demand for accommodation,
preferably located in a semi-rural area. As the most accessible villages have
filled up to the extent that no new housing is allowed, improvements in the
technology of transport and increased real-wage levels have allowed even
further decentralization and the extension of commuting into more distant
rural areas. As this urban wave moves outwards, the rural population
decline of the past century is stemmed by the flow of new ex-urban migrants.
These dormitory settlements, growing almost solely because of outmigration from central cities, are the metropolitan villages,[18] tentatively defined
as villages where more than 20 per cent. of the workforce is employed in
towns and cities.

Within the United Kingdom, London is clearly exceptional. Early
planning restrictions, the massive size of its workforce, the almost unique
use of extensive rail journeys to work[19] and the larger proportion of rich
people for whom travelling costs are less important, have meant that there
are far more metropolitan villages, both inside and outside the green belt,
than around any other world city. In addition, the first good account of the
development of such villages came from Hertfordshire,[20] although there
are now sufficient general accounts of various aspects of metropolitan
village development around both London and provincial cities to enable
some general statements, hypotheses and conclusions to be made on the
social and spatial characteristics of the metropolitan villages.[21]

Spatially, the key characteristic of the metropolitan village is its accessibility to a centre of urban employment. Villages, such as East Horsley in
Surrey and Radlett in Hertfordshire, that were on railway lines were
becoming residential dormitories before the war; except where the preserva-
tory influence of the green belt has constrained postwar development, most
of these villages are now small towns. Since the war the car has become
more important as the main means of commuting, except around London,
where it continues to play a secondary and servicing role to the railway.
The movement towards universal car ownership has increased the accessibility of many hitherto remote villages and enabled residential development
in the interstices between the suburban lines around London and between

the major roads and railways outside other cities. There is little research on preferred maximum journey-to-work times; conventional wisdom suggests a maximum of an hour, yet many rapidly growing villages in more remote parishes of England can only be reached from central cities in almost twice this time. The conventional maximum is clearly unsatisfactory, at least in the case of London. Furthermore, an hour by train or car on different kinds of road and in different traffic conditions results in wide distance variations. Clearly, where the workplace is not in the central city, or the railway line is electrified or the road is a motorway, then a remote village is more easily accessible. The social characteristics of individual villages are closely related to the time required and transport cost for the journey to work; relative inaccessibility is likely to result in a larger number of commuters of higher social class and a greater proportion of established villagers working locally.

Variations in accessibility are not the only constraints on the development of metropolitan villages. There are certain institutional restrictions, such as prevention of any form of residential development in a few villages preserved because of their particular contribution to the rural landscape. Again, restriction on the expansion of sewerage systems is probably a critical restraint on the construction of much new housing, particularly in villages. Yet if new development is prevented there are no restrictions on changes of occupants, as old villagers die or move away. Conceptions of rural life also affect the demand to live in particular kinds of villages; those that are the most picturesquely rural and surrounded by fine countryside are most eagerly sought after. The mining villages, within easy commuting distance of many northern cities, are studiously avoided by the urban commuters and retain their historic social compositions, although the decline of local employment may mean that they become metropolitan villages by default as the workforce is obliged to commute to more distant employment. Spatially the metropolitan villages are distributed in proportion to their accessibility from the central city, modified by particular institutional and social demands.

Metropolitan villages are seen therefore as little more than small, detached portions of suburbia; but there are certain distinctions, since separation is usually distinct and maintained by planning restrictions. The restrictive influence of legislation effectively preserves much of the historical, physical form of the village and prevents large-scale population increases in the foreseeable future. In consequence, house prices rise as the historical village is maintained; the status of village residence, seen even in the continuing desirability of such urban places as Highgate and Dulwich, where estate agents are well aware of the name's emotive value,[22] is seen also in the indiscriminate application of the term 'village' to old village nuclei and to such new settlements as New Ash Green. The absence of

4

industry in almost all metropolitan villages results, to an even greater extent than in suburbs, in the separation of residential and industrial land; villages are comparable with those high-status suburbs that contain no industry. This kind of parallel suggests the value of comparing the social and demographic composition of metropolitan villages with the established suburbs, yet the paucity of information on established suburbs militates against even the most simple comparisons.

In Britain established suburbs which form part of the continuous build-up areas of large cities have attracted surprisingly little serious geographical, economic or sociological attention. Indeed, apparently the only geographical study of a single suburb in the United Kingdom was, in a very real sense, long ago and far away from the mainstream of British life.[23] Subsequently there have been more studies, especially around London, concentrated more specifically on the sociology of suburbia.[24] In North America, where private suburbia is not paralleled by public suburbia, interest in the 'green ghettoes dedicated to the élite and segregated by class and space'[25] has been more concentrated and sustained.[26] Consequently, generalizations derived from existing research are likely to be extremely limited in their applicability within Britain; popular literature describes modern private suburbs as communities in which conformity and homogeneity are unusually concentrated,[27] the implication being that the move from city to suburb initiates certain changes; they are a second 'melting pot'. However, the obverse of this, that incipient change precipitated outward-migration, is at least as plausible. Moreover, in detail, suburban conformity and homogeneity is almost certainly a myth.

The characteristics of North American suburbs that have been cited most frequently[28] are first, that suburbs are more likely to be dormitories; second, that they are quite far away from the workplaces in the central city; third, that they are newer and more modern than the central city and designed for the car rather than the pedestrian; fourth, that they consist of single-family rather than multi-family structures and are therefore less dense; fifth, that their populations are younger, more likely to be married, with higher incomes and white-collar occupations. This is essentially true also of British suburbs with the important exception of those containing local authority estates which may have a high proportion of multi-family structures and tend to be less dependent on the car. The major, if rather sterile, point of debate is still the degree of conformity and homogeneity expected and found in suburbs and, more important, what this means, how significant it is and how it might be measured. There are real social, economic (and political) distinctions between separate suburbs, especially between private and public estates, yet the lack of detailed research prevents any examination of the small-scale variations which certainly exist; there is considerable scope for research on the macro- and micro-ecology of suburbia, yet unless this is closely tied to the operation of the whole urban residential system it is unlikely to be particularly fruitful.

At this stage, therefore, similarities and differences between villages and suburbs are liable to be both qualitative and largely subjective; inter-village comparison is more susceptible to substantive examination. The minimal definition of a metropolitan village means that there are a large number of such villages with only one common feature, a division between urban commuters and a local labour force. This division parallels and often underlines a further difference between the old-established and the new residents, and it is these distinctions that give the metropolitan villages their specific character and unique characteristics.

Housing and Mobility in Metropolitan Villages

It is the metropolitan village housing situation that at least partially determines its social and demographic characteristics. Housing, and particularly certain kinds of desirable detached and semi-detached housing, is a scarce resource, and individual households are unable to compete equally for this resource. There are essentially three kinds of housing situation: first, the local authority systems where accommodation is owned and allocated by local authorities according to such criteria as length of residence, workplace, household size and present housing situation; second, privately-owned housing, often flats, rented to individuals at 'free market' rents; and third, privately-owned or mortgaged housing, where individuals are already owners of the property or are becoming so. These are three of the possible kinds of housing class[29] and they are the three with most general significance. Nevertheless, the second is almost non-existent in metropolitan villages although a parallel category of tied accommodation, where accommodation is rented (or given free) to an individual and his family as long as he performs a specified job, is more important in many of these semi-rural areas. (Historically, tied houses and cottages have come to be associated with agricultural occupations; yet because of the decline in the agricultural labour force, coupled with the poor quality of much of this housing, they are now declining rapidly.)

Because of the low rate of mobility between these different housing systems, the spatial distribution of housing reflects very closely the kind of people who can and will live in a particular area. The evolution of the two basic kinds of housing system in metropolitan villages is critical to an examination of the social, demographic and organizational characteristics of the local population. Privately-owned housing has always existed, yet it is only in the present century that the sale and resale of housing has become a major service industry, with the growth of building societies and estate agencies. Almost paradoxically, during the depression of the 1930s, at least in the London area, building societies became more popular as basic deposits and loan interest rates fell.[30] At the same time real costs of building fell, so that the 1930s became a major period of housing construction and no more so than in the earliest metropolitan villages. Hence, before the Second World War, almost all railway stations within 30 km of central London, and many stations at lesser distances from provincial cities, were surrounded by growing estates of high quality residential accommodation. The 'freeze' on expansion of these villages, with the imposition of green-belt policies since the Second World War, has meant that additions to the housing stock have come largely from infilling and from rounding-off, which add variable but small amounts of new housing. As a result, their prewar status has been partially maintained. Beyond the green belts postwar development has continued steadily, and the most rapidly-growing villages since the war have been those at greater distances from the central city. Partially because of greater postwar pressures and demands on space, houses and gardens here have been smaller. Village status is reduced. Nevertheless, what is most important about this housing system is that, although it appears to operate in a local framework, with local builders and estate agents and advertisements in local papers, the demand is both regional (being based primarily in the central city) and national (as a result of job-location changes). For the suburb it has been argued 'that the prices of houses act as a social sieve through which drop each homogeneous segment of the population round the edge of the towns'.[31] For those metropolitan villages that are closest to the cities, exactly the same is true.

The local authority housing system is substantially different. Modern local authority housing resulted from the Housing, Town Planning etc. Act of 1919, which made the first provision for a statutory basis to planning. In almost all the areas around large cities the housing authorities are the Rural District Councils and these soon constructed their first estates; in the rural areas, small estates were built, usually outside the old village, and they became a distinct morphological component of the rural landscape. Local authorities have virtual autonomy in the selection of tenants for their houses; there is no statutory income limit nor residential qualification that authorities must observe. The only statutory provision is that they should give 'reasonable preference to persons who are occupying insanitary or overcrowded conditions'.[32] However, there are generally uniform priorities. Single persons are usually excluded, as are those with annual incomes over a prescribed maximum, usually at present between £1,250 and £1,500. Secondary qualifications are health, eviction or insecurity of tenure, overcrowded accommodation and isolation. Between the two world wars, the Parish Councils were entitled to appoint representatives to discuss with the Rural District Council the selection of tenants for local authority housing in their parish. Now Parish Councils have been bypassed; the local authority housing market has become slightly wider, yet it is fundamentally different from the market for owner-occupied accommodation in its specifically local organization.

Guildford Rural District, for example, organizes local authority housing in a large number of metropolitan villages to the south of London. Virtually all the occupants of these houses work in the district; many have lived and worked there all their lives. Yet, because there is almost no industry in the Rural District and agricultural employment is increasingly unimportant, there has never been a massive demand for housing in the area. However, because of financial restrictions on local authority expenditure on housing, even the present demand cannot be satisfied by rapid loca authority housing construction, and a long semi-permanent waiting list is a feature

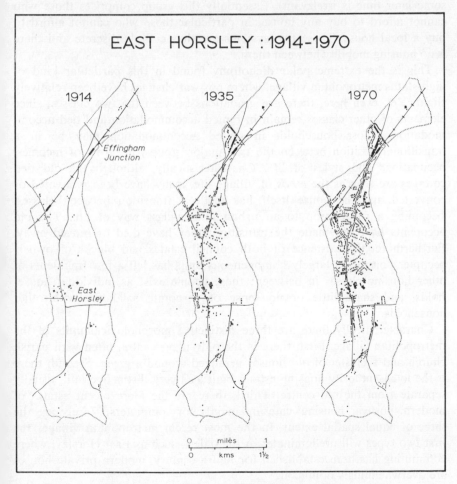

Figure 5–2 Expansion of East Horsley, 1914–70

even of areas like this, although they are some distance from the major areas of housing stress. Consequently, within Guildford Rural District, only 16 per cent. of the housing stock is owned by the local authority; within some villages it is much less than half this figure.

In a village like East Horsley (Figures 5–1 and 5–2), between Guildford and London, the two systems operate in a parallel but completely reverse direction. By the beginning of 1971 access to the owner-occupier system was restricted by house prices and mortgage policies to people with large incomes (or a large amount of capital) because house prices were almost entirely above £10,000. Access to the local authority system is dependent on local attachment and is restricted to those with very small annual incomes (although after the initial allocation of a council house, a large increase at some later time is irrelevant). Essentially this group comprises those who cannot afford to buy any house, in particular those who cannot afford to buy a local house. These two systems are thus entirely discrete and there is no housing mobility between them.

This is the extreme polar dichotomy found in this particular kind of high-status metropolitan village, where postwar changes have been relatively slight. Yet, even here, there are gradations between the two classes, since elements of other classes remain in rented accommodation and tied accommodation. Those households in rented accommodation may be in a transitional position between the two major groups, in terms of incomes, occupations and styles of life. Characteristically, although the old tied cottages are seen as the *ethos* of village life, many have been renovated or converted and the house itself has made a transition between classes, becoming a rustic prop to an urban middle-class way of life. The old occupants have not made the transition; they have died or moved away. Furthermore, the existence of both council estates and blocks of owner-occupier housing as largely homogeneous units has left a few fragments of other housing classes in between; these people exist as individual households, and share little or no sense of corporate solidarity with other households.

Characteristically there are three distinctive morphological units of the metropolitan village. First, there is the old village centre, often with parish church and a cluster of old houses arranged around a green. Second, there is the local authority housing estate, built as a very distinctive unit, usually separate from the old centre. Third, there are the more recent estates of modern, postwar housing, catering mainly for commuters. Rarely are the three of equal spatial extent. In the most recent metropolitan villages the first two types will predominate; in the oldest, such as East Horsley, where commuting has been established for half a century, modern private houses are overwhelmingly dominant.

Council-house occupants work locally and generally earn wages below the national average; their inability to move outside the local authority system means that they are also unable to move far geographically. Their only moves will be within council accommodation to different kinds of property at particular stages in their life cycles; where particular villages or estates offer a range of property these people are unlikely to move long distances. Only five of the sixty-two council households in East Horsley had previously lived outside the Rural District.

Owner-occupiers largely work in the nearest large city and earn wages above the national average; subject to certain financial restrictions and self-imposed restrictions, like accessibility to particular churches, relatives or schools, they are free to live in any area within commuting distance of their workplace. No authority restricts the distance of their move. Of the sixty-five owner-occupier households which arrived in East Horsley between 1961 and 1966, only eleven came from within the Rural District.

It is the differences between these two major groups and the latent hostility between them that characterizes the metropolitan village. Distinctions between old and new residents, however defined, are almost entirely subsumed in this relationship. These differences may be characterized by the differential demographic and socio-economic structure of the two groups. Obvious difficulties of sampling, analysis and classification prevent formal comparisons at most stages, but the research time-span of six years from 1964 to 1970 suggests that at least short-term temporal changes are insignificant.

In all the metropolitan villages there was a similar age structure among the newest immigrant groups. The recent immigrants were always younger on average than the total population and the established residents were older. Only in Swanley, Kent (where 10 per cent. of the immigrants were over sixty, compared with 17 per cent. of the established residents) was there a large percentage of elderly migrants.[33] In all areas, the majority of

Table 5–1. Age structure of population, East Horsley, Surrey

Age groups	Newcomers (%) (1967–9)	Population (%) (1966)
0–9	22·1	12·4
10–19	11·8	12·9
20–29	10·7	9·2
30–39	17·5	10·5
40–49	16·6	16·2
50–59	10·8	19·7
60–69	8·5	10·5
70+	2·0	9·6
Total	100·0 (n=553)	100·0 (n=3700)

Source: Author's survey

migrants consisted of young adults and young children, and for both established residents and new immigrants the mean age was lower in the more working-class areas[34] and higher in such middle-class areas as Otford and Kemsing, Kent, and East Horsley, Surrey (Table 5–1).

Households with small incomes (or high non-housing expenditures) are deterred from buying houses in areas like this until they can earn a higher income. In addition, the middle-class areas contain relatively few council houses, where new residents are always much younger than either those in private houses or the average village population. In the most exclusive villages, mainly those within the green belt, house prices are so expensive that even some commuters are excluded and are forced to live beyond the outer edge of the green belt.

Incidence of migration in most cases falls sharply above the age of forty, but may increase immediately after retirement age (although the metropolitan villages tend not to be retirement centres, precisely because of the high cost of housing dependent on the villages' now unwanted accessibility). Almost without exception, the new immigrants form simple nuclear households; extended families and single individuals are extremely rare and even rarer are overseas immigrant households. In addition, few of the new immigrants have relatives in the area.

In all metropolitan villages the dominant migration direction is outwards from the central city, with a large amount of evidence suggesting that the movement is from the nearest part of that city. In Hertfordshire immigrants to Radlett came from Hampstead, Highgate, Edgware and Wembley.[35] For most villages in Kent, Bexley and Bromley are important feeder areas, whilst in Surrey, the outer south-west London suburbs are important, although in those areas with highest socio-economic status and most distant from London, the migration direction appears more random. (There is insufficient evidence around any other city to draw similar conclusions; limited observations suggest that the idea of sectoral migration can be extended to metropolitan villages.) It is not clear to what extent the move to a metropolitan village is a second stage of movement out from central London, but the low percentages of migrants moving directly from the more central London boroughs to such high-status villages as East Horsley, Tewin and Radlett suggests that the suburb is one stepping-stone to a high-status village. It is possible, therefore, that there should also be migration from low-status villages to high-status villages; but although there is some evidence for this, especially in Surrey, it represents only a small percentage of all moves.[36] Migration appears dominantly sectoral, as envisaged by Hoyt, yet the resultant veneer of owner-occupiers approximates to the concentric rings of Burgess; Hoyt has inevitably described process, Burgess has described stage.

Analysis of the reasons for migration gives further indications of the processes involved in suburbanization and urban growth. Within Britain little attention has been paid to motivation, and surveys have rarely distinguished between 'push' and 'pull' factors, although this seems especially important in the metropolitan villages where migration decisions connected with changed employment location are of restricted importance. East Horsley again provides some specific information on the motives of migrants (Table 5–2).

Table 5–2. Main influence on migration of owner-occupiers, East Horsley, Surrey

	Pull	Push
Work/job location	4	35
House/land available	14	—
House value	1	1
Large/small/special house	13	13
Country/area/health/quiet	39	5
Friends/relatives	4	2
Transport facilities	22	13
Retirement	—	5
None/don't know	1	17
Other	2	9
	100%	100%
(n=139)		

Source: Author's survey

In interpreting a table like this it should be recalled that, if all reasons other than just first choices were analysed, an entirely different result might emerge, since most location decisions are a result of several factors. Yet the distinction between the two columns is sufficiently marked to suggest that surveys demanding only the 'reasons' for migration are likely to be unrewarding, although the results of other surveys appear to refer to pull rather than push factors. The role of transport, linking the 'rural' village with the city is particularly clear, and in this case the high status of the village is surely reflected in the high proportion of respondents who were unable to state any reason for leaving their previous house. Attempts to compare migratory moves with different metropolitan villages are fraught with uncertainty, hence little is known of the decision processes of different kinds of migrants or the whole nature of the 'mover-stayer' dichotomy. It has not been established which individuals within the household are primarily responsible for migration decisions, what time is available for house selection and what are the space-searching procedures likely to be involved. The individual concerned or the time available may be much more important, if less tangible, than more specific and apparently rational post-migration justifications.

There is little reliable information on what people want of their potential homes and, in the absence of free choice, the true preferences of different sectors of the population are difficult to determine. Some discontent is inevitable where housing is a key index of social status, hence there is a high level of demand for the kind of house that is available in the metropolitan villages. Nevertheless, migration is not a simple response to objective social and economic conditions; for residential location, as for industrial location, there can be only a limited number of optimal locations at any one time. Consequently optimal choice may not even be possible where these locations are already filled and no homes are available. For that matter, as the decision-makers have only limited information on housing, commuting, social organizations and so on, an optimal choice is highly unlikely. Observations suggest that the decision-maker negotiates for an environment of relative certainty, to the extent that there is a tendency to postpone decisions; and uncertainty is reduced by the imitation of the successful decisions of others in similar situations. This kind of limitation tends therefore to lead to social segregation, notwithstanding the detailed inter- and intra-village location decision which is largely a matter of chance.

Housing classes are reflected, too, in social and economic differentials.[37] In all metropolitan villages where this topic has been examined, newcomers show a heavy bias towards socio-economic groups 1 and 2,[38] but this is variable according to the location of the village. The nearest villages to the city contain greater proportions of groups 1 and 2, because of their earlier construction, the better quality and greater expense of housing. In the London area, for example, Radlett was described as a 'dormitory' for professional and business men, and 65 per cent of newcomers to East Horsley were in these two groups.

Social Organization of Metropolitan Villages

The most recent newcomers to metropolitan villages are from a high socio-economic group and have high educational status, they are owner-occupiers and they are younger than the established village households. Their spatial separation within the villages is related to the date of house construction; the more recently that estates of new houses have been built the more confined to these are the newcomers. Where, as in East Horsley, most house building was completed before 1960, more recent migrants are scattered throughout the village where old houses become vacant, and the only new houses are built separately in a limited number of vacant plots. Spatial segregation is most clearly defined in the council estates, which are often morphologically distinct and separated by a considerable distance from the remainder of the village. In most metropolitan villages there are important divisions between the newest residents of highest social class and the residents, usually old-established, of council estates; in the older-established metropolitan villages, there may be groups of prewar commuters who fill a social position between the other two extreme groups. The old-established nature of these early commuters has worked towards a sharp social-class dichotomy in several such villages, between the owner-occupiers and the council tenants, where spatial separation often parallels the situation in contiguous suburbs, only on a smaller scale. In newer metropolitan villages, however, there are also many households in the lower socio-economic groups who are not in council houses and who have not yet been priced out of the owner-occupier market. There are no indications yet that metropolitan villages are part of an invasion and succession cycle with higher-class residents gradually giving way to lower-class residents; even in the metropolitan villages with the cheapest house prices commuters from lower socio-economic groups are not yet pushing out higher-group residents. The invasion-succession process is still entirely uni-directional as residents from higher social classes take over the villages and homes of lower-class residents.

In terms of social organization, therefore, it is interesting to examine the way in which the social life and pretensions of the newcomers differ from those of the established residents (particularly those living in council estates) and how the social life of the villages has changed and adapted to meet the demands of the newcomers. In the rural village of Gosforth, Cumberland, some two decades ago, individuals at the upper end of the social scale played an important leading role in village life and a rough hierarchy existed from the squire to the parish agricultural labourers.[39] The last trace of this hierarchy in Surrey's metropolitan villages was probably around 1953, when street and parish parties were organized to celebrate the Coronation.[40] Since then, the village populations have generally become too large to form a single hierarchy and the wellknown people in the villages may not now be those who play an important role in village life, but are those who are wellknown for a particular contribution to national affairs. Instead of a hierarchy dependent upon a small group of leaders or an individual (a relic of a period when almost all social and economic activity was confined to the village) the metropolitan village is segmented into various groups and, more important, contains a large proportion of people who have no interest in the village apart from residence. The parish council is no substitute for the traditional squire.

The social organizations existing in a particular metropolitan village are obviously related to the social composition of that village. In East Horsley, for example, out of over twenty social organizations only a vestigial Young Farmers' Club is indicative of a rural location. The massive concentration of the population of this village in the upper socio-economic groups has produced several theatrical and musical groups culminating in the Horsley Society of Arts, none of which perform any village-level integrative function, existing rather for particular subgroups of the middle class. Meanwhile, the local organizations designed to fulfil possible demands from council-house tenants are a limited number of sports clubs, the Seniors' Club and the British Legion. These are declining, in the same way that the interwar Working Men's Club folded up, whilst the Music Society, the Arts Society and the strangely middle-class Horticultural Society survive. Similar patterns are modified elsewhere; where there is a limited influx of middle-class commuters, these are expected to play important roles in village society[41] but where they are a majority, their reorganization and reshaping of existing social organizations is resented.

Yet even more remarkable in these new metropolitan villages is the proliferation of amenity societies. In 1957 in England there were about two hundred local amenity societies; in 1968 there were about six hundred.[42] Expansion continues and for Horsley a clearly-defined hierarchy exists. At the top is the Surrey Amenity Council, an umbrella organization founded in 1951. The essential constituents of the Council are the local Surrey societies, of which the Horsley Countryside Preservation Society is one. Founded in 1956, by April 1970 it had some 1,900 members in the parish. Many other parishes in Surrey have a similar organization, functioning in a similar way. For East Horsley and four other neighbouring parishes there is a further umbrella organization, the Five Villages Association, founded in 1969, specifically in opposition to Surrey County Council proposals to route a motorway through the parishes. This Association grew exceptionally rapidly, keeping pace with changing proposals. Below this is the Ockham Road Protection Association, founded in 1965, with a membership of over 1,200, dedicated to improving both the safety and beauty of the main road through the parish. Finally, several individual roads are represented by a number of small societies, principally concerned with maintenance, but also with amenity. The significance of this hierarchy[43] is, first, that it is probably uniquely well developed within England; second, that the large membership of the various organizations contains no council householders; third, that the organizations are relatively successful; and fourth, that there is nothing comparable in villages which have become metropolitan villages since 1945.

The new residents and the old council-house tenants have clearly different attitudes to amenity and planning. The commuters are content with metropolitan village life; the village is certainly large enough and has enough social organizations either in the village or within range of a short car-journey. These people do not want to see further expansion of the village, whilst council-house tenants find few and expensive shops, poor school facilities and a lack of social organizations. Further expansion would result in a greater local population and ultimately more shops and playing spaces for children. It is in this remarkable and clear dichotomy that the problem of participation in planning is crystallized; the demands of council-house tenants are the exact opposite of those in private houses. Indeed, in the smallest villages, which often have the highest status, an influx of the upper-middle class actually results in a loss of facilities; East Clandon, in Surrey, with a population of 250, lost both its primary school and village shop following the change of occupants that followed the steady conversion of tied cottages to owner-occupied houses.

The different kinds of social organization are paralleled in different kinds of spatial organization. Fundamental to this is the journey to work, the urban commuter versus the local man, and the railway-user versus the cyclist or pedestrian. Reality is, as always, more complex than the stereo-type. Around British cities other than London, railways are relatively unimportant for commuting, whilst, because of the limited number of workplaces, local journeys within rural districts may be long and complex. Where local public transport is inadequate these local journeys may, from necessity, produce some two-car council households.[44] The absence of social provision in many metropolitan villages has meant that shopping trips and demands on professional services must often be made elsewhere. Local shopping facilities are poor or expensive; distant shopping facilities demand either a second car or an expensive and inconvenient journey by public transport. Local variations in the provision of services and transport are so variable that it is difficult to arrive at general conclusions; neverthe-less the distance of many services from most villages imposes a severe financial constraint on their accessibility for the lowest-paid workers in the villages.

Despite the participation of new commuters in village social organization and their stimulation of new local activities, their social links are rarely confined to the village and are as likely to be with other members of spatially dispersed 'non-place' communities,[45] either in cities or in other villages. In contrast, the social networks of the council-house tenants are more likely to be restricted to the village of residence whilst, at the same time, the social links between the two groups are likely to be confined to economic relations, either through gardening or domestic help. This kind of dual social organization, coupled with a patron-client relationship be-tween groups, is not the basis of a unified village community.[46] Metropolitan villages at best exhibit the coexistence rather than the integration of social groups; any single social hierarchy has clearly disappeared. They represent a residential location, too, that often meets only the needs of some members of a particular social class at a particular point in the life-cycle.

International Parallels

The metropolitan village is essentially a product of the stringent planning regulations that have limited urban growth around the outer edge of the continuous built-up area of large cities. Since neither of these conditions occur to the same extent elsewhere, the phenomenon is primarily British; yet around many other cities of the developed world there are incipient examples and parallel forms. In North America, the relentless spread of urbanization gradually engulfs the rural areas around the cities, but the new small-scale suburbs are not greatly constrained by planning regulations and often coalesce to spread suburbanization. There is little organizational opposition to this and less formal opposition is reduced by the prices paid for land to be developed; the ubiquity of owner-occupied housing outside the American central city, and the more general absence of old-established villages and hamlets, result in little social conflict from the whole process. In addition, the absolute dominance of the highway and the car in America allows a more sprawling suburbia than the more densely developed metropolitan villages that are more closely tied to the railways around London.

If the free enterprise system of the United States and the formless urban sprawl that has resulted may be contrasted with the United Kingdom, how much more severe is the contrast with the countries of eastern Europe where nationalization of the housing market and declared attempts to remove housing inequalities might be expected to produce a radically different situation. The limited amount of information available[47] does suggest a general increase in social heterogeneity within cities rather than the increased segregation of the west and also indicates that there are no parallels with western metropolitan villages. Rigorous centralized planning, the lack of capital for private-enterprise housing and inadequate public or private transportation beyond the city boundary are more than sufficient to prevent the emergence of this essentially capitalist phenomenon. However, the slow rate of urban housing construction, coupled with a more rapid expansion of urban job opportunities, has created a new and disadvantaged class of rural commuters. These people live in villages or farms beyond the outskirts of big cities because of restriction on immigration to the cities. They spend long hours commuting but are deprived of many of the privileges afforded by the network of urban community services, such as education and entertainment facilities.

In less developed countries, the situation is slightly different. The main barrier to the emergence of metropolitan villages is neither rigorous planning nor, in many cases, lack of capital, but the still prevalent and almost universal conception that the 'good life' is in the city. Even the expatriates, always amongst the most wealthy in these growing cities, are unwilling to move out, partly because of the complete absence of even the most rudimentary service provisions in almost all villages, but also, and perhaps more significantly, because of their own conceptions of an urban life-style. Villages close to major cities in all developing countries[48] exhibit two main characteristics: they are closely affected by ideas and innovations flowing from that city, and they provide a permanent labour force by migration or a temporary labour force by commuting to supplement that of the city. None of these commuters are ever former urban residents. The metropolitan village is far from being even an ideal.

Conclusion

The metropolitan village is seen therefore as essentially a product of a developed capitalist society; yet the polarized class composition of the village, often considered to be its main characteristic, is seen only in the most rigorously-planned situations where village suburbanization has been in progress for several decades. Villages where urban pressures have been more recent, and hence more restricted, exhibit a social class composition that is more heterogeneous than many parts of towns and cities. It is only in exceptional circumstances that the metropolitan village even approximates to the homegeneity of the city suburb and, if the village exists for one category of people as a rather pleasant and remote suburb, for others it remains a place of work and residence with a conspicuous absence of social services and amenities. Within a limited distance from cities there exists a kind of village that may be of very variable composition as a result of a variety of social forces directed either from the central city or from the local region, of which by far the most important is the nature of and access to the housing market.

Although the metropolitan village is in a particular kind of spatial location, its characteristics are a result of external social processes, such as the political forces that determine the flow of money in the economy or influence the size and shape of local authority regions, the composition of their planning committees and so on. Parallel to these are the economic constraints of bank rates, investment decisions and mortgage restrictions. It is an examination of these factors that provides a basis for examining the underlying rate of suburbanization in metropolitan villages and the ultimate social composition of such villages. Small-scale planning decisions and the decisions of individual households are subject to numerous and variable national economic constraints; yet it would be erroneous to suggest that social forces and spatial structure are unimportant. Spatial structure is critical to all social and economic links, and analysis of social and spatial organization within the village, through the response of villages to different rates of influx of migrants and the formation and maintenance of social networks within the village, has detailed implications for the planning of

such villages. If a micro-spatial model of the development and organization
of metropolitan villages is impossible, it is because the most important
forces that influence their growth and character are spatial and almost
entirely national, yet their influence is temporally and spatially variable.
The metropolitan village is an integral part of the city and, more important,
of the nation; its process and pattern of development can only be seen in
relation to regional and national changes.

Further Reading

A readable account of the history and social characteristics of the modern
residential suburb is D. C. Thorns, *Suburbia* (London, 1972) whilst a valuable
theoretical introduction is provided by C. Bell and H. Newby, *Community
Studies* (London, 1972).

The most detailed account of an American suburb is that of H. J. Gans, *The
Levittowners* (New York, 1967) whilst P. Hall 'The Urban Culture and the
Suburban Culture', in R. Wells and C. Walton (eds.) *Man in the City of the
Future* (London, 1968), 99–145, sets this account in a national and international
context.

At present the most useful published study of any metropolitan village is
contained in R. E. Pahl, *Urbs in Rure: The Metropolitan Fringe in Hertfordshire* (London, 1965) and R. E. Pahl, *Whose City?* (London, 1970). However the
present London bias is offset substantially by P. Ambrose, *The Quiet Revolution: Social Change in a Sussex Village 1871-1971* (London, 1974) which analyses
recent changes in the village of Ringmer.

References

1. W. Scharer, 'Die Suburbane von Zurich', *Geographica Helvetica* **11** (1956),
   1–46: 11.
2. Accurate data on decentralization of employment from the central city to
   the suburbs is not readily available largely because census information
   rarely differentiates employment data at this level. Pahl, for example,
   notes how it is only particular kinds of employment that can be decentralized
   (R. E. Pahl, 'Poverty and the urban system', in M. Chisholm and G.
   Manners (eds.), *Spatial Policy Problems of the British Economy* (Cambridge,
   1971), 132, yet most cities have a considerable range of offices and factories
   on their city fringes.
3. M. Young and P. Wilmott, *Family and Kinship in East London* (London,
   1957).
4. B. H. Berger, *Working Class Suburb* (Berkeley and Los Angeles, 1966).
5. H. Gans, *The Levittowners* (New York, 1967).
6. S. Donaldson, *The Suburban Myth* (New York, 1969).
7. C. Bell, *Middle Class Families* (London, 1969), 127–8.
8. There is no reason why one should not be formulated in terms of the percentage of space given over to residential land use, within 1 kilometre
   squares of the city, but this would seem to serve no useful purpose other
   than an arid academic exercise.

9. A. S. Sturt, 'The relationship between distance and commuting to central London', *Discussion Paper* **25** (LSE Graduate Geography Department, 1968); and R. Leigh, 'Journey to work definitions of the London region', *Discussion Paper* **7** (LSE Graduate Geography Department, 1967).

10. K. G. Grytzell, 'The demarcation of comparable city areas by means of population density', *Lund Studies in Geography Series B* **25** (1963).

11. M. Waugh, 'Suburban growth in north-west Kent, 1861–1961' (Unpublished Ph.D. thesis, University of London, London, 1968).

12. See Chapter 4.

13. See D. Thomas, *London's Green Belt* (London, 1970).

14. See J. H. Johnson, 'The suburban expansion of housing in London, 1918–1939', in J. T. Coppock and H. C. Prince (eds.) *Greater London* (London, 1964), 162–4.

15. See J. T. Coppock, 'A General View of London and its Environs', in Coppock and Prince, *op. cit.*, 38.

16. Before 1967 British new towns had not been expected to grow to a size of over 100,000 but a 'second generation' of new towns was then inaugurated when Milton Keynes was designated a new city with a final target population of around 250,000; others of city size followed. Nevertheless by December 1971 even the earliest new towns, Harlow and Basildon, had reached populations of 79,000 and 85,000 respectively.

17. The village of New Ash Green was built midway between Gravesend and Sevenoaks in the London green belt after the Minister of Housing had overruled his inspector's recommendations and approved the development of an entirely new village. Construction began in 1967 and by 1971 it had a population of approximately 1,000 people. However, the initial attempt to build an 'integrated, balanced community' fell through in 1969 when the Greater London Council abandoned its plans to participate in this private-enterprise village by constructing houses for their own tenants. Consequently it is now predominantly middle class. (See references in note 21.)

18. The term 'metropolitan village' appears to have been first coined by F. I. Masser and D. C. Stroud, 'The Metropolitan Village', *Town Planning Rev.*, **36** (1965), 111–24. It is important that this be distinguished from the 'urban' village which should only refer to communities *within* an urban area: see J. Connell, 'Urban Villages and Social Networks', *Occasional Papers* **11** (Department of Geography, University College, London, 1970).

19. It might perhaps be hypothesized that the sheer awfulness of London's environment, coupled with the undoubted attractions of such peripheral rural areas as the Chilterns and the Downs, are a further significant factor.

20. R. E. Pahl, *Urbs in Rure: The Metropolitan Fringe in Hertfordshire* (London, 1965); and R. E. Pahl, *Whose City?* (London, 1970), Chapters 1–5.

21. The more important works dealing with some or all aspects of village life that supplement Pahl's original work in Hertfordshire are as follows: For Reading, R. Crichton, *Commuters' Village* (London, 1965); for Liverpool, Masser and Stroud, *op. cit.*; for Leicester, N. Elias and J. L. Scotson, *The Established and the Outsiders* (London, 1965); for Nottingham, D. C. Thorns, 'The changing system of rural stratification', *Sociol. Rur.* **8** (1968), 161–78; for Bristol, H. E. Bracey, *Neighbours* (London, 1964); for Worcester, E. Radford, *The New Villagers* (London, 1970); for Glasgow, P. Green, 'Drymen; village growth and community problems', *Sociol. Rur.*, **4** (1964), 52–62; and also for Aberystwyth, G. J. Lewis, 'Suburbanization in

Rural Wales: a case study', in H. M. Carter and W. K. D. Davies (eds.), *Urban Essays: Studies in the Geography of Wales* (London, 1970), 144–76. Around London there is for Kent, Kent County Council, *Kent Development Plan, Quinquennial Review, 1963,* Report of the Survey and Analysis, Part 4, Vol. 3 (Maidstone, 1966); G. Popplestone, 'Conflict and Mediating Roles in Expanding Settlements', *Sociol. Rev.* **15** (1967), 339–55, and for the special case of New Ash Green, J. Barr, 'Status village', *New Society* **371** (30 October, 1969), 677–80 and H. Sachs, 'A study of New Ash Green' (Unpublished seminar paper, CES, March 1971, mimeographed, 51 pp.). For Hertfordshire there is also J. T. Coppock, 'Dormitory settlements around London', in Coppock and Prince, *op. cit.,* 265–91, and for Surrey, J. Connell, 'Green belt county', *New Society* **439** (25 February 1971), 304–6. This is here supplemented by data from two unpublished sources: for Leeds, J. Connell, 'Pool in Wharfedale: a pilot study', (Unpublished, mimeographed 21 pp., September 1968), and for Surrey, J. Connell, 'Aspects of Housing and Migration in Central Surrey' (Unpublished Ph.D. thesis, University of London, London, 1973). In addition to work of much slighter content, there are additional theses that throw light on metropolitan villages especially in Kent and Sussex, most of which are listed in J. Connell. Much of this chapter attempts to synthesize these accounts but with special reference to East Horsley, Surrey.

22. J. Eyles, 'The inhabitants' images of Highgate Village – an example of a perception measurement technique', *Discussion Paper* **15** (LSE Graduate Geography Department, 1968).

23. J. H. Johnson, 'The geography of a Belfast suburb', *Irish Geography* **3** (1956), 150–61.

24. Bell, *op. cit.,* on West Swansea; Young and Willmott, *op. cit.,* on 'Greenleigh' and P. Willmott and M. Young, *Family and Class in a London Suburb* (London, 1960), on Woodford. Geographically these may be supplemented only by three unpublished theses, all curiously on Kent suburbs of Greater London: M. C. Carr, 'The growth and characteristics of a metropolitan suburb: Bexley Borough, North West Kent, 1880–1963' (Unpublished Ph.D. thesis, University of London, London, 1971); B. Taylor, 'Bromley, Beckenham and Penge, Kent since 1750' (Unpublished Ph.D. thesis, University of London, London, 1966); M. Waugh, 'Suburban Growth in North West Kent' (Unpublished Ph.D. thesis, University of London, London, 1968).

25. L. Mumford, *The City in History* (London, 1963), 493.

26. The most important of these is Gans, *op. cit.,* but many earlier works, some in a much less theoretical vein, have been extremely influential, notably Berger, *op. cit.,* W. H. Whyte, *The Organization Man* (New York, 1957), W. M. Dobriner (ed.), *The Suburban Community* (New York, 1958) and, in Canada, J. R. Seeley, R. A. Sim and E. W. Loosley, *Crestwood Heights: a North American Suburb* (Toronto, 1956) and S. D. Clark, *The Suburban Society* (Toronto, 1966). Much of this is usefully reviewed by P. Hall, 'The Urban Culture and the Suburban Culture', in R. Wells and C. Walton (eds.), *Man in the City of the Future* (London, 1968) and also by W. Bell, 'The city, the suburb and a theory of social choice', in S. Greer, D. L. McGrath, D. W. Minar and P. Orleans (eds.) *The New Urbanization* (New York, 1968). In western Europe there has also been little geographical analysis of suburban growth. A limited number of studies has largely concentrated on villages that have been engulfed by urban expansion to become suburbs, for example, R. T. and B. G. Anderson, *The Vanishing Village: a Danish mari-*

time community (Seattle, 1964) and also J. David, 'L'Evolution d'une commune suburbaine de l'agglomeration Grenobloise', *Revue de Geographie Alpine* **59** (1971), 141–8.

27. H. J. Gans, 'Urbanism and Suburbanism as ways of life: a re-evaluation of definitions', in A. M. Rose (ed.) *Human Behaviour and Social Processes* (London, 1962).

28. O. D. Duncan and A. J. Reiss, *Social Characteristics of Rural and Urban Communities, 1950* (New York, 1956), 131.

29. This term was first formulated by Rex and Moore in their study of primarily immigrant housing in central Birmingham, J. A. Rex and R. Moore, *Race, Community and Conflict* (London, 1967).

30. Johnson, *op. cit.* (1964), 157.

31. Bell, *op. cit.*, 129.

32. J. B. Cullingworth, *Housing and Local Government* (London, 1966), 121.

33. Kent C. C., *Kent Development Plan, Quinquennial Review 1963*, Report, Part 4, Vol. 3 (Maidstone, 1966).

34. Defined according to socio-economic groups (see note 38).

35. Coppock, *op. cit.*, 289.

36. It would be tempting, but a little unwise, to envisage John Goldthorpe's comments as being appropriate to metropolitan villages: 'In the largest cities like London it is said that the average income rises by steps of £100 or £200 a year with each railway station along the suburban lines as you go out from the centre – finishing up at Epsom, where the millionaires live conveniently near the racecourse'. J. E. Goldthorpe, *Introduction to Sociology* (London, 1968), 153.

37. The official method of social stratification used by the Registrar General is to identify a number of socio-economic groups by using the occupation of the head of the household as a guide to position in a group. Although this grouping is not synonymous with social class, nor is it indicative of status or of individual subjective assessment of class, it does indicate a measure of social position and economic status. Nevertheless, by assuming that social structure can be explained effectively in terms of occupational distribution, the adoption of the official classification enables comparison both with census material and between village studies.

38. The six groups are roughly defined as follows:
   Group 1. Professional workers, employees or self-employed, engaged in work which would normally require qualifications of university degree standard.
   Group 2. Employers and managers in central and local government, industry, commerce and farming (with employees).
   Group 3. Foremen and supervisors in manual work, skilled manual workers and all people (including farmers) working on their own account.
   Group 4. Employees in clerical, sales and security occupations and other non-manual employees.
   Group 5. Semi-skilled manual workers and agricultural workers; employees engaged in service occupations concerned with food, drink, clothing and other personal needs.
   Group 6. Unskilled manual workers, members of the armed forces and all persons with inadequately stated incomes.
   Precise details of these groups are given in the *Classification of Occupations 1960* (HMSO, London, 1964). In this paper, 'middle class' loosely refers to Groups 1, 2 and 3, and 'working class' to Groups 4, 5 and 6.

39. W. M. Williams, *The Sociology of an English Village: Gosforth* (London, 1950).
40. Connell, *op. cit.*, 305.
41. R. Frankenberg, *Village on the Border* (London, 1957); and Popplestone, *op. cit.*, **341**.
42. J. Barr, 'The amenity protesters', *New Society* **305** (1 August 1968), 152–5.
43. J. Connell, 'The preservation of central Surrey', *Town and Country Planning* **40** (1972), 265–8.
44. H. D. Clout and R. J. Munton, 'The problem bus', *Town and Country Planning* **39** (1971), 112–16.
45. M. Webber, 'Order in diversity: community without propinquity', in L. Wingo (ed.), *Cities and Space* (Baltimore, 1963). This is a unique and idiosyncratic interpretation of community, yet the concept is interesting.
46. The social and economic links underlying, the spatial organization of communities form an emergent field deserving of more general geographical attention. See J. Connell, 'Social networks in urban society', in *Social Patterns in Cities* (Institute of British Geographers, Special Publication no. 5, 1973), 41–52.
47. See, for example, J. Musil, 'The development of Prague's ecological structure', in R. E. Pahl (ed.), *Readings in Urban Sociology* (Oxford, 1968), 232–59.
48. See, for example, in three different areas, H. B. Barclay, *Buuri al Lamaab: A Suburban Village in the Sudan* (Ithaca, 1964); J. Connell, 'Mahmood Abad and Talebabad: villages in transition', in J. Connell (ed.) *Semnan: Persian City and Region* (London, 1970); and M. S. A. Rao, *Urbanization and Social Change: a Study of a Rural Community on a Metropolitan Fringe* (New Delhi, 1970).

CHAPTER 6

The Growth of Second-Home Ownership: An Example of Seasonal Suburbanization

HUGH D. CLOUT

Numerous urban studies have analysed the spatial expansion of residential areas around the nuclei of many of the world's cities, as successive advances in public and private transportation have permitted a separation between place of work and place of residence. The resultant patterning of modern cities in the developed world includes not only continuously built-up sub-urbia but also more distant commuter settlements which retain a large proportion of rural landscape features but function as parts of the 'dispersed city'.[1] Such residential areas, or suburbs, display great variation in their morphology, chronology of development and socio-economic structure but they share the common characteristic of being composed of primary resid-ences, namely housing that is occupied continuously apart from vacation periods. Theories of urban and regional development have been generated from the distribution of such primary residences with associated population densities decreasing outwards from central points of concentration.[2] How-ever, an additional form of accommodation for urbanites has risen to importance in the last few decades, involving the seasonal or part-time occupance of other than primary places of residence.

The Diversity of Second Homes

This 'secondary' category comprises both static and mobile dwellings which are sited beyond the city's built-up limits and are inhabited regularly for week-ends, public holidays and annual vacations. In fact, caravans and other forms of mobile dwelling will be excluded from the following discus-sion. Only static types of seasonal dwelling will be considered under the general term of 'second home'. Even so, a wide range of dwellings must be included since national traditions of second-home development vary enormously. In regions such as western Europe, with long histories of dense rural occupance and recent depopulation, most second homes are converted farm or fishing cottages. Specially constructed villas and chalets for leisure-time use are relatively few in number except around very popular resorts. This situation will undoubtedly change in the future, as the demand for second homes in popular areas will exceed the supply of cottages falling vacant and will have to be satisfied by specially planned estates of recreational housing. Such a stage has already been reached in North America where '. . . whole cities of cottages flourish in summer and are almost emptied of people in the winter'.[3] In Queensland, Australia, new structures predominate over converted property but very few second homes, apart from commercial flats, are architect-designed.[4] Visual and functional similarities between areas of second-home construction and primary suburban zones close to the rural-urban fringe have been reported in many parts of the developed world.[5]

Second homes merit geographical attention for two main reasons. First, they add new and distinctive features to the already complex assemblage of residential areas around urban cores, thereby transporting 'the city' and its inhabitants into the countryside for substantial periods each year. Second, the seasonal presence of second-home occupants gives rise to important social and economic changes in host communities. In short, the proliferation of second homes provides important support for Wirth's conclusion that some form of urbanism will eventually predominate in all types of settlement.[6] The following discussion will briefly consider examples of second-home development in the past and contemporary contrasts in the occupation of leisure-time housing. It will then comment on the spatial organization of second homes around urban centres and outline some of the social and economic implications of second-home establishment in rural areas.

The Growing Popularity of Second Homes

The popularization and proliferation of second homes is essentially a post-1945 phenomenon, resulting from the combination of sufficient income for non-essential items and sufficient time away from work to allow this income to be spent on leisure-time activities. Specific motives for acquisition include capital accumulation, fashion following, status attainment and the desire to engage in non-urban recreation. Improvements in public and private transportation have allowed these ambitions to be realized.[7]

Nevertheless, small numbers of second homes existed around Europe and North American cities at much earlier dates, but their occupation was a privilege reserved for a small and affluent section of society. Members of the Swedish nobility started to establish summer residences around Stock-holm in the early seventeenth century and their example was emulated by middle-class businessmen during the nineteenth century.[8] Daniel Defoe, travelling through the English counties of Surrey and Essex close to London in the 1720s, found '. . . handsom large houses . . . being chiefly for the habitation of the richest citizens, such as . . . are able to keep two houses, one in the country and one in the city'.[9] The town of Epsom in Surrey functioned as a seasonal suburb for the affluent. 'In the winter this is no place for pleasure indeed; as it is full of mirth and gaiety in the summer, so the prospect of the winter presents you with little but good houses shut up, and windows fasten'd; the families remov'd . . . the people out of the town.'[10] Later in the eighteenth century, Arthur Young recorded many examples of luxurious second homes around the provincial cities of France. He noted in his journal that the merchant classes of Rouen '. . . are right to have country villas, to get out of this great, ugly, stinking, close and ill-built town which is full of nothing but development and industry'.[11] Paris was ringed with second homes on an even grander scale.[12] In 1840 the settlement of Auteuil, now part of inner Paris, was described in the follow-ing terms. '. . . For six months of the year the streets are empty, the doors closed and the houses silent. The inhabitants are in Paris where they spend the winter.'[13] Similar examples could be reported around many European cities.

This highly restricted nature of second-home occupation has been broken down since the Second World War. Melvin Webber, in his consideration of planning beyond the industrial age, has suggested the shape of things to come. 'Those persons who will be able to afford spaciousness and high geographic mobility will also be able to claim both, and these cannot be supplied in the . . . urban packages we have been offering. Multi-house and multi-car families will use far more space than we have been accustomed to provide.'[14] The recent proliferation of second homes in many developed countries of the world presents an early phase in the leisure-time strengthen-ing of functional inter-relationships between cities and their zones of in-fluence which will intensify and become increasingly widespread in the remainder of the twentieth century and beyond.

In spite of its importance, the establishment of second homes has received little attention from geographers and has not been inserted into theories of urban and regional growth. Most studies have been descriptive rather than analytical or predictive in nature and have considered second-home occupation as a specialized branch of tourism. This may have been a valid approach in the past, but the growing popularization of second homes, and the increasing lengths of time being spent in them by large numbers of people, demand serious recognition and would justify the inclusion of seasonal residences in studies of urban growth. Traditionally-recognized but always nebulous distinctions between 'rural' and 'urban' phenomena need reconsideration in the light of second-home development.

Following Wolfe's pioneer work in Ontario, Mercer has recently argued that '. . . both countryside and resort settlements should be viewed simply as highly specialized ecological extensions of the city, constituting . . . the city's living space'.[15] This approach will be adopted in the following discussion, which will consider second-home occupation as a temporary but nonetheless recognizable form of suburbanization. Primary urbanization permitted a spatial separation between place of work and place of rest within the built-up city. Second-home occupation has introduced a new dimension to this process, allowing the urbanite to change his environment completely on a regular and repeated basis, rather than simply moving from one part of the city to another as a result of his journey to and from work. In regions with long experience of second-home occupation, such as the Canadian province of Ontario, 'going up to the cottage' in peri-urban areas is accepted as part of normal residential activity by many families.[16] It is not considered to be 'vacationing', which is equated with seasonal movements to more distant areas.

The temporal distinction between the occupation of primary and secondary residences is contracting, and will continue to do so as working weeks became even shorter in the future. Second homes within easy access of urban centres are already being occupied by urbanites for two and increasingly three nights each week virtually throughout the year. But more remote areas are suitable for second-home occupation during long vacations when considerable lengths of travelling time represent only a very small proportion of the total recreation experience. Another more complex type of occupation involves the whole family staying in its second home during the father's official paid holiday but with the mother and children remaining there throughout the whole period when schools are closed to be joined by the father each week-end. Part-of-the-year residences have developed in France, Scandinavia and North America and are occupied by at least some members of the family for up to three consecutive summer months each year.

National Contrasts in Second-Home Development

In 1964 Wolfe reported that inadequate attention had been paid in recreational research to the million second homes that he considered to exist in the United States at that time.[17] His criticism could have been applied equally well to research in other parts of the developed world. During the last few years, however, investigations have been undertaken in several countries, although the number of articles produced is small by comparison with studies of other aspects of recreation or of the growth of suburban areas. One of the reasons for such a sparsity of research is undoubtedly the shortage of reliable information on the number and distribution of second homes. Nevertheless, an assemblage of available statistics and local investigations suggests that striking national contrasts exist in the volume of second-home occupation, linked in part at least to differing traditions of urban living. It is not surprising that alternative, or even compensatory, residential accommodation in the form of second homes is widely sought in countries with high proportions of apartment dwellers. By contrast, the British tradition of lower-density suburban development, in the form of detached or semi-detached houses with individual gardens, has allowed something of the spaciousness of rural living to be achieved inside the margins of the built-up city.[18] Differences in the length of paid vacations also vary greatly between countries. For example, holidays with pay of at least one month each year are universal in France but this is not yet the case in Britain.[19]

No comprehensive figures exist for second homes in Britain. Questions on this topic were not included in the most recent (1971) census. It was, however, estimated that only 1 per cent. of British households possessed second homes in 1967, and that the volume of holidays spent in them was insignificant by comparison with experience in other western European countries (Table 6–1). A few years later a Wye College study estimated that in 1971 there were between 180,000 and 200,000 'built' second homes in England and Wales, 70 per cent. of which were on the coast. If static caravans were included the total would rise to between 300,000 and 350,000, but even then only 2 per cent. of households had access to second homes.[20]

Table 6–1.   Estimated percentage of vacations spent by city dwellers in second homes, *c*. 1960

United Kingdom	'insignificant'
Belgium	10
West Germany	1
Netherlands	2
Sweden	25
France	10

Source: F. Cribier, *Les Résidences secondaires et le tourisme dans la Somme* (Amients, 1968), 7

Detailed information on house occupation in Sweden is available from local tax registers, and in generalized form from a national inventory which listed 300,000 second homes in 1962 and showed marked concentrations close to Göteborg, Stockholm and other large cities (Figure 6–1).[21] This figure was probably an underestimate, since 400,000 second homes were in existence in 1967 and were used by one in every five urban households

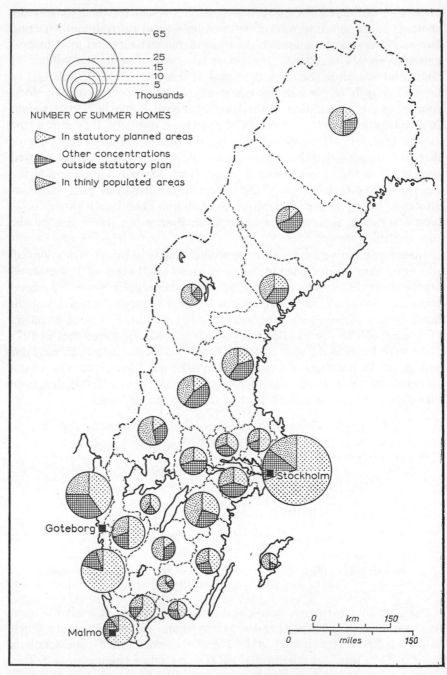

Figure 6–1   Second homes in Sweden, 1962 (based on Norrbom [1966], 64)

in the country.[22] By 1969 the number had risen to 450,000.[23] The use of both a primary and a second home is well established as an important feature of Swedish living habits. The same is true for Denmark and Norway, with 145,000 and 190,000 second homes respectively in 1969 and in Belgium there were 53,700 second homes in 1961.[24]

Census data in the United States do not relate specifically to second homes, but indirect information derived from associated housing categories has been of value in their identification. Hart has used figures for 'seasonally vacant non-farm dwelling units' from the 1960 Census of Housing to prepare a map of second homes in the north-eastern United States.[25] Ragatz produced a nationwide estimate from the same source by adding 'other seasonally vacant units' to 'units held for occasional use' and subtracting those 'vacant for migratory workers'.[26] By using an index of concentration, the importance of second homes in the total housing stock emerged for states in the north-east, around the Great Lakes, and in parts of the Rockies (Figure 6–2). More recent information from a survey of

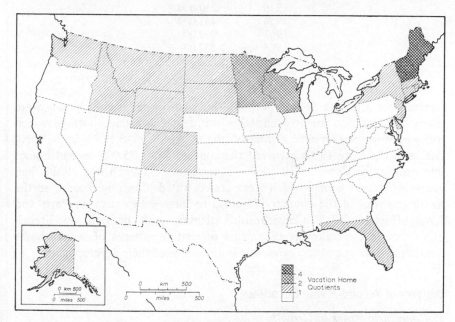

Figure 6–2   States with vacation-home quotients of over 1·00, United States, 1960

Vacation-home quotient for States is defined as: $V_i/C_i \div V_t/C_t$ where
V_i = number of vacation homes in an individual state
C_i = total housing units in an individual state
V_t = number of vacation homes in the United States
C_t = number of housing units in the United States
(based on figures in Ragatz [1970a], 118)

telephone users allowed the same author to estimate that 3 million families in the United States (5 per cent. of the total) owned 'vacation homes', narrowly defined as buildings 'originally constructed for the purpose of leisure-time activities'.[27] Vacation homes comprised 5 per cent. of the total housing stock in the late 1960s and one in every ten new residences being constructed was a vacation house. Numbers were estimated to be rising by between 100,000 and 200,000 each year, and could reach 300,000 by the late 1970s. If converted agricultural properties were to be included the total number of properties involved would be considerably higher.

By contrast with estimates derived from indirect sources, questions on second homes have been asked in recent French censuses and their results, together with a series of official estimates, may be used to depict changing numbers since 1938 (Table 6–2). Reductions were recorded during and

Table 6–2.   Second homes in France, 1938–68

1938	320,000
1946	250,000
1954	447,000
1962	960,000
1968	1,232,000

Source: M. A. Brier, *Les Résidences secondaires* (Paris, 1970), 2

immediately after the Second World War, when some second homes were taken over for permanent occupation during the housing shortage which followed wartime bombing. Similarly, the return of *pieds noirs* from North Africa in the early 1960s involved the conversion of 25,000 second homes into primary residences.[28] In 1967, 18 per cent. of French households had access to second homes which were concentrated along the coasts, in the mountains and in the countryside close to large cities such as Paris and Lyons (Figure 6–3).[29] Considerable attention will be paid to French experience in the following discussion of spatial patterns of second-home location and the social and economic implications of their development.

Patterns of Second-Home Location

1. *Concentric Rings of Growth*

Limited opportunities for personal mobility prior to the automobile age restricted the establishment of second homes to areas which were only a few kilometres beyond the edge of the built-up city, yet sufficiently distant to allow their occupants to escape to a different 'non-urban' environment. Thus, in the early 1900s, large numbers of Parisian-owned second homes were found in the contiguous *départements* of Seine-et-Marne and Seine-et-Oise.[30]

Similarly, luxurious second homes were being constructed right on the outskirts of Prague for affluent members of urban society.[31]

At a very broad level of generalization, a concentric-ring pattern of second homes might be recognized as one moved outwards from suburbia, composed of primary residences, to a week-end dormitory zone and then,

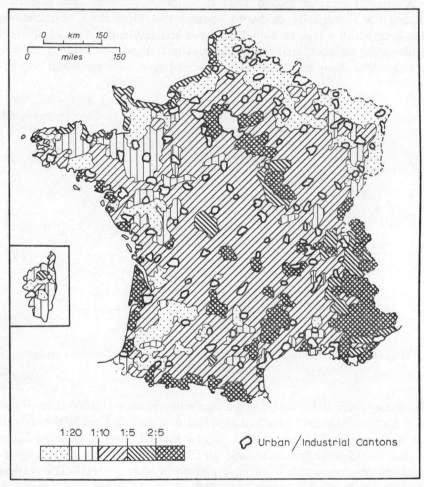

Figure 6–3   Ratio of second homes to permanent residences in rural France, 1962

at a greater distance, to a summer dormitory zone.[32] Mead has depicted '. . . a summer Stockholm, a summer Oslo and a summer Helsinki to which the urban resident migrates for up to three months of the year' and Ragatz has identified 'somewhat mis-shapen' concentric rings of seasonal suburbs around cities in the north-eastern United States.[33] Differences in the

diameters of these rings depend on a variety of factors, including the stage
of transport development reached at a given point in time, the volume of
demand for second homes emanating from central cities, national variations
in the perception of distance (linked to car comfort and road quality), and
a number of local features.

A detailed study of second-home development between 1900 and 1960
around the French city of Lyons showed that three rings of increasing
diameter, which served to bound the week-end residential zone at different
dates, could be associated with advances in transport technology (Figure
6–4(a).[34] The changing distribution of second homes for week-end occupa-

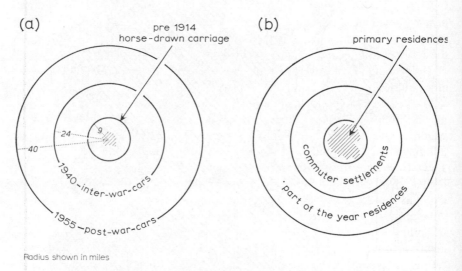

Figure 6–4   Concentric-ring pattern of second-home development around
Lyons, 1900–60

tion during these sixty years showed that a maximum travelling time of one
hour for the single journey was acceptable to Lyonnais citizens throughout
the study period. This was not to suggest that this particular expenditure
of time would prove critical around all cities and at all periods, but something roughly comparable must have applied in other contexts. The earliest
ring identified around Lyons extended up to 15 kilometres from the
city centre and corresponded to one hour's travelling time in the era of the
horse-drawn carriage prior to 1914. A second ring, with a maximum radius
of 40 kilometres, characterized the interwar period when private cars were
being widely purchased. During the 1950s cars were more powerful and
reliable than previously and the radius of week-end suburbs extended out
55 to 65 kilometres. A similar evolutionary model has been proposed for
Queensland, Australia, where an initial 'proximal' phase of second-home

establishment close to urban areas was succeeded by a 'distal' phase, made possible by advances in transport technology and the construction of good, hard-surfaced highways.[35]

If such a concentric-ring pattern is to present even a crude approximation to the actual evolution of peri-urban second homes, it needs to be internally dynamic and incorporate changing residential functions within successive zones of first and second homes. The Lyons study showed that by the 1950s the continuously built-up city had expanded to engulf many of the early twentieth-century week-end suburbs which had become primarily residential areas (Figure 6–4(b). Similarly, more distant settlements, which had functioned as week-end suburbs in the interwar period, later contained primary residences for commuters employed in Lyons. Such changes in the function of housing units account for the apparently anomalous decline in the numbers of second homes recorded in recent years in peri-urban areas of France, while the overall trend has been for second homes to become more numerous.

Marked variations exist in the breadth of rings of second homes arranged around different central cities. These variations are linked not only to conditions of supply and demand for second homes, but also to national differences in road quality, perception of distance and willingness to travel. Thus Europeans generally travel shorter distances to reach their second homes than North Americans or Australians. Superimposed upon such national variations is the fact that large demands for second homes emanating from big cities push week-end suburbs far out into their zones of influence as proximal areas become saturated. Taking the French example again in some detail, Paris exercises a blanketing effect over rural properties falling vacant throughout the inner Paris Basin, so that the capital's week-end suburbs now extend over 160 kilometres from Notre Dame and may involve three hours' driving time or more to reach them.[36] The proportion of second homes owned by Parisians declines in a series of concentric bands with increasing distance from Paris, but to the west of the capital week-end suburbs with more than 75 per cent. of all second homes occupied by Parisians reach as far as the Channel coast (Figure 6–5).[37] By contrast with the broad zone of second homes around Paris, French provincial cities with up to one million inhabitants dominate week-end suburbs up to 100 kilometres distant which are reached after one and a half or two hours' drive.[38] Cities with less inhabitants command smaller zones of influence, with maximum radii of 50 kilometres being normal for cities with under 100,000 residents.

Similar short-distance movements are recorded in other parts of Europe. In the early 1960s, 65 per cent. of second homes in Sweden were located less than 50 kilometres from their owners' permanent residences and in Denmark 80 per cent. were under 65 kilometres away.[39] Wibberley has noted a proliferation of second homes in close proximity to the edges of built-up areas in Britain.[40] In a similar fashion, Gardavsky emphasized locational inertia in the survival of second homes very close to the city of Prague, even in areas where the environment has been severely degraded by the air and water pollution which partly stems from the second homes themselves. Because of such high densities of second homes '. . . it follows that they represent a type of environment which does not differ very much in quality from a town setting. . . . These recreational municipalities affect the natural environment to such an extent that they practically negate recreation as such.'[41]

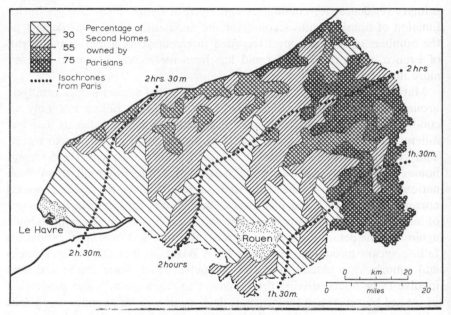

Figure 6–5   Percentage of second homes occupied by Parisians in Seine-Maritime *départment*, 1962

By contrast with such a restricted scale of week-end mobility in Europe, far longer distances are acceptable in the broader and more highly motorized environments of North America and Australia, with up to 320 kilometres between first and second homes being considered a reasonable drive for a week-end. However, Ragatz believed that if North Americans were permitted the choice and were not subject to the inflated prices of second homes close to large urban areas, most would select to drive no more than 150 or 250 kilometres to their week-end residences.[42] This opinion may be correct but the observed pattern of second-home location is more widespread (Table 6–3). Tombaugh sought to rationalize

Table 6–3.   Distance between second homes and primary residences
of households, Michigan

Kilometres	Percentage
less than 40	9
40–79	13
80–159	12
160–319	30
320–479	21
480–639	6
640 and over	9

Source: L. W. Tombaugh, 'Factors influencing vacation home
location', *Jn. Leis. Res.* **2** (1970), 54–63: 57

this distribution, and especially the small proportion of second homes in Michigan that were less than 40 kilometres from the owners' primary residences, in terms of a preference by highly mobile North Americans for a distinct separation between their first and second homes. '. . . It is likely that the urge to "get away from it all", to change environments for a short time, excludes some zones around the primary residence.'[43]

Seasonal suburbanization does not only involve 'average' choices and behaviour patterns. Wolfe has argued that 'all cities have people of high momentum and people of low momentum. The former are better educated, have more interesting jobs and higher income, are less tied down by young children – in a word are more affluent and more mobile – than the latter.'[44] The spatial behaviour of high-momentum people is different from their low-momentum neighbours, taking them to cottages sited at greater distances away from their first homes. The examples cited merely represent conditions at the time of investigation. Patterns of second-home development are constantly changing. If one excludes the possibility of estates of leisure-time homes being built to cater for major urban centres, it is not inconceivable that Europeans may have to look almost as far afield in the next few decades for their second homes as many North Americans do at present. But it would of course be naïve to assume that trends already commonplace in North America will affect Europe in exactly the same fashion in the future.

2. *Sectoral and Nuclear Growth*

The concentric-ring pattern offers a useful generalization to describe the evolution of second homes acquired for leisure-time use. A close correlation is implied between distance from demand centre and type of use, but in fact discrete residential zones of influence for exclusive use over either week-ends or long vacations may not be identified. With increasing distance from central cities it is more likely that second homes will be used for long vacations rather than for week-ends, but a study of behaviour patterns shows that '. . . many people take their vacations well within the "usual" week-end or day-trip zone, especially if such time is spent in privately-owned and frequently-visited holiday homes'.[45] Half of all second homes in Sweden in the early 1960s were used for both week-ends and vacations, and around the French cities of Lyons and Saint-Etienne the proportion was even higher (Table 6–4).[46]

Table 6–4. Use of second homes by residents of Lyons and Saint-Etienne (percentage)

Weekends and vacations	62
Vacations only	20
Weekends only	18

Source: 'Loisirs – aire métropolitaine Lyon/Saint-Etienne', *Les Cahiers de l'OREAM* **6** (1968), 1–20: 16

Perhaps the major drawback of the concentric-ring generalization is that it assumes the existence of an homogeneous peri-urban environment uniformly endowed with sites for second-home establishment. This is far from the case in reality. Recreational and residential hinterlands are made up of sectors with different conditions of access and hence of varying suitability for second homes. In addition, specifically 'attractive' nuclei are perceived within recreational hinterlands by urban residents seeking to acquire second homes. Such points of attraction may correspond with features in the physical landscape but they may also derive from a variety of cultural attributes.

The location of railways and highways away from an urban demand centre tends to distort the pattern of second homes into a series of sectors and also extends radii of development further away from the central city than might normally be expected. Such points are well exemplified by the proliferation of second homes along main roads and railways leading westwards, eastwards and especially south-eastwards from central Paris (Figure 6–6).

The existence of particular site conditions perceived to be attractive is important in suggesting where old cottages may be sought for renovation as second homes and planning permission be requested for new villas to be built. At a very simplified level, areas of dissected terrain with sunny hillsides prove popular but plateau areas with broad, treeless landscapes are far less favoured.[47] Natural and man-made water surfaces form particularly

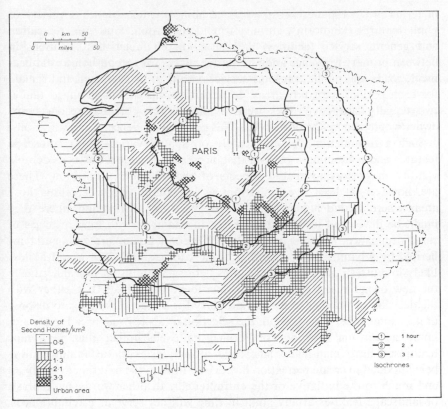

Figure 6–6 Density of second homes per square kilometre in the Paris Basin, 1962

attractive environments. Hence rivers, coasts, natural lakeshores and even the margins of reservoirs held back by hydro-electric power barrages are of great importance. In Marsden's words '. . . water is *the* multi-function recreation resource, activities on, under or by it appealing to all ages'.[48] This opinion was confirmed by Tombaugh, who showed that 89 per cent. of Michigan's second homes were located within five minutes' walk from water surfaces.[49] Other important factors affecting real distributions of second homes include the existing settlement pattern, namely the location of houses and farm buildings which might fall vacant and become available for conversion; and, second, the precise location of sites where planning permission has been granted for developing estates of specially-constructed homes.

In order to facilitate his modelling of second-home development in central Sweden, Aldskogius formulated the concept of 'recreational place utility' which is a composite measure summarizing individuals' perception of sites in terms of their preference for second-home living.[50] Hence a variety of point features (landforms, surface water, vegetation, land use, recreation and general service facilities) and situation characteristics (relationship between primary residence and alternative places for second-home establishment, roads and public transport services) need to be evaluated and ranked for each part of the study areas. In general terms, it was assumed that if two equally 'attractive' sites were available, the potential second-home owner would choose the one closer to his primary residence.

Such a formulation, relying heavily on spatial variations in landscape features and containing a built-in distance-decay function, has considerable validity in portraying spatial aspects of second-home acquisition. There are, however, at least five limitations to its suitability for depicting those areas where second homes have already been established and where they might be developed in the future. First, in countries with long histories of rural occupance, suitable properties for second homes are frequently inherited by urbanites. This occurs in France, for example, but would be less likely in Australia or the United States.[51] In such an instance of inheritance the new owner is not confronted with a locational choice, but rather with the decision of whether to use the property for a second home or to dispose of it in some other way. Second, the selection of a site or an area for second-home acquisition may be conditioned by social rather than landscape features. Third, man-made landscape attractions, such as minor valleys being flooded to create recreation lakes, owe little to the natural environment and much to the initiative of the entrepreneur. In other words, an analysis of landscape features at any point in time will not serve as a reliable basis for predicting the sites of second homes in the future. Fourth, growing numbers of second homes are being constructed on special estates whose attractiveness depends to a large extent on effective advertising. Finally, land-use planning controls are becoming more rigorous in many countries and will condition future patterns of second-home development to a far greater degree than in the past.

The social attractions of particular areas for developing second homes take on many forms which will be illustrated in the context of France. Strength of sentimental attachment to one's birthplace helps to explain many instances of second-home establishment far from the owner's primary residence. Thus large numbers of people born in the Massif Central but currently living in Paris have acquired second homes in distant parts of the Aveyron and Cantal massifs for vacation use and for eventual retirement.[52] In addition, certain areas appeal to distinct groups in French society for social or cultural reasons. One of the clearest examples is provided by the large numbers of Protestants from many parts of France who have acquired second homes in south-eastern parts of the Massif Central where a Protestant majority is found among the local population.[53]

Wolfe's analysis of second homes around Toronto showed that '. . . the zonation of the city finds a rough extension in the zonation of summer resorts. Thus the people from poorer districts, when they own cottages, own them in resorts that are close to the city; those from well-to-do districts are able to range further afield, to less closely-settled areas with better recreational endowments.'[54] But the fashionability of week-end suburbs changes through time. 'Areas close to the city were fashionable when only the well-to-do could afford cottages, and became less fashionable as leisure, recreation, and cottage-owning became more democratized. Similarly, well-to-do gentile cottages have abandoned once fashionable resorts as Jews have begun to move in.'[55] Toronto's second-home-owning Jews were '. . . segregated into specifically Jewish resorts. . . . Here again the zonation of the city is extended to the country and the social and economic stratification of the Jewish city is paralleled in its summer resorts.'[56]

A further social factor behind the distribution of week-end suburbs is the fact that supplying second homes has become an important aspect of commercial real-estate business in many parts of the developed world. Family attachment to rural sources of outmigration will surely decrease in importance, but one can envisage that other social features will influence the development of week-end suburbs in the future. Variations in the social desirability of different areas, resulting from formal advertising and the diffusion of information between actual and aspiring second-home owners, will probably be the most significant. As Barbier noted '. . . at the beginning, the second-homes movement was linked to rural depopulation and stemmed essentially from the countryside; now it stems from the demands of the town'.[57]

Social and Economic Implications of Second-Home Establishment

The temporary influx of urban dwellers to week-end and seasonal suburbs leads to important modifications in the social and economic conditions of the host communities. One assumes, on balance, that city-dwellers benefit from their stay in second homes, even though the journeys involved in reaching them may have been nerve-racking. Many studies suggest that establishing second homes bings advantages to rural areas. Ragatz has argued that '. . . the possibility of expanding the vacation-house market as an alternative to land uses which are either obsolete (farming, mining) or impossible to attract to rural areas (manufacturing, industry, commerce) . . . seems like a rational alternative to investigate for the advancement of regional economic development'.[58] Positive effects of second-home development in the North American context include opportunities to sell off surplus buildings and land; to provide local communities with additional tax inputs; and to derive other benefits from expenditures on local services such as grocery stores, restaurants, building and supply businesses.

This optimistic point of view may be valid in some circumstances but it must be remembered that disadvantages as well as benefits accrue from second-home development. Additional public utilities may have to be provided and it is possible that unfinished, do-it-yourself, second homes could create rural slums. However, in the North American case, Ragatz could conclude that '. . . contributions to the local tax base and expenditure patterns would seem to outweigh the costs of whatever additional public services might be required. . . . The negative implications of a seasonal economy would appear to be secondary to its positive contributions.'[59] Such a conclusion is open to some debate as the following discussions of second homes in Wales and France will show. It would, of course, be unwise to imagine that reactions to second-home establishment in any one region would be replicated in detail in other parts of the world. Great variations in reaction must be expected, linked to a wide range of variables which includes the size of the second-home colony in relation to the number of full-time residents, the degree of self-containment exhibited by the week-end suburb, the amount of local economic deprivation and hence reliance on non-agricultural sources of income, and the attitudes of key members of host communities towards outsiders.

In Britain members of the Welsh Language Society have expressed their opposition to the sale of cottages in Wales for use as second homes by interrupting auction proceedings. Their immediate concern has been over the purchase of Welsh cottages by *English* cityfolk who leave them empty apart from week-ends and holiday times. Prices of houses in some rural areas have become so inflated that young couples have been unable to acquire a dwelling in their home area. Welsh culture, some would argue, has been threatened by even further dilution as the English invaded. In addition, there is the fact that in Britain the transformation of many ramshackle cottages into tidy second homes has been made possible by money grants from the Central Exchequer under the 1969 Housing Improvement Act. Such help was really intended to improve primary residences but second homes were not ruled out. Urban second-home occupants were aware of such grants and applied more readily than their country cousins. Rural dwellers were not in fact being denied financial help for improving their homes, but the use of public money for ' luxury ' leisure-time accommodation understandably raised much controversy in rural Britain. Members of Parliament for central Wales and other country constituencies have argued that claims for improving first homes should receive priority treatment. But on the credit side it must be remembered that second-homers in Wales, as in other parts of Britain, pay full contributions to local rates even though their homes are not occupied throughout the year. Such payments provide money to local authorities to improve council housing, education, health, welfare and other services that are not required by second homers but are necessary for permanent residents. Sums in the order of four million pounds are spent each year by the owners of an estimated 8,700 second homes in rural Wales on house purchase, payment of rates and acquisition of local goods and services.

Some permanent country dwellers in France have also experienced disadvantages following the establishment of second homes. Even though the agricultural population is decreasing, there are growing demands to provide housing for farming families in advanced agricultural regions such as the Paris Basin, where one-third of French second homes are also located and pressures are perhaps strongest for the conversion of cottages to week-end use.[60] Large, extended farming households are becoming a thing of the past and young agricultural families expect a house of their own. This is not possible for many lower-income farm workers, who are not housed by their employers since landlords can make impressive profits by selling even ramshackle cottages to city dwellers. Rented accommodation for farm workers has become very rare in country areas affected by week-end suburbanization. This reduced availability of housing for permanent occupation provides a new and powerful contributory reason for agricultural workers to leave the land.

In some instances, selling cottages and land to urbanites for leisure-time use in peri-urban areas permits an influx of capital into the countryside. This is not always the case. If a sale is handled through an estate agent a proportion of the sum obtained will not return to the vendor who, in any case, may be an absentee landlord living in an urban area. Nevertheless, a new type of settlement geography is developing around the major cities of France and, one suspects, elsewhere in the world, as the number of week-enders increases but the permanent population of the countryside declines. Such a contraction hastens the disappearance of village schools and other services which, in turn, encourages further outmigration of permanent residents.

Urbanites occupying second homes primarily for week-ends create new expenses which, in France at least, have to be met very largely by the permanent rural population. Week-enders generally stock up with provisions before leaving the city on Friday and, as a result, purchase little at village shops. But it is the responsibility of village authorities to arrange for garbage to be cleared away on Monday. In farming areas close to Paris, severe competition for limited supplies of piped water develops over week-ends throughout the year but especially in the summer months. To the countryman's eyes at least, temporary residents are prodigal in their use of water, demanding supplies to fill swimming pools, clean cars and water flower gardens at the same time as farmers attempt to irrigate crops and water livestock. Such clashes of interest can only be resolved by sinking new wells and providing additional piped supplies. But the extra equipment may be required for only a few dozen days each year so that, for the rest of the time, the village has a surplus capacity. At present, the greater part of the charge for such utilities has to be met by local taxpayers, who are members of a permanent community.

On balance, the development of week-end suburbs in the Paris Basin does not benefit the agricultural population. Housing is taken over that might have been used by farm workers. New houses are constructed and landscaped gardens laid out on plots of land abstracted from agricultural use but which might prove vital for property rationalization or farm enlargement in the future. Vast quantities of water are consumed and extra tax burdens placed on full-time residents. Week-enders do not benefit village shopkeepers who, even if they are willing to cater for the urbanites' more exotic tastes, cannot do so at supermarket prices. Week-enders, in the Paris Basin at least, rarely buy provisions from local farmers who, as modern operators, have little for sale at the farmgate. This would not be the case in more remote and economically-critical areas where second-home residents stay for the whole summer and buy dairy products and vegetables from local mixed farmers who can derive profits from such sales.

Further clashes of interest may develop between locals and second-home occupants in week-end suburbs since the services of local builders and workmen are sought by both groups but to the satisfaction of neither. Week-enders complain that local builders and plumbers are slow and inefficient. Farmers complain that garagemen prefer to service city-dwellers' cars and ignore pleas to repair farm machinery. But some additional jobs are created in response to the establishment of week-end suburbs. Builders are kept busy in renovation and construction work but their heavy lorries damage local roads and place further charges on the permanent residents. Labourers are required by nurserymen and landscape gardeners to modify the environment by cosmetic treatment and thereby permit week-enders to realize their conceptions of rurality. Such jobs, together with part-time housekeeping and gardening, form welcome additions to limited ranges of local employment.

As already suggested, opinions on the desirability of second homes in rural areas depend, among other factors, on the degree of local economic crisis. One obtains an impression of general dissatisfaction from permanent residents around Paris and their complaints seem well founded. Certainly local taxes are imposed very lightly on second-home occupants in France and then only after several years of occupation. Unfavourable reactions do not derive in such proportions from areas where economic conditions are more critical, since economic benefits can come to progressive individuals and 'open' communities who choose to take advantage of the presence of second-home occupants. Differences in attitude towards urbanites separate progressives from more backward-looking rural dwellers, and can provide a powerful mechanism provoking the disintegration of rural communities.

Contrasting basic attitudes must be borne in mind when considering local reactions to second-home residents. Nevertheless, three-quarters of village mayors responding to a questionnaire circulated in the French Massif Central agreed that advantages from second-home establishment outweighed disadvantages.[61] Increased trade for local shopkeepers was the most important benefit resulting from second-home families spending their long vacations in the region. The second most frequently recorded advantage was the seasonal increase in activity and social life from which all other advantages (and disadvantages) stemmed. Some villages experienced marked improvements in visual appearance as second homes were constructed, old buildings renovated, and a special effort made by all-year residents to keep their settlements tidy.

Few mayors recorded any disadvantages arising from second-home occupation. Some noted technical and economic problems such as the need to provide piped water, mains drainage and electricity to second homes. Other disadvantages for some sections of the population stemmed from the fact that the local area was no longer perceived simply as a stretch of terrain where agricultural activities took place but had taken on new attributes as a series of points in recreational space. Landowners realized that by selling land, houses and outbuildings for second-home development they could obtain sums of money that would have been unthinkable from the sale of property for agricultural purposes. A new, urban-derived system of values was being applied, to the advantage of landowners and village progressives but to the detriment of agricultural labourers in search of housing and of farmers trying to enlarge their holdings.

The social results of second-home development are of two contrasting, indeed conflicting, types. The temporary presence of urbanites among country dwellers increases their exposure to urban-derived or 'national' systems of information and values which are already diffused through the mass media. Income derived from the sale of property or services to city folk allows some country-dwellers to improve their material lot and continue to live in the countryside rather more comfortably than before. For others, the acquisition of capital provides the necessary financial support to pay for a total abandonment of country life through cityward migration. This second type of reaction is particularly characteristic of young country-dwellers who may acquire new skills by serving second-home occupants and other tourists, but then realize that these skills can only be put to full use, and their aspirations be satisfied, through migration to the city. Contrasting flows of population thus result, as young people, especially those with initiative, move away from the land, and urbanites move in the reverse direction in search of rest and recreation.

Temporary flows of people to the countryside at week-ends and during vacations may be transformed into a more permanent repeopling process, as retired folk sell their city property and use their former second homes as first homes. Purchase with a view to eventual retirement is certainly an important factor in explaining second-home acquisition. However, it must be remembered that an inflow of retired people does not compensate for the loss of a balanced age structure through depopulation. To take the argument one stage further, inheritance of second-home property, rather than agricultural cottages, may become highly significant for future generations. This phenomenon already affects the United States, with a well-established second-home tradition but with the absence of the type of rural 'roots' that may be traced for many city dwellers in Continental Europe. 'Inheritance' rather than 'purchase' factors may acquire added importance in explaining future distributions of second homes. In any case, contacts between town and country will be strengthened with children regularly spending time in the parental second home.

Conclusion

The proliferation of second homes involves just one aspect of a complex process described by Rambaud as '. . . the dispersion of the town into the countryside'.[62] The rural-urban fringe, where built-up land gives way to more open forms of land use on the edge of the city, is no longer the single 'cutting edge' of urban expansion.[63] This role is also performed by second homes, either dispersed among farmhouses and primary residences in the existing settlement pattern or located in specially constructed new estates. Growing demands for leisure-time homes will require effective management programmes to provide necessary services and utilities such as roads, electricity, piped water and mains drainage. Strategies of second-home concentration provide by far the cheapest solution.[64] Land-use zoning schemes for agricultural rationalization and afforestation would not be impeded. Scattered examples of modern architecture would not offend the eye. The great paradox seems to be that new 'rural' agglomerations are being conceived – micro-towns! This certainly suits the planner, the landscape preservationist and some week-enders, but one feels that this is just what other week-enders are trying to escape from as they drive out of the city on Friday nights. The European image of the 'second home' as a converted farm cottage is already an anachronism in North America and will become so increasingly in Europe. In the next few decades, seasonal suburbanization will not only gather pace but take on a new form and dimension far removed from the existing pattern of rural settlement.

Further Reading

H. Aldskogius, 'Modelling the evolution of settlement patterns: two studies of vacation-house settlement', *Geogr. Reg. Stud. Uppsala* **6** (1969), 1–108.

C. L. Bielkus, A. W. Rogers and G. P. Wibberley, *Second Homes in England and Wales* (Wye College, 1973).

R. J. Burby, T. G. Donnelly and S. F. Weiss, 'Vacation-home location: a model for simulating the residential development of rural recreation areas', *Regional Studies* **6** (1972), 431–39.

F. Cribier, *La grande migration d'été des citadins en France* (Paris, 1969).

P. Downing and M. Dower, *Second Homes in England and Wales* (Dartington Amenity Research Trust, Countryside Commission, London, 1973).

V. Gardavsky, 'Recreational hinterland of a city taking Prague as an example', *Acta Univ. Carol. Geogr.* **1** (1960), 3–29.

R. L. Ragatz, 'Vacation housing: a missing component in urban and regional theory', *Land Econ.* **46** (1970a), 118–26.

R. L. Ragatz, 'Vacation homes in the northeastern United States: seasonality in population distribution', *Ann. Assoc. Amer. Geogr.* **60** (1970b), 447–55.

L. W. Tombaugh, 'Factors influencing vacation-home location', *Jn. Leis. Res.* **2** (1970), 54–63.

R. I. Wolfe, 'Summer cottagers in Ontario', *Econ. Geogr.* **27** (1951), 10–32

R. I. Wolfe, 'Vacation homes, environmental preferences and spatial behaviour', *Jn. Leis. Res.* **2** (1970), 85–7.

References

1. See, for example, R. E. Pahl, 'Class and commuting in English commuter villages', *Sociol. Rur.* **5** (1965), 5–23; and 'The rural/urban continuum', *Sociol. Rur.* **6** (1966), 299–329.
2. R. L. Ragatz, 'Vacation housing: a missing component in urban and regional theory', *Land Econ.* **46** (1970a), 118–26: 118; and 'Vacation homes in the northeastern United States: seasonality in population distribution', *Ann. Assoc. Amer. Geogr.* **60** (1970b), 447–55: 447.
3. R. I. Wolfe, 'Recreational travel: the new migration', *Can. Geogr.* **10** (1966), 1–14: 3.
4. B. S. Marsden, 'Holiday homescapes of Queensland', *Aust. Geogr. Stud.* **7** (1969), 57–73: 69; the importance of construction of new second homes is outlined in H. D. Clout, 'Second homes in the United States', *Tijdschrift Voor Economische en Sociale Geografie* **63** (1972), 393–401; and in J. M. Hall, 'Europe's seaside: a landscape of leisure', *Built Environment* **2** (1973), 215–8.
5. See, for example, *Ibid.*, 68; and V. Gardavsky, 'Recreational hinterland of a city taking Prague as an example', *Acta Univ. Carol. Geogr.* **1** (1969), 3–29: 9.
6. Quoted by H. J. Gans, 'Urbanism and suburbanism as ways of life', in R. E. Pahl (ed.) *Readings in Urban Sociology* (Oxford, 1968), 115.
7. R. L. Ragatz, *op. cit.* (1970a), 119.
8. B. Hedenstierna, 'Fran grosshandar villa till fritidsby', *Kust och Hav: Ymer Arsbok* (1967), 122–46.
9. D. Defoe, *A Tour through the Whole Island of Great Britain* (London, 1962), I, 6 (first published 1724–6).
10. *Ibid.*, **162**.
11. A. Young, *Travels in France* (London, 1889), 113 (first published 1792).

12. F. Cribier, *La Grand migration d'été des citadins en France* (Paris, 1969) 28; and J. Bastié, *La Croissance de la banlieue parisienne* (Paris, 1964), 64.

13. Quoted in A. Demangeon, *France: économique et humaine* (Paris, 1948), II, 199; see also A. Chatelain, 'Les migrations temporaires de détente et de loisirs des Parisiens, XVIIe–XXe siècles', *Etudes de la Region Parisienne* **44** (1970), 27–32 and 45 (1971), 31–8.

14. M. M. Webber, 'Planning in an environment of change: Part I, Beyond the industrial age', *Tn. Plann. Rev.* **39** (1968), 179–95: 194.

15. D. C. Mercer, 'Urban recreational hinterland: a review and example', *Prof. Geogr.* **22** (1970), 74–8: 77. Indeed the characteristics of second-home suburbs correspond with most of the following features recognized for primary suburbs: young married occupants with children; middle-class status; low population density; open space; see S. F. Fava, 'Suburbanism as a way of life', *Amer. Soc. Rev.* **21** (1956), 33–8.

16. R. I. Wolfe, *op. cit.*, 10.

17. R. I. Wolfe, 'Perspective on outdoor recreation', *Geog. Rev.* **54** (1964), 203–38: 218.

18. R. E. Pahl, *op. cit.* (1966), 269.

19. F. Cribier, *op. cit.*, 41–52.

20. J. Barr, 'A two-home democracy', *New Society* (1967), 313-15: 313; C. L. Bielkus, A. W. Rogers and G. P. Wibberley, *Second Homes in England and Wales* (Wye College, 1973); P. Downing and M. Dower, *Second Homes in England and Wales* (Dartington Amenity Research Trust, Countryside Commission, London, 1973); A. Goss, 'A site for second homes', *Built Environment* **2** (1973), 451–3; A. W. Rogers, 'Home from home', *New Society* (1973), 372. Regional examples of second homes are examined in the above references and in more detail in: Carmarthenshire County Planning Department, *Survey of Second Homes in Carmarthenshire* (Carmarthen, 1973); Caernarvonshire County Planning Department, *Survey of Second Homes in Caernarvonshire* (Caernarvon, 1973); C. Jacobs, 'Second homes in Denbighshire', *County of Denbigh tourism and recreation research report* **3** (1972), 1-60; I. Martin, 'The second-home dream', *New Society* (1972), 349–52.

21. C. E. Norrbom, 'Outdoor recreation in Sweden', *Sociol. Rur.* **6** (1966), 56–73: 64.

22. H. Aldskogius, 'Vacation house settlement in the Siljan region', *Geogr. Annlr.* **49B** (1967), 69–96: 69.

23. R. J. S. Hookway and J. Davidson, *Leisure: Problems and Prospects for the Environment* (London, 1970), 7.

24 For second homes in other European countries see: Anon., 'Cottages in Schleswig-Holstein', *Landscape* **15** (1972), 8; J. Claude, 'L'urbanisation des campagnes en Ardenne liégeoise', *Bulletin de la Société d'Etudes Géographiques* **41** (1972), 133–56; H. Carstensen, 'Bau- und planungsrechtliche Probleme zum Wochendhaus: Dargestellt am Beispiel Schleswig-Holstein' *Raumforschung und Raumordnung* **23** (1965), 29–32; J. De Wilde, 'Résidences secondaires et tourisme de week-end en milieu rural', *Revue Belge de Géographie* **92** (1968), 5–55; F. Dussart and C. Fourez, 'Les résidences secondaires en Ardenne', in F. Dussart (ed.), *L'habitat et les paysages ruraux d'Europe* (Liège, 1971), 103–15; G. A. Hoekveld, 'The Netherlands in Western Europe', *Tijdschrift Voor Economische en Sociale Geografie* **63** (1972), 129–48: 147; M. Ruggieri, 'Modificazioni degli abitati Abruzzesi, con particolare riferimento all' Abruzzo aquilano', *Bollettino della Società Geografica*

Italiana **10** (1972), 487–505: 505; J. Vendrell-Vidal, 'Viviendas secundarias en España', *FIABCI Reporter* (August 1971), 23–3; B. Vielzeuf, ' Le tourisme balnéaire du lac Balaton', *Bulletin de la Société Languedocienne de Géographie* **92** (1969), 115–38: 122; G. Werkman, 'Tweede woningen in Nederland', *Bouw* **41** (1971), 1454–6.

25. J. F. Hart, 'The three R's of rural northeastern United States', *Can. Geogr.* **7** (1963), 13–22: 18. Second homes in the northeast United States are also discussed in J. D. Black, *Rural Economy of New England: A Regional Study* (Cambridge, Mass., 1950), 609–15 and 759–60; R. N. Brown, 'Economic impact of second-home communities: a case study of Lake Latonka, Pennsylvania', *U.S. Dept. of Agricultural Economics Research Service, ESR – 452* (1970), 1–24; G. K. Lewis, 'Population change in northern New England', *Ann. Assoc. Amer. Geogr.* **62** (1972), 307–22; and U.S. Department of the Interior Bureau of Outdoor Recreation, *Northern New England Vacation Home Study 1966* (Washington, D.C., 1967), 1–12).

26. R. L. Ragatz, *op. cit.* (1970a), 120; a sample study of second homes in the United States is presented in U.S. Bureau of the Census, 'Second homes in the United States', *Current Housing Reports Series H – 121* **16** (1969), 1–38.

27. R. L. Ragatz, *op. cit.* (1970a), 118 and 120.

28. M. A. Brier, *Les Résidences secondaires* (Paris, 1970), 21.

29. P. Le Roux, 'Les Résidences secondaires des Français en Juin 1967', *Etud. Conjoncture, Suppl.* **5** (1968), 1–35: 5; and H. D. Clout 'Second homes in France', *Jn. Tn. Plann. Inst.* **55** (1969), 440–3 (contains a bibliography of French language material on second homes for the 1960s). Second homes as elements of the urbanization of the countryside are discussed in J. Antoine and J. Aglietta, 'La résidence secondaire, phénomène urbain?', *2000* **2** (1969), 16–22.

30. F. Cribier, *op. cit.* (1969), 271.

31. V. Gardavsky, *op. cit.*, 5.

32. R. I. Wolfe, 'Summer cottagers in Ontario', *Econ. Geogr.* **27** (1951), 10–32: 29; and R. L. Ragatz, *op. cit.* (1970a), 118.

33. W. R. Mead, *An Economic Geography of the Scandinavian States and Finland* (London, 1958), 81; and R. L. Ragatz, *op. cit.* (1970b), 452. See also S. G. Ljungdhal, 'Sommar-Stockholm', *Ymer* **2** (1938), 218–42 for the development of second homes around that city in the second half of the nineteenth century and the early years of the twentieth century.

34. R. Jean, 'La Repartition des résidences secondaires dans l'environnement d'une grande agglomération urbaine' (Lyons: Circonscription d'Action Régionale Rhône-Alpes, n.d., Mimeographed).

35. B. S. Marsden, *op. cit.*, 65–6.

36. F. Cribier, *op. cit.* (1968), 56.

37. D. Clary, 'Les Résidences secondaires de tourisme en Seine-Maritime', *Etudes Normandes* **67** (1968), 1–12; and 'Quelques remarques sur les résidences secondaires en Normandie d'après le recensement de 1968', *Etudes Normandes* **73** (1969), 1–11; and S. Hate and G. Ampe, 'Les Résidences secondaires en Haute-Normandie: les résidences secondaires dans l'Eure au 1.1. 1967' (Rouen: Mission d'Etudes pour l'Aménagement de la Basse Vallee de la Seine, 1968, Mimeographed).

38. F. Cribier, *op. cit.* (1968), 61.

39. R. J. S. Hookway and J. Davidson, *op. cit.*, **7**.
40. G. Wibberley, 'Rural Planning in Britain: a study in contrast and conflict', Inaugural lecture at University College, London, delivered 27 May, 1971.
41. V. Gardavsky, *op. cit.*, 24. See also T. Neubauer, 'Probleme der Naherholung für die Prager Bevölkerung im mitteleren Moldautal', *Erdkunde* **27** (1973), 69–75.
42. R. L. Ragatz, *op. cit.* (1970b), 453.
43. L. W. Tombaugh, 'Factors influencing vacation-home location', *Jn. Leis. Res.* **2** (1970). 54–63:56.
44. R. L. Wolfe, 'Vacation homes, environmental preferences and spatial behaviour', *Jn. Leis. Res.* **2** (1970), 85–7: 87.
45. D. C. Mercer, *op. cit.*, 75.
46. 'Loisirs – aire métropolitaine Lyon/Saint-Etienne', *Les Cahiers de l'OREAM* **6** (1968), 1–20: 16.
47. F. Cribier, 'Les Résidences secondaire du Bassin Parisien', in text accompanying *Atlas de Paris et de la Régon Parisienne* (Paris, 196), 907.
48. B. S. Marsden, *op. cit.*, 67.
49. L. W. Tombaugh, *op. cit.*, 56. Waterside planning problems associated with second homes in Ontario are examined by R. Jaakson, 'Recreation zoning and lake planning', *Tn. Plann. Rev.* **43** (1972), 41–55.
50. H. Aldskogius, 'Modelling the evolution of settlement patterns: two studies of vacation house settlement', *Geogr. Reg. Stud. Uppsala* **6** (1969), 1–108: 44–6. Another interesting attempt at modelling second-home establishment as a component of real estate is presented by R. J. Burby, T. G. Donnelly and S. F. Weiss, 'Vacation-home location: a model for simulating the residential development of rural recreation areas', *Regional Studies* **6** (1972), 421–39. But for a critical examination of techniques for modelling vacation travel see R. I. Wolfe, *op. cit.* (1970), 85–7.
51. H. D. Clout, 'Social aspects of second-home occupation in the Auvergne', *Plann. Outl.* **9** (1970), 33–49: 37–9.
52. H. D. Clout, 'Second homes in the Auvergne', *Geogrl. Rev.* **61** (1971), 530–53; and R. Beteille, 'Résidences secondaires en milieu rural:l'exemple du bassin rouergat du Viaur', *Revue Géogr. Pyrénées S.-Quest.* **41** (1970), 159–76: 168–9.
53. H. D. Clout, *op. cit.* (1970), 42.
54. R. I. Wolfe, *op. cit.* (1951), 29.
55. *Ibid.*
56. *Ibid.*, 30.
57. B. Barbier, 'Logements de vacances et résidences secondaires dans le Sud-Est méditerranéen', *Bull. Ass. Géogr. fr.* **344–5** (1966), 2–11: 2.
58. R. L. Ragatz, *op. cit.* (1970a), 119. A vigorous defence of second homes as elements for improving social and economic conditions in depopulated rural areas is found in B. Barbier, *Villes et centres des Alpes du Sud: étude de reseau urbain* (Gap, 1968), 274. But a rather more critical evaluation is presented by J. Jung, *L'aménagement de l'espace rural: une illusion économique* (Paris, 1971), 221–2.
59. *Ibid.*, 126.
60. F. Cribier, '300,000 résidences secondaires', *Urbanisme* **96–7** (1966), 97–101.
61. H. D. Clout, *op. cit.* (1970), 43–8.

62. P. Rambaud, 'Tourisme et urbanisation des campagnes', *Sociol Rur.* **7** (1967), 311–34: 311.
63. G. V. Fuguitt, 'The city and the countryside', *Sociol. Rur.* **28** (1963), 246–61: 257.
64. The case for purpose-built second homes in Britain is examined in R. A. Mordey, 'Second homes: a positive approach?', *Town and Country Planning*, **40** (1972), 269–71.

CHAPTER 7

Urban Manufacturing: A View from the Fringe

PETER A. WOOD

Most general texts on urban geography acknowledge the significance of manufacturing for modern urban growth and make some attempt to trace its structure and location patterns within and between cities. Unfortunately, the degree of systematic understanding which they provide about the operation of industrial enterprise in the urban system is not particularly impressive. One important reason for this is that successful manufacturing activity does not solely depend upon extensive urban development. Conversely, towns and cities may prosper without resorting to large-scale manufacturing production. Murphy summarizes these difficulties in another way:

Is there a city manufacturing structure such as [can be] described for retailing? This is hardly to be expected. Retailing is predominantly local in its appeal, so it benefits from nearness to customers; it follows that demand should result in similar responses to like situations throughout the city. Manufacturing would probably result in repetitive developments of this sort if it were entirely for local consumption . . . but of course, such is not the case.[1]

Further complications, reflected in the geographical patterns of industry within towns and cities, are associated with the inertia of land-use ownership and control. Physical morphology is therefore seldom a direct result of current patterns of activity. Thus Berry and Horton preface an extensive historical account of the evolution of industrial patterns in Chicago with the comment: 'the complexity of these [historical] events and their impact on the spatial distribution of industry within cities make it difficult to establish a theoretical basis for intra-urban industrial location'.[2]

Table 7–1. Classification schemes of manufacturing in cities

By areas: (R. E. Murphy)	By industries: (A. R. Pred)
A *Older manufacturing districts in central areas* e.g. port industries, rail access, water power sites	A *Ubiquitous industries concentrated near CBD* linked to wholesale functions, serving metropolitan markets; on perimeter of CBD, e.g. food industries
B *CBD manufacturing* e.g. light manufacturing, printing, newspapers, garments ('loft type')	B *Generally located communication economy' industries* need face-to-face contact be-between sellers and buyers, e.g. lawyers, advertising agencies, brokers, printing
C *Scattered factories in residential areas* mainly light industry and local service industries (pre-zoning regulations)	C *Local market industries with local raw material sources* includes use of local semi-finished goods and bi-products; near centre of city and, more recently, on the periphery
D *Industrial districts resulting from clearance and redevelopment*	D *Non-local market industries of high value products* random location in the metropolis, e.g. computers, pharmaceuticals
E *Outlying industrial areas* recent origin, on or near edge of city, large areas, modern industries; includes waterfront belts and:	E *Non-centrally located communication economy industries* need to cluster for the sharing of scientific or technical information, although not in the CBD, e.g. electronics and aerospace industries
Organized industrial areas single large firms or small-medium sized plants; includes industrial parks (i.e. organized by single agency); rail or freeway oriented, sometimes inside city area	F *Non-local market industries on the waterfront* e.g. heavy raw materials industries, petroleum refining
	G *Industries oriented towards national markets* bulky finished goods, near transportation facilities

Sources: R. E. Murphy, *The American City: an Urban Geography* (New York, 1966); A. R. Pred, 'The intra-metropolitan location of American manufacturing', *Ann. Assoc. Amer. Geogr.* **54** (1961)

Both the wide operating horizons of urban manufacturing and the legacy of its past land-use needs, therefore, seem to have confined theoretical statements about it to the types of descriptive generalization shown in Table 7–1. Murphy's scheme simply categorizes types of industrial area in and around a typical city. Figure 7–1 is an elaboration of the patterns which he defines. Pred's definition of industries is based upon the type of market which they serve (local or national), their possible dependence on local or imported materials, or the significance to them of communications between enterprises.[3] In spite of his strictures against earlier attempts to generalize about intra-urban patterns of manufacturing location,[4] the logicality which

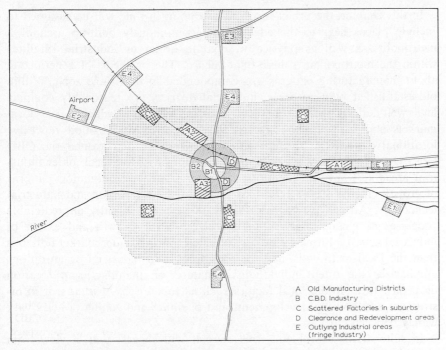

A   Old Manufacturing Districts
B   C.B.D. Industry
C   Scattered Factories in suburbs
D   Clearance and Redevelopment areas
E   Outlying Industrial areas
     (fringe Industry)

Figure 7–1   Generalized industrial locations in a large city

(A) Old manufacturing districts
    1. port industries
    2. rail access
    3. old water-power sites
(B) Central business district manufacturing
    1. within CBD
    2. around edges of CBD
(C) Scattered factories in the suburbs (sometimes marking former edges of the city)
(D) Clearance and redevelopment areas in old parts of the city
(E) Outlying industrial areas
    1. port industries
    2. airport-oriented industries
    3. satellite communities
    4. road and rail transport oriented industries
       (based on a classificatory scheme in Murphy [1966], 340)

Pred claims for his scheme is not very clear. There appears to be considerable overlap between the categories and too heavy reliance is placed on the significance of 'communication economies' as determinants of intra-urban location patterns outside the Central Business District (CBD).

The Urban Fringe as a Milieu for Manufacturing Growth

In this chapter, the urban fringe at any point in time will be assumed to include places near to the edge of the continuously built-up area of a metropolis, as well as physically separate urban or industrial satellites within the metropolitan sphere of influence. The problems of generalizing about manufacturing patterns are compounded in the fringe zone. Within old-established built-up areas, industrial districts are reasonably compact and well-defined. Many of them contain industries which serve local markets and, as Murphy suggests, this sector tends to exhibit repetitive locational patterns in different cities, especially in and around the CBD (see Figure 7–1). Even where markets are not primarily local, older industrial areas still have an identifiable history from which common patterns of growth emerge, based upon past phases of transportation and industrial technology. Around the edges of cities, however, apparently unpredictable processes of change are still taking place in the growth and extent of industrial activity. Firms are usually oriented towards wider market horizons than the local metropolis, and the size of modern industrial organizations emphasizes the often individualistic nature of manufacturing location decisions. In addition, local factors such as topography, patterns of infrastructure and housing development, and planning and zoning policies vary widely between cities.

In spite of these problems, this chapter will suggest that 'a view from the fringe' may provide a solution to the *impasse* which confines our generalized understanding of locational processes in urban manufacturing. Such a view releases the interpretation of manufacturing trends in and around cities from too close an association with conventional ideas about the 'urban system'. These ideas are dominated by the urban core as their central point of reference, and it will be argued that the concept of the core-dominated city cannot provide an adequate framework for explaining contemporary developments on the metropolitan fringe.[5] The inadequacy of this model of the typical city is most glaring for the analysis of manufacturing, since many important aspects of industrial organization are not nowadays closely determined by accessibility to the central urban market.

Another consequence of adopting a view from the fringe is the focusing of attention upon contemporary locational processes. This removes some of the confusion caused by the legacy of past industrial growth in the city, while also drawing attention to the various sources of industrial change that contribute to economic growth in different parts of a metropolitan area. For example, manufacturing expansion may be brought about through the *in situ* growth of established plant capacity, the relocation of firms and the setting up of branches from elsewhere, or through the seedbed growth of new establishments. The historical basis of urban manufacturing patterns can also be viewed in this light, since each of these sources of change makes a different contribution as industrial areas proceed from growth to stability and then relative decline. Most inner suburban industrial areas, now hemmed in by subsequent urban growth, originated as a part of the urban fringe in a similar manner to modern urban fringe manufacturing.

In summary, the urban fringe has provided the milieu for manufacturing growth since the mid-nineteenth century, so that current developments may be regarded simply as a continuation of long-established trends. Metropolitan satellite areas still rely to a large extent upon manufacturing for local employment, even though many residents there travel elsewhere to work.[6] Concern for the processes of manufacturing location change in cities, rather than for the neat classification of established land-use patterns, should therefore draw attention away from the urban core and towards the urban periphery, away from elaboration of the conventional 'urban system' to an examination of the contemporary 'industrial system'.

Decentralization of Industry – A Valid Model?

Unfortunately, empirical evidence with which to explore the origins and character of manufacturing growth in various parts of metropolitan areas is not readily available. This is one consequence of the assumptions which have pervaded their analysis in the past. Nevertheless, the nature of modern growth processes around the urban fringe can quite easily be established, simply by extending the reasoning of conventional core-dominated models of urban manufacturing change. Probably the most influential of these in recent years has been that of Moses and Williamson.[7] They hypothesize a simple situation in which a city core is surrounded by a satellite or residential zone and examine the processes of land-use change between these two areas during the past century. They point out that such a model results in rent and wage gradients which provide the lowest factor costs for manufacturing in the outer zone. Thus metropolitan manufacturing would have been decentralized in competition with other land uses even in the nineteenth century, but for the constraining role of transportation. The high cost of moving freight compared with moving people within the city, combined with high inter-urban rail transportation costs, are invoked as the primary reasons for urban concentration during the nineteenth century.

Low transport costs in the city core thus outweighed the low factor costs which have always been available for manufacturing on the urban fringe.

Moses and Williamson suggest that decentralization has followed transportation developments during the twentieth century, incidentally confirming Pred's remark that, 'even by the late nineteenth century, evidence was accumulating to show that the paramount industrial importance of the core of the emerging metropolises was a temporary phenomenon'.[8] The growth of road haulage first reduced intra-urban ties to rail and water sites, and later, with the building of long-distance highways, allowed more inter-urban traffic to move by road. Satellite areas also became more attractive because public and private road transport enabled employers to recruit labour from wider areas, in effect allowing them to create their own labour markets which functioned independently of core-dominated mass transportation systems. Improvements in methods of rapid personal communication, such as the telephone, also reduced the dependence of firms upon close proximity to each other for day-to-day transactions.

All of these trends have been well documented since the First World War in North America and western Europe and have reached overwhelming importance since 1945. It is thus not surprising that many industrial firms in metropolitan fringe areas were originally located in city cores and later migrated outwards. After three-quarters of a century of this process of 'decentralization', however, it is surely legitimate to enquire whether other processes of change and sources of growth originating in the fringe zone itself have now achieved greater significance for the explanation of manufacturing trends.

The results of the empirical analysis by Moses and Williamson of the setting-up of new plants and branches in the Chicago metropolitan area also raise the same question. The authors emphasize that the old city areas inevitably possessed most industrial employment at the beginning of the century. They demonstrate that in the 1950s and 1960s the number of firms that already existed in different zones of the metropolitan area provides much the most effective predictor of the industrial movement generated by each zone. Allowing for this factor, Moses and Williamson show that the propensity for plants to move out of different areas of Chicago was more or less constant in the period from 1950 to 1964. Their primary conclusion about the mid-twentieth-century situation was that variations in the characteristics of the destination areas were the most significant factors in explaining the pattern of industrial movements.

Even while confining their attention only to plant relocations, and thus disregarding other sources of growth in the metropolitan fringe, Moses and Williamson implicitly demonstrate how the edge of the city has generated an amount of industrial movement equivalent to the metropolitan core, allowing for its relative established size. They also suggest, like Pred, that decentralization from the city cores has merely been a transitional phase during which the tight concentrations of nineteenth-century industry may have supplied no more stimulus to growth in surrounding areas than would have been expected, given the core size, its former importance and its physical obsolescence. On the other hand, for many decades suburban and satellite areas around large cities have not only experienced rapid growth of indigenous firms (whatever their first origins), but have also provided a benign environment for the growth of new firms and for the attraction of increased investment from other regions. In these circumstances it is no longer sensible to regard outer metropolitan areas merely as industrial satellites of the central city. In fact, *they* have been the key regions for modern industrial growth during most of the twentieth century. Nevertheless, the best known analyses of urban industry since the Second World War have seemed content to perpetuate a core-dominated interpretation of urban industrial growth, in which decentralization to the fringe zones has not simply been regarded as a *description* of the aggregate trend, but has also been elevated to the status of an *explanation* of how firms make locational decisions within the city system.

This last distinction is important, since the trend towards a more scattered distribution of industry around modern cities cannot be denied. The *process* of decentralization, however, is a specific model which should be accepted only if it provides the most satisfactory available framework for explaining manufacturing location changes in a metropolitan context. A crucial assumption of the decentralization model, as exemplified by Moses and Williamson, is that the availability of transportation, land and external economies varies systematically away from the city core and that their changing use by manufacturing has resulted in the major locational trend of urban industry during this century; that is, in decentralization. Unfortunately, the core of the metropolis is not necessarily an important reference point for the locational choices of modern manufacturing firms and, in any case, many other facets of production, in addition to transportation, land availability and external economies, may outweigh these influences in locating new manufacturing capacity. Thus, although certain manufacturing industries may have behaved according to the assumptions of the decentralization model at certain times, it does not adequately represent the general processes of locational change in the mid-twentieth century.

Decentralization: the Persistence of a Myth

During the postwar period the tendency for industry to become more widely dispersed has frequently been discussed and analysed, following its general recognition in the 1930s.[9] The work of Woodbury, Kitagewa and Bogue, and Reeder[10] was particularly influential in the early 1950s, and their example has pervaded discussion of the changing patterns of metropolitan industry ever since, with its emphasis on the measurement of decentralization. This is not a retrospective criticism of their work. Rather, it reveals the failure of subsequent writers to build upon the conceptual and methodological foundations which they laid. The reason for the perpetuation of the decentralization 'myth' is due partly to the fascination of research workers with statistical trends, rather than with actual processes of locational choice by manufacturers. Also, the obvious elegance of a model which is based upon a straightforward trade-off between accessibility to the city centre and land availability has been extremely attractive. This principle, after all, has served as a very useful basis for generalizing about other aspects of urban life, such as residential land use and service industries. The preoccupation with decentralization arose also from what Woodbury himself, in 1953, summarized as, 'a constant admixture of analysis of facts and trends with advocacy of certain objectives and goals'.[11] Dispersion of population and employment has certainly constituted an important objective for social planners on both sides of the Atlantic. The traditions set up by Ebenezer Howard in Britain and the New Deal in the United States urge decentralization as a recipe for solving the social and environmental problems of large cities.[12] Thus the measurement of trends has usually been directed towards rates of decentralization, in order to examine the efficacy of these policies. A further policy theme which reinforced the pressure for decentralization in the 1950s arose from the presumed vulnerability of large cities to nuclear attack.[13]

Woodbury also complained about the ill-defined nature of the industrial and urban processes at work in industrial decentralization, pointing out that there was no standardized view of how it should be measured and little attempt to co-ordinate the time periods and geographical scales over which it was operating. In fact, little of substance has since been added to Woodbury's discussion in the Urban Redevelopment Study. He took up the example of D.B. Creamer in the 1930s and exhaustively discussed the processes of decentralization in terms both of factory and employment diffusion from major cities to their hinterlands and of the relative dispersion of manufacturing over the whole of the United States. One of his most significant conclusions, which anticipated Moses and Williamson, was that the forces pushing industry out of old industrial areas were of diminishing importance in relation to the attractions and advantages of the new locations.[14] Also emphasized was the continuing need to study the experience and requirements of different kinds and groupings of plants, different industries and different urban regions. Little of this type of detailed study has in fact been carried out during the past twenty years. Most of the analyses of general urban trends in manufacturing since the early 1950s have followed the examples either of Kitagewa and Bogue or of Reeder.[15]

The first of these two studies was a large-scale statistical analysis, comparing American industrial growth in central cities and the surrounding parts of their metropolitan areas. The authors analysed data for the periods 1929–39 and 1939–47. The degree of 'centralization' or 'suburbanization' measured by the differential growth patterns was also statistically related to population changes, industrial specialization and other characteristics of the Standard Metropolitan Areas (SMAs), and deviations in the degrees of suburbanization were explained in terms of local conditions. Changing suburbanization (both increasing and decreasing) appeared to be most rapid in metropolitan areas where current population growth was high compared with the recent past. Neither the density of the central city nor the size of the SMA were significantly related to the centralization or suburbanization of manufacturing, suggesting again that the pushes administered by congestion and land competition were not crucial in determining the rate of suburbanization.[16] Thus Kitagewa and Bogue undertook an aggregate statistical study and interpreted changes of manufacturing distribution in terms of a suburbanization process from central city cores. This interpretation was, of course, implicit in the formulation of their analysis of aggregate trends from the beginning.

Reeder's study was of one city, Chicago, and examined, first, the movement of industrial establishments outwards from the central city to the rest of the SMA between 1936 and 1950; second, the location of new establishments in the Outer Metropolitan Area (OMA); and, third, the relationship between industrial and population changes in the whole Chicago area. He showed that movements from the city were mainly directed to nearby areas of the urban fringe, although more widespread movements seemed to be taking place during the postwar years. Also, the appreciable movements from outside the SMA tended to locate farther away from the central city than moves by decentralized industries. Unfortunately, Reeder had no information about the total numbers of establishments in the core or outer zones of the SMA, so that he was unable to establish the relative importance of industrial movement from or to each area. He made an 'informed guess' that there was proportionately greater movement from the core to the periphery and concluded that centrifugal movement both from Chicago and from the larger satellite industrial areas would be a continuing trend.[17] His own evidence, however, reveals that during the study period, 521 new establishments were set up in the outer SMA compared with only 323 which moved out from Chicago.[18] No information was available about movements within the outer zone or about the setting-up of new firms there, and it was not possible to relate the moves from Chicago to its overwhelming established importance. And yet Reeder was able to summarize his analysis of changes in Chicago in terms of 'decentralization' and 'centrifugal' movements.[19]

More recently, in 1965, Meyer, Kain and Wohl included a statistical survey of central city/SMA differentials of employment growth in the thirty-nine largest metropolitan areas of the United States, excluding New York, between 1947/8 and 1958.[20] As an analysis of aggregate patterns this compared with that of Kitagewa and Bogue. Manufacturing was shown to have declined by 0·6 per cent. per annum between 1947 and 1958, while increasing by 15 per cent. per annum in the metropolitan rings. Twenty-four of the central cities had a decline of manufacturing employment during the period (twenty-nine between 1954 and 1958), while only four metropolitan rings declined at the same time (nine between 1954 and 1958). Although these data allowed a comparison of the differential growth trends between different activities, they added nothing to the understanding of the sources and processes of suburban industrial growth. Unfortunately, as in Reeder's work, a decentralization 'hypothesis' is judged to have been verified for many urban activities, including manufacturing.[21] The likelihood that much of the suburban industrial growth had nothing to do with the outward movement of establishments or of job opportunities from the old cities is not discussed.

Modern studies of particular cities have tended to depend heavily upon regression analyses of the relationships between employment or establishment relocation and other changes in the urban system. Logan's analysis of local government divisions of the Sydney metropolitan area sought to correlate changes in manufacturing employment between 1954 and 1961 with other variables, such as population change, local manufacturing job ratios,* industrial land availability, distance from the CBD and industrial investment in buildings.[22] The best 'explanation' of manufacturing growth seemed to be provided by population growth in the preceding period (1947–54), indicating a lag effect in the growth of manufacturing employment following general urban expansion. Areas of labour 'surplus' (low job ratios) generally had most growth, indicating perhaps how residential zones in the outer metropolitan areas attracted firms because of the ready availability of labour. In another study, Logan proceeds from the promising assumption that conventional models of city structure provide little understanding of entrepreneurial behaviour, and reports on a survey of a large sample of manufacturing firms in Sydney in 1962 and 1963.[23] His conclusions are, however, disappointing. A strongly-developed concentric pattern of industrial land values per acre is taken as evidence of the importance of accessibility to centrally-located transport terminals and other facilities.[24] Transfer costs to the metropolitan market and other centrally-located services are balanced against the economies of scale which may be available on large suburban sites. Substitution between various inputs derived from the city system is

* Number of manufacturing jobs
  ─────────────────────────────
  Number of locally resident workers

regarded as the critical principle for understanding the locational decisions of manufacturing firms within an urban area. Logan's approach is therefore based upon the decentralization model, which is open to the general criticisms put forward in this chapter. A hint of special pleading for the decentralization theme is evident in his discussion of industrial land rents, since their concentric pattern surely results from competition with other land users and tells us nothing about the general desire of manufacturing to locate near the centre of the city. The situation of Australian cities, however, may be somewhat peculiar because of their overwhelming dominance over both regional and national economic activity. Logan's general theoretical statements are of interest, since they draw attention to the purposeful manner in which entrepreneurs may substitute the production and locational economies available at different places. The centre-dominated pattern which he claims to have resulted for Australian cities may not, however, be the necessary result of similar behaviour in more widely urbanized regions, such as in western Europe or the eastern United States.

Both the analyses of aggregate statistical trends and the examination of particular metropolises such as Chicago or Sydney have, perhaps unconsciously, tended to reinforce the acceptance of a decentralization model of metropolitan manufacturing growth. In spite of considerable indirect evidence to the contrary during the past twenty years, ranging from Woodbury's conclusions to those of Moses and Williamson, growth in the metropolitan fringe areas seems usually to be regarded as the result of a process of movement away from the restraining conditions of old city areas. It is important to accept the fact that this may indeed be the case in certain circumstances. Conditions in Australia and probably in many parts of North America represent a stage of urban-industrial evolution in which the dominance of central cities has not yet been challenged for long enough to question the apparent validity of the decentralization model (the situation of cities in the developing world not being considered here). One generally searches in vain, however, for some suggestion that this situation may be simply a state of transition from the nineteenth-century city, or that there is a need to investigate the sources of industrial growth in and around cities without anticipating the strength of the influence of the local urban core.

An Alternative Approach to Metropolitan Industry

Until recently the study of the changing distribution of manufacturing in and around cities has been less exhaustively pursued in Britain than in North America or Australia. Most attention has instead been concentrated upon inter-regional balances of employment growth, and upon movements

of firms between different parts of the country, to assess the effect of
government policies on the declining economies of the old coalfield and
industrial areas. The effectiveness of particular planning measures has also
preoccupied the study of intra-regional growth, especially in the examination of the growth of new and expanded towns around London.[25]

In the late 1960s, however, some evidence has become available which
allows the processes of industrial growth and change in and around London
to be examined in more detail than before.[26] Although this information is in
many ways incomplete, it allows a more objective view to be taken of industrial growth in a metropolitan context than does other published information. It allows alternative hypotheses about manufacturing location trends to
be tentatively considered, and in particular it permits us to assess interpretations of manufacturing relocation which do not necessarily depend upon
the orientation of entrepreneurial decision-making to the city centre.

Several writers in recent years have advocated the study of industrial
location change as a bi-product of investment decision-making within
firms.[27] As an approach to industrial location theory, this has a number
of advantages as well as some disadvantages. In examining urban manufacturing it should allow the direct and indirect influence of the urban core
to be placed in the context of all the other relevant location factors for
different industries at particular places and times. The locational consequences of investment decisions can be examined at the scale of the
individual firm, operating in a metropolitan context or elsewhere. In
addition, certain generalizations can also be deduced concerning the likely
aggregate behaviour of industry. An example of such a generalization
might simply state that firms tend to minimize the distance of new investment from their existing plant. Since most locational decisions take the
form of an increment to existing capital investment and the desire is
generally to secure an 'optimum' return on this total investment, there is a
strong tendency for firms to favour the reorganization and expansion of
existing plant if site conditions allow, or alternatively the setting-up of a
branch nearby. Only in a minority of cases, where major schemes of
development are envisaged and the return on capital may be judged over
a longer than normal period, will major relocations be possible, either in
large branches or to new plants at some distance.

Keeble, in analysing manufacturing movement from south-east England
and the West Midlands between 1945 and 1965,[28] found that a relatively
simple distance-based gravity model explained the volume of jobs created
by migrant firms over a range of distances, including those to areas well
beyond the metropolitan fringe of the exporting regions. An explanation
of this aggregate 'distance-decay' relationship which is also applicable at
the scale of the individual firm, can probably be most convincingly couched
in terms of the management of capital investment. One important feature

of this evidence is its independence of any specifically 'urban' process. Thus, in the case of the evidence of Moses and Williamson cited earlier, an explanation, derived from the wish of the large number of firms in central Chicago to relocate plant nearby so as to optimize the return on their total capital investment in all locations, is perfectly adequate in itself. Decentralization patterns will emerge from this process in the case of a highly-centralized city where industry is seeking to grow, and sectoral movement to established suburban industrial areas is also compatible with the same process of selection. Equally, however, this reasoning provides a framework for a view of metropolitan trends from the fringe. Such a framework would categorize the sources of manufacturing growth in the metropolitan fringe in the following manner :

1. Local firms will grow *in situ*, as long as existing land capacity allows. Fringe areas are likely to possess space in which firms can expand or reorganize production.
2. Relocations of plants and setting-up of branches will come mostly from nearby locations. Thus the main source of relocation movement will be firms already in the fringe zone itself.
3. In-movements of manufacturing capacity will take place mainly from large manufacturing centres nearby (according to simple 'gravity principles' of new investment location). Thus, a large established urban area is likely to contribute considerable new capacity, regardless of any specifically urban process associated, for example, with accessibility changes or land-rent gradients.
4. There will also be some probability that plants will be set up from elsewhere in the nation or from overseas, according to the general attractiveness of the urban region within the national economic framework. Depending on the nature of the existing industry in the area, there will also be some seedbed growth of new enterprises within the urban fringe.

Until recently these alternative sources of growth have not been investigated in different parts of metropolitan areas. As fuller information becomes available, however, the balance of change around the fringe due to 'decentralizing' industry and to the other possible sources will be seen to vary between different metropolitan areas and is also likely to change through time in a manner which is of considerable research interest. It seems probable, for example, that decentralization has been of diminishing importance in recent decades. On the other hand, planning policies which encourage this movement may have boosted the contribution of metropolitan industry to growth in certain sectors of the metropolitan fringe.

Recent Empirical Evidence: the Case of South-East England

South-east England is conventionally defined as the official standard region (see Figure 7–3, p. 145) which, as Keeble and Hauser explain, 'very roughly circumscribes a London-focused functional unit'.[29] At its centre is the administrative area of Greater London, which will be taken to represent the continuously built-up metropolitan core of the region. In the 1970 *Strategic Plan for the South East*,[30] the region outside London was divided between the Outer Metropolitan Area (OMA) and the Outer South East (OSE) (see Figure 7–4, pp. 146–7). The former of these corresponds to the immediate satellite area of London but the metropolis has a variable influence over much of the region. This should not allow attention to be diverted from the fact that many areas of both the OMA and the OSE have very well-developed economic and social functions of their own.

The major finding which recent surveys of the London metropolis have in common, in spite of widely differing resources and aims, is that manufacturing firms in and around the metropolis have been highly mobile in the relocation of their investment since the Second World War. The surveys also share an important limitation for the purposes of this discussion in that they provide relatively little detailed information about sources of manufacturing growth for different zones and sectors. Even for industrial movement itself, which has been quite closely examined, the differing scope of the surveys has confused the resulting impression. Keeble, for example, studied the important north-west sector of suburban London and discovered, not surprisingly, that firms from there are tending to move radially outwards from the centre in order to find space to grow.[31] In fact, relocation has taken place to all parts of Britain and firms moving to the metropolitan fringe form part of a more extensive movement beyond the influence of the metropolitan area. His 'dual population hypothesis' may have some validity in distinguishing between types of firm which have indulged in short- and long-distance movement,[32] although the influence of planning legislation in producing this pattern cannot be discounted.

Two official surveys, less specifically focused than Keeble's, have produced useful general data but also have severe limitations in providing a full picture of manufacturing growth. The 'Howard Report', published by the Board of Trade, examined for the whole of Britain the origins of establishments opened between 1945 and 1965 in both new and old premises.[33] The country was divided into fifty areas and the setting-up of a new plant or a branch was counted as a 'move' if it took place in a different area from the parent factory. The survey was confined to plants with more than ten employees. The acquisition of other firms, or the setting-up of completely new firms, was not included in the survey. It also specifically excluded the growth of plant capacity *in situ*. The main difficulty of this survey is its coarse geographical scale, since it was primarily intended as a national survey. Thus the south-east of England around London, for example, was divided into only seven zones and moves within these were not counted.

A much more detailed survey was also carried out in the late 1960s as part of the research for the South East Joint Planning Team's *Strategic Plan for the South East*.[34] Within its brief, this is the most comprehensive study so far of industrial change within and around the London metropolis. The scale of geographical analysis was quite detailed (although, as usual, less so in the metropolitan fringe zone than elsewhere) and the examination of industrial moves was set in the context of a wider survey of industrial trends in the region. Its major limitation as a sample survey, however, was the restriction of its findings to firms with over a hundred employees.

The Strategic Plan report indicated the importance of relocation in contributing towards industrial change in the London region, by showing that nearly half of its sample of 3,270 establishments had moved between 1945 and 1968.[35] They provided 36 per cent. of the 1968 manufacturing employment in the region. Sixty per cent. of these moves were over distances of less than 32 kilometres and 30 per cent. were within London itself (defined as the area of the Greater London Council (GLC) and roughly corresponding to the continuously built-up area of London). The majority of these short-distance moves would not have been counted by the Board of Trade survey. Its comprehensive data for the longer-distance movement of plants with more than ten employees indicate that, between 1945 and 1965, 825 firms moved within the south-east region, accounting for 206,000 jobs, while 221,000 jobs were provided by the 723 firms which moved to the rest of the United Kingdom from the region.[36] Only 104 firms moved into the south-east region and 17,000 of the 32,000 jobs generated by these were in the 48 plants set up by overseas firms. These sketchy pieces of information at least indicate the considerable significance of industrial movement in and around London in the postwar period.

The first generalization that can be made about the pattern of movement is that it has been local in nature (more than half of the moves were within the subregions defined by the strategic plan). The less frequent, longer distance moves seem to show a radial pattern, from the established industrial areas of inner London to the rest of the south-east region. Unfortunately, long-distance moves which do not conform to this radial flow are obscured by the large size of the areal units that are used to subdivide the region outside London. Other information about processes of industrial growth outside London itself is difficult to glean from the Strategic Plan evidence. Newly-established plants do not appear to grow significantly faster in the metropolitan fringe (OMA) or outer region (OSE) than in the older metropolitan area.[37] On the other hand, the OMA does seem to support a more frequent seedbed establishment of new enterprise.[38] Nine per cent. of the new factories in the survey housed new firms, but this proportion was least (3 per cent.) in the inner London area and most (12 per cent.) in the OMA.

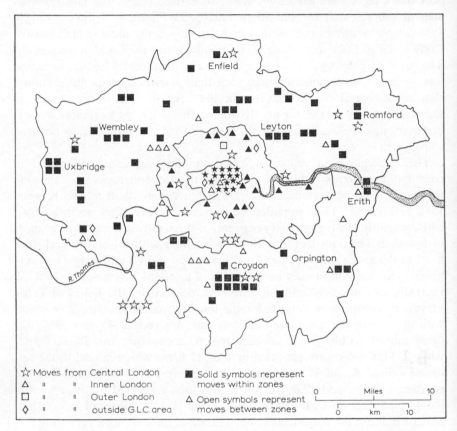

Figure 7–2 Location of new manufacturing establishments, Greater London, 1945–69; the map shows factories with more than a hundred employees in 1968, which had been set up since 1945; the establishments are classified by their area of origin, and include those that involved a transfer of premises, those produced by setting up new branches, and completely new enterprises (based on *Strategic Plan for the South East*, sample of relocated plants)

In the key growth industries of engineering and electrical goods (SIC Order VI), the proportion of new enterprises was 11 per cent. overall and 16 per cent. in the OMA. The outer areas of the region (OSE) contained fewer new firms. The survey excluded small firms and the sample size was quite small, so that these results are no more than indicative of the metropolitan fringe as the main area of manufacturing innovation. A further point was that 72 per cent. of the sample of new enterprises set up in the region since 1945 had been absorbed by other firms by 1968.

The maps and diagrams derived from the Strategic Plan provide some perspective on the geographical character of the movement patterns. The maps (Figures 7–2 and 7–3) show moves of the sample firms between zones

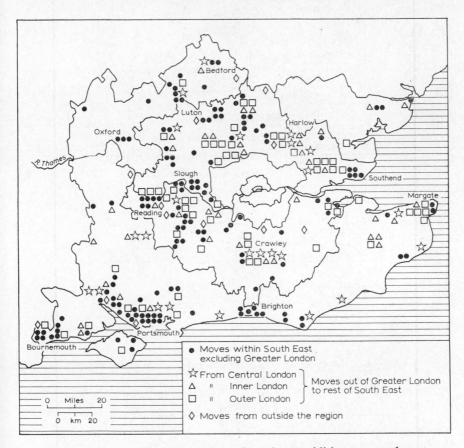

Figure 7–3 Location of new manufacturing establishments, south-east England, 1945–68 (constructed on same basis as Figure 7–2)

(open symbols), indicating in a rather crude fashion the radial element in the movement.[39] The dark symbols indicate moves within the defined zones, many of which were in fact very localized in their relocation. Nevertheless, the large element of intra-zone movement shown is a useful antidote to the assumption that decentralization is the key process of change. Rather surprisingly this is particularly true in suburban London (outer GLC area), and in certain sectors of the fringe (OMA) zone. The map for the whole of

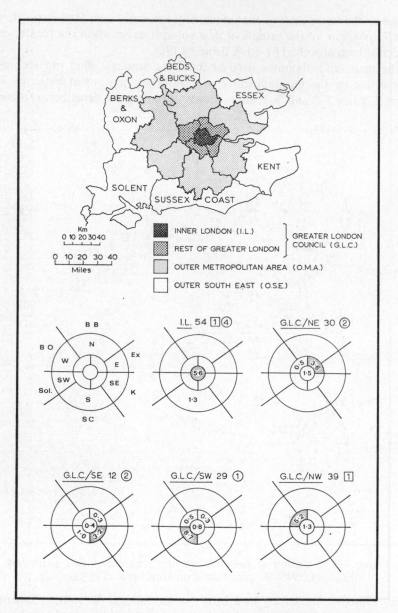

Figure 7–4 Origin of manufacturing plants moving to various areas of
south-east England; each diagram indicates, for each destination area, the
sample number of new plants moving from other areas of the south east
between 1945 and 1968, as a percentage of the total number of industrial
establishments in the origin area in 1948; the caption to each diagram

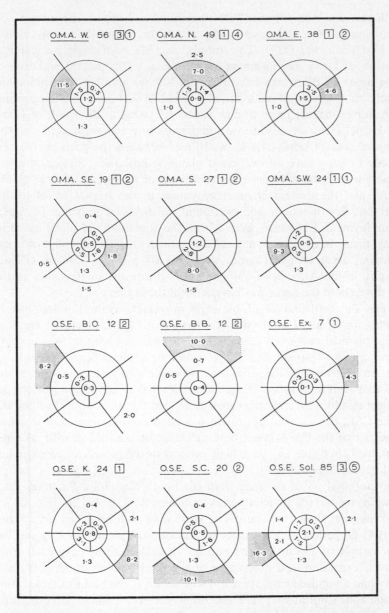

indicates the name of the destination area, the sample number of in-migrating plants, the number of plant moves from the United Kingdom outside south-east England (in a square), the number of plants set up from more than one other origin area ('multiple transfers' in a circle) (based on *Strategic Plan for the South East, Studies,* Volume 5 [Appendix B]) south-east England (Figure 7–3) distinguishes between moves out of the various parts of London and moves within the rest of the region (including the OMA and the OSE). The 'moves' include both complete changes of location and the establishment of branches. The pattern indicates that some areas of the fringe have received a large number of London firms, mainly as a result of national and local government planning policies. Such moves include those to new towns (Crawley to the south of London, and Hemel Hempstead, Harlow and Basildon to the north) and also to the Margate area of north-east Kent. Moves between the parts of the region outside London have also reflected planning initiatives, for example in the attraction of firms to replace the run-down of naval employment at Portsmouth and the movement of employment to the coastal resort towns of Brighton, Bournemouth and Southend, with their problems of seasonal unemployment. Elsewhere, even within the constraints of planning policies, many firms have set up new establishments in the already prosperous industrial areas of the Thames valley to the west of London (Reading-Slough), in the Aldershot-Camberley-Guildford area to the south of these, and throughout the north-western sector of the region.

Thus the contribution of outward movement from London has been greatest, in terms of establishments with more than a hundred employees, in the planned new-town communities, as was intended at their inception. Elsewhere in suburban and fringe London, a much larger proportion of firms have come from the same zone. In other words, there is some evidence here that well-established fringe industries have themselves generated the greatest stimulus for industrial growth around the metropolis. Farther afield, in the OSE, this element of growth has been even stronger. Other evidence suggests that the OMA is not only favoured by seedbed growth, as already mentioned, but also enjoys a high proportion of growth of manufacturing employment *in situ*.[40]

Further analysis of the data from the South East Joint Planning Team's research report on manufacturing movement is given in Figure 7–4.[41] Each diagram shows the sources of large new establishments set up during the 1945-68 period in the various subdivisions of south-east England based on a sample of 536 firms. The number of sample firms from each zone of origin is expressed as a proportion of the total number of firms there with more than a hundred employees in 1948 (which is the best available estimate of each zone's initial size). The diagrams therefore estimate the contribution of the different zones in and around the metropolis in relation to what might be 'expected' from their established industrial importance. Inner London, for example, has contributed some plants to all zones in the south-east region, but in no case has this contribution formed a higher proportion of its 1948 population of large firms than have 'local' moves. Further, only in the rest of the GLC area (excluding the south-eastern sector) did Inner London contribute more than any other outside zone, when allowance is made for its large established size. In view of both the overcrowding and obsolescence of the Inner London industrial areas and the persistence of the decentralization hypothesis, this is rather remarkable.

As was evident from the earlier maps (Figures 7–2 and 7–3), the establishment of new plants in the rest of the GLC areas has taken place from varied sources, mostly within the same zone. This area has also contributed to most other parts of the south east, especially to the OMA. Here again, however, a high proportion of new plants in the sample originated from 'local' sources, if the potential number of contribution firms in each zone is taken into account. Only in the eastern and south-eastern sectors of the OMA did the contribution of GLC firms (from the north-eastern and south-eastern sectors, respectively) approach the significance of local moves.

In many respects, this evidence is not very satisfactory. It does not provide the comprehensiveness of information about sources of growth in the different sectors of the London region that would ideally be required. The sample is not large enough for detailed patterns to be reliably discerned and in any case the areal subdivisions of the region are rather coarse, especially outside London itself. It is also possible that some of the 'local' moves may include a radial or decentralizing component which has been hidden by this generalization of detail. On the other hand, the exclusion of small firms no doubt underestimates the importance of short-distance, 'local' moves, and these would augment the pattern of such moves amongst the large firms in the sample. The absence of information on the sizes of establishments locating in different areas also leaves many questions about the significance of the different components of change unanswered.[42]

Thus, even in the case of this unusually comprehensive and in many ways very useful study, the bias introduced by a concentration upon movement of plants and by the tacit assumption that decentralization from London provides the chief basis for this, precludes the further use of the data for the investigation of metropolitan manufacturing trends. Obviously, this analysis shows an element of outward movement but, in the context of the historical situation, it is not particularly overwhelming. Even when *in situ* and seedbed growth are not taken into account, the analysis of movement alone points to indigenous forces within the fringe as the chief basis of industrial expansion there.

Conclusion

This chapter began as a view of urban manufacturing industry from the metropolitan fringe, and it has been critical of much of the systematic literature which deals with patterns of urban manufacturing location. Too much of both the theoretical discussion and the gathering of information has tended to confirm underlying assumptions, rather than subject them to critical appraisal. Too often aggregate statistical relationships have been employed to confirm one interpretation of intra-metropolitan changes (i.e. decentralization), without adding a great deal to our understanding of this process and without considering alternative mechanisms. Policy issues have also clouded the discussion and a core-dominated model of the city system still haunts economists, geographers and planners alike. And yet this model is generally agreed to be out-of-date for many urban functions both in North American and European conurbations. There is a lengthy documentation of the metropolitan fringe as the zone of most rapid industrial growth over many decades, not simply as a reception area for refugee firms from the urban core. In western Europe planning may have modified the trend, but fringe growth was already well established before official attempts at control were introduced after the last war. In any case, the imperatives of modern industrial and transportation technology have been actively accommodated by the planner in organizing industrial estates associated with satellite communities.

This chapter suggests that a different, and perhaps more objective, view of manufacturing growth processes around the metropolitan periphery in the 1960s and 1970s would probably provide some surprising results. Such processes of change cannot be explained in terms of hypothetical transport costs, rent gradients or even communications networks, least of all those which are oriented towards the nearest metropolitan CBD. They have to be appraised in terms of all the factors influencing the investment decisions made by industrialists. These will be determined partly by the existing patterns of operations within firms and partly by external pressures upon their production systems. A heavy weight of inertia acts through the first of these, so that incremental adjustments in the established pattern of location (leading to both growth and decline) are the most likely form of change in all parts of the metropolis. As well as general economic forces operating at a national and regional level, the milieu of the metropolitan fringe may form a part of the external influences upon the pattern of investment in manufacturing. For example, it was pointed out in the *Strategic Plan for the South East* that, since labour is particularly scarce in the region, its availability is an important factor which might encourage the success of new developments.[43] Similarly, where land-use planning controls are generally strict, the ready availability of suitable land is likely to attract firms to local areas. Only in such rather negative ways does the specifically metropolitan or urban context of modern manufacturing influence its changing patterns of production. Overall, the *Strategic Plan* could not identify any major advantage offered by one part of the south east compared to other parts of the region.[44]

In fact, the differential attractions of places are becoming less important as the road transportation, public utilities, labour supply and communications facilities, that at one time were only associated with large cities, have become almost ubiquitously available in countries with highly-developed spatial economies. Obviously, some industries have specific needs which may only be found in certain locations, including sites near the centres of large urban areas. Also, the decentralization of some plants from these large established centres is likely to form one component of the pattern of locational change that results from investment decision processes in manufacturing. Many other trends in the location of productive resources, however, may also result, especially since the pattern of established industry is nowadays so scattered around major cities.

The significance of this more general view of metropolitan manufacturing change emerges most strongly when its planning implications are considered. In Britain, as also in France, Italy and Scandinavia, much attention has been devoted to the encouragement of relatively long-distance movements by industry. For the purpose of reducing regional disparities on a national scale, this is obviously necessary as at least one part of any regional development programme. Within regions, however, the growth of the metropolitan fringe in south-eastern England, and also around other cities, nowadays provides a source of industrial growth for the development of established communities and the expansion of new communities which is not tied to relatively long-distance movement out of the metropolis. Although these radial moves can make some contribution, they are the most difficult moves with which to initiate a policy, because of the distances involved and the disturbances caused to the operation of the firms. On the other hand, many of these difficulties would be overcome by exploiting the growth potential of existing and often long-established centres of industrial activity in the fringe zone itself. Regional strategies need to harness the considerable growth capabilities of the metropolitan fringe, rather than remain pre-occupied with the more difficult task of attracting firms from farther afield. The experience of North America suggests that longer-distance moves from the metropolitan centre will make their contribution after attractive centres of growth in the fringe have become established. The underlying trend towards a more dispersed pattern of life in the metropolitan community is already well established and likely to continue. In these ways a view from the fringe may release planners as well as urban theorists from the mental constraints of the nineteenth-century city.

Further Reading

There is virtually nothing written which directly develops the theme explored in this chapter, which has criticized generally adopted approaches to the study of urban fringe manufacturing. The list of references to the chapter will provide an extended bibliography, but those new to this subject will find it useful to begin by reading some of the general surveys of urban manufacturing.

A wellknown article by a geographer is A. R. Pred, 'The intra-metropolitan location of American manufacturing', *Ann. Assoc. Amer. Geogr.* **54** (1961), 165–80.

A parallel article by economists is L. Moses and H. F. Williamson Jr., 'The location of economic activity in cities', *Amer. Econ. Rev.* **62** (1967), 211-22.

A modern approach to urban manufacturing which recognizes the complexity of the changing pattern of urban manufacturing is W. F. Lever, 'The intra-urban movement of manufacturing: a Markov approach', *Trans. Inst. Br. Geogr.* **56,** (1972), 21–38.

References

1. R. E. Murphy, *The American City: an Urban Geography* (New York, 1966), 340–1.
2. B. J. L. Berry and F. E. Horton, *Geographical Perspectives on Urban Systems* (Englewood Cliffs, 1970), 459.
3. A. R. Pred, 'The intra-metropolitan location of American manufacturing', *Ann. Assoc. Amer. Geogr.* **54** (1961), 165–80.
4. Including the transportation-based analyses of Alfred Weber, R. M. Haig, A. Losch, R. M. Hurd, H. Hoyt and R. U. Ratcliff, and the graphic representations of E. W. Burgess, H. Hoyt, C. D. Harris and E. L. Ullman and W. Isard. Pred favoured the type of categorization of urban manufacturing suggested by B. Chinitz, *Freight and the Metropolis* (Cambridge, Mass., 1960).
5. Pred mentions this point, *op. cit.,* 171.
6. This is emphasized in H. Blumenfeld, 'The urban pattern', *Ann. Amer. Acad. Pol. and Soc. Sci.* **352** (1964), 74–83: 'Now, industrial workers are predominant and growing in number primarily in the satellite towns of the metropolitan regions'.
7. L. Moses and H. F. Williamson, Jnr., 'The location of economic activity in cities', *Amer. Econ. Rev.* **62** (1967), 211–22.
8. A. R. Pred, *op. cit.,* 168.
9. See particularly: T. E. Thompson, *Location of Manufacturers, 1899–1929* (Washington D.C., 1933); and D. B. Creamer, *Is Industry Decentralizing?* (Philadelphia, 1935).
10. C. Woodbury, *The Future of Cities and Urban Redevelopment* (Chicago, 1953), Part II, 'Industrial location and urban redevelopment' contains an exhaustive review of earlier work and a discussion of industrial decentralization; E. Kitagewa and D. J. Bogue, *Suburbanization of Manufacturing Activities within Standard Metropolitan Areas* (Scripps Foundation, Maimi University, 1955); L. Reeder, 'Industrial location trends in Chicago in comparison to population growth', *Land. Econ.* **30** (1954), 177–82; L. Reeder, 'Industrial decentralization as a factor in rural-urban fringe development', *Land Econ.* **31** (1955), 275–80. See also A. H. Hawley, *The Changing Shape of Metropolitan America: Decentralization since 1920* (Glencoe, 1965); L. F. Schnore, 'Metropolitan growth and decentralization', *Am. J. Sociol.* **63** (1957), 171–80.
11. C. Woodbury, *op. cit.,* 206.
12. *Ibid.,* 205.
13. *Ibid.* Part II, Chapter IV, 'Security considerations in industrial location', 166–204; and L. Reeder, *op. cit.* (1955), 277.

14. C. Woodbury, *op. cit.*, 287.

15. See note 10. A number of general works and studies of particular metropolitan areas were also published, the best known of which were B. Chinitz, *City and Suburb* (Englewood Cliffs, 1964); J. Gottman, *Megalopolis: The Urbanized Northeastern Seaboard of the United States* (Cambridge, Mass., 1961), Chapter 9, especially 482–95; E. M. Hoover and R. Vernon, *Anatomy of a Metropolis* (Cambridge, Mass., 1959) especially Chapters 1–3 and 9; R. M. Lichtenberg, *One-Tenth of a Nation* (Cambridge, Mass., 1960); G. A. Wissinck, *American Cities in Perspective: With Special Reference to the Development of Their Fringe Zones* (Amsterdam, 1962); W. Zelinski, 'Has America been decentralizing? The evidence for the 1933–1954 period', *Econ. Geog.* **38** (1962), 251–69; M. Hall (ed.) *Made in New York* (Cambridge, Mass., 1959); and I. Lowry, *Portrait of a Region* (Pittsburg, 1963).

16. E. Kitagewa and D. J. Bogue, *op. cit.*, 68.

17. L. Reeder, *op. cit.* (1955), 277.

18. *Ibid.*, Table 1.

19. A study of the Chicago metropolitan area by M. W. Reinemann for a similar time period came to the conclusion that 'the primary increase in the suburban zone represents new industrial establishments'. See M. W. Reinemann, 'The pattern and distribution of manufacturing in the Chicago area', *Econ. Geog.* **36** (1960), 144.

20. J. R. Meyer, J. F. Kain and M. Wohl, *The Urban Transportation Problem* (Cambridge, Mass., 1965), Chapter 3.

21. *Ibid.*, 54.

22. M. L. Logan, 'Manufacturing decentralization in the Sydney metropolitan area', *Econ. Geog.* **40** (1964), 151–62.

23. M. L. Logan, 'Locational behaviour of manufacturing firms in urban areas', *Ann. Assoc. Amer. Geogr.* **56** (1966), 451–66.

24. *Ibid.*, 458.

25. The copious literature on British regional planning is concisely summarized in G. McCrone, *Regional Policy in Britain* (London, 1969). The location of manufacturing is more specifically discussed in Sarah C. Orr, 'Regional economic planning and location of industry' Chapter 2 in Sarah C. Orr and J. B. Cullingworth, *Regional and Urban Studies* (London, 1969); and D. E. Keeble, 'Employment mobility in Britain', in M. Chisholm and G. Manners (eds.), *Spatial Policy Problems of the British Economy* (Cambridge, 1971), 24–68.

26. Work is also in progress in and around at least two other British conurbations. For Birmingham see B. M. D. Smith, 'The administration of industrial overspill', *Occasional Paper* **22** (University of Birmingham, Centre for Urban and Regional Studies, Birmingham, 1972); for Glasgow see W. F. Lever, 'The intra-urban movement of manufacturing: a Markov approach', *Trans. Inst. Br. Geogr.* **56** (1972), 21–38.

27. The locational decision processes of manufacturing firms have been widely discussed by location theorsts in recent years. See especially P. M. Townroe, 'Industrial location decisions', *Occasional Paper* **15** (University of Birmingham, Centre for Urban and Regional Studies, 1971); P. Dicken, 'Some aspects of the decision-making behaviour of business organizations', *Econ. Geog.* **47** (1971), 426–37.

28. D. E. Keeble, *op. cit.*, 53–65.

29. D. E. Keeble and D. P. Hauser, 'Spatial analysis of manufacturing growth in outer South East England 1960–67', *Regional Studies* **5** (1971), 231.

30. South East Joint Planning Team, *Strategic Plan for the South East* (London, 1970).

31. D. E. Keeble, 'Industrial decentralization and the Metropolis: the north-west London case', *Trans. Inst. Br. Geogr.* **44** (1968), 1–55.

32. D. E. Keeble, *op. cit.* (1971), 42–7. The 'dual population hypothesis' states that postwar movement of manufacturing activity in Britain may basically be divided into long-distance, large-establishment movement to high un-employment peripheral regions and short-distance, small-establishment urban overspill movement around major conurbations (42).

33. R. S. Howard, *The Movement of Manufacturing Industry in the United Kingdom, 1945–65* (Board of Trade, London, 1968).

34. South East Joint Planning Team *op. cit.*; South East Joint Planning Team, *Strategic Plan for the South East: Studies, Volume 5: Report of Economic Consultants Ltd* (London, 1971).

35. South East Joint Planning Team, *op. cit.* (1970), paragraph 2.41.

36. R. S. Howard, *op. cit.,* Appendix B.

37. South East Joint Planning Team, *op. cit.* (1971), Tables B66 and B72.

38. *Ibid.* Appendix A, Table A17 and paragraphs 69–71, p. 26.

39. Figures 7–2 and 7–3 are modified versions of Figures 10 and 11 from the *Strategic Plan for the South East.*

40. Keeble and Hauser, *op. cit.,* 229, show that manufacturing employment in south-east England outside Greater London grew by over 400,000 workers between 1951 and 1966, to a total of 1,155,000. Their maps (especially Figures 5 and 7) show that, at least for the period 1960–7, the OMA was the major beneficiary of these changes. The growth rate for the south-east outside London amounted to 3·4 per cent. per annum, representing 53 per cent. of the total growth in manufacturing employment for the whole of England and Wales during the period. The Howard Report, *op. cit.,* p. 16, paragraph 51, suggests that 194,000 jobs resulted from moves to south-east England from Greater London. Unfortunately, in its data the reception region includes East Anglia and this number presumably also includes movement within Greater London itself. Thus an accurate figure of employment growth in the OMA and OSE areas due to the in-migration of firms alone is not readily available.

41. These data are taken from an origin/destination matrix of the sample of 536 firms with over 100 employees, discussed in South East Joint Planning Team, *op. cit.* (1971).

42. In South East Joint Planning Team, *op. cit.* (1971), Tables A19 and A20 indicate that larger plants in the survey sample tend to be set up over longer distances, as branches rather than as complete transfers of location. The mean employment size of the sample of moved factories was largest in the OMA (650 for branches, 420 for transfers) and smallest in Inner London (500 and 300).

43. South East Joint Planning Team, *op. cit.* (1971), paragraph 58.

44. *Ibid.,* paragraph 49.

CHAPTER 8

The Suburbanization of Retail Activity

JOHN A. DAWSON

The Process of Suburbanization

Retail enterprise is diffused from the city centre as a city grows and suburbs develop. Within the small town it is possible to find a single point with a level of accessibility which is acceptable to all consumers of all types of retail service. Shops are located at or close to this central point. As the city area increases, distances and journey times to a single centre become too long to be acceptable to all consumers and pressures build up for the development of non-central shopping areas. With a more numerous and a more heterogeneous urban population the pressures are further increased by a widening range of consumer demands. These pressures are relieved by suburban shop developments. Both the precise location and the timing of these developments reflect the operation of a complex equation involving both customer accessibility and the varied needs of different types of shops to attract sufficient sales in order to operate at a profit.

As any city grows so retail-service provision takes on an organized form, resulting from the interplay of consumer behaviour and retail economics. In recent years a third force has emerged, which sometimes works with and strengthens the other processes but sometimes works against them. This is the conscious effort of land-use planners to regularize shop distributions. Powers of land-use control allow the implementation of policies which can effectively stop the development of suburban retail centres or alternatively can positively encourage them. The locational decentralization of shops is a logical concomitant of the forces of consumer behaviour and economics of retailing, working within an expanding urban economy, but, in Britain at least, the variety of land-use controls available to local and central government can regulate and even negate this natural process.

Within most cities, economic, social and political forces have produced great variation in the character of retail land use. A wealth of empirical study has shown this variety in all parts of the world.[1] In western-type cities the supply of retail services frequently has a *nodal form* with the provision of well-defined series of spatially-separate shop groups. The demand for retail services, however, has a *regional form,* with a shop's customers usually living within a region which has the shop as its focus. It is the resolution of nodal supply with regional demand which provides retail activity with an overall spatial structure.

Many attempts have been made to define this spatial structure for particular cities or to search for order within the structure.[2] The cross-fertilization of urban-rent theory and classical central-place theory has provided, for example, a basis for attempts to explain the pattern of different sized centres. Areas of shopping activity have been defined and placed into discrete groups, based on the number of retail functions each centre performs.[3] Such studies inevitably distinguish a Central Business District (CBD), and a sequence of less important centres scattered through the city. Whilst such theories can be useful in studies of patterns prior to about 1950, increasingly theory and reality have parted company. Changes in the processes of both retailing and consumer behaviour have occurred beyond the ambit of the classical theories. And additionally, the policies of urban planners are often determined with only scant reference to current urban economic theory. The explanation of urban retail structure thus needs a firmer theoretical basis than one built simply on measures of the functional complexity of centres. The size of shops, their organization and type of trading must be taken into consideration if some sort of taxonomy of retail centres is to be meaningful. Some recent studies have shied away from the size-group shibbileth and have become concerned with individual processes operating within the urban retail system. Some of these processes are non-spatial and fall beyond the usual sphere of interest of the geographer; others fall more clearly within the usual confines of geography. Studies of the retailer's increased emphasis on selecting shop locations in the suburbs is an example of this latter type.

In essence the suburbanization of retail activity is the means by which the consumer demands of a relocated population are satisfied by profit-making retail enterprises, located in the suburbs but operated within a legal and administrative framework controlled by urban planners. The process is one of growth, both in retail demand and in retail supply.

Reasons for the Suburbanization of Retailing

1. *The Decentralization of Consumer Demand*

The primary factor responsible for the growth of suburban retail activity is the decentralization of demand. From 1950 to 1960, in the United States, total population numbers rose by 18 per cent., but the suburban population increased by 40 per cent. Increases of a similar order have occurred in parts of suburban Europe. From 1961 to 1971 over a quarter of the fifty-two metropolitan areas identified in England and Wales had population increases of over 25 per cent. in their outer metropolitan zones, compared with decreases or minimal increases in their inner metropolitan areas.[4] On a more detailed level, work in Nottingham indicates the considerable effective decentralization of demand in this medium-sized English city.[5]

The economic and social character of the burgeoning suburban population is as important as its growing size. In American cities it is the middle-class white population with its above average income that has long been pre-eminent in the residential occupation of the city fringe. In an early study of suburban shopping centres, Rolph indicated the influence of consumer income on levels of retail investment.[6] Prosperous consumers move away from the central area and attract after them a major sector of urban retail activity. In European cities there is evidence of a similar situation. Even as early as 1950, maps of average income per head in Stockholm show a strong differential between centre and suburbs.[7] Furthermore work on some non-western cities again shows a decentralization of upper- and middle-income families; currently in Japanese cities it is the newly-emerging middle class that is settling in the suburbs. Whilst the suburban retail demand is a reflection of the characteristics of the population moving to the suburbs, the suburban way of life in turn influences the population after it has settled in the suburbs. The consumer's economic horizon is widened and his demands become more sophisticated with movement to the outer city. As Duncan indicates, 'an appetite for better things, partly generated by social emulation, has created desires for better quality merchandise and improved retailer services'.[8]

Although the general implications of the growth of suburban population numbers are common to most urbanized societies, there are variations in the general patterns. In the United States, consumers in the new suburbs which grew in the 1950s had neither fixed shopping habits nor inherited behaviour patterns, as the new suburbs frequently began life with barely adequate retail provision. The movement of department-store branches from bases in the central area took advantage of this situation and was able to play a formative role in determining suburban shopping behaviour. Johnston and Rimmer have suggested that the suburbs of Australian cities in the mid-1960s were essentially in a similar state to their North American counterparts ten years earlier.[9] Around European cities, however, a different situation has arisen with suburban growth often occurring as infilling among existing villages or small towns which had shopping centres already established. New suburban dwellers thus found a pre-existing framework of journey-to-shop patterns into which they often fitted. In such environments it is the small, existing centres which have benefited most from the growth in suburban population.

2. *Increased Personal Mobility*

The second major reason behind the recent growth of suburban retailing is a change in consumer behaviour, especially in European and North American based societies, resulting from increased personal mobility. One of the roles of the car is that of a shopping basket on wheels. The central-area shopping facilities in most cities have developed in association with public transport, but with the massive use of private transport these city centres can no longer provide the services demanded by consumers. In 1970, over 80 per cent. of families in the United States owned a car; in the United Kingdom the corresponding figure was over 50 per cent. Both these average figures underestimate car ownership in the suburbs, with their higher income levels. Even more telling are figures for families with two cars, since the two-car consumer will use a car for almost all shopping trips. In the United Kingdom slightly less than 10 per cent. of families fall into this category, and the figure approaches 30 per cent. in the United States. Again it is the suburban population which is prominent in two-car ownership.

Transportation studies in Europe and North America have indicated that upwards of 15 per cent. of home-based car trips are shopping trips. This high level of shopping mobility has in its wake a change in consumer-buying behaviour. Some shopping trips develop into family excursions with a willingness to travel quite long distances to a shopping centre uncongested by motor vehicles. As Johnston and Rimmer point out: 'with a vehicle, factors other than mere distance affect the choice of centre, such as congenial shopping environment and ease of parking. In addition the consumer . . . may wish to avoid the drudgery of several shopping trips per week and complete all purchases for a seven-day period during a single outing.'[10]

3. *Central Area Decline*

The concomitant of increased retail investment in the suburbs is a decrease in investment in the central area. Once begun, the decline of attractiveness of a shopping centre is difficult to halt, and central-area blight can act as a major 'push' factor encouraging the decentralization of retail activity. Most inner metropolitan areas have a declining total population. Between 1961 and 1971 several British cities show a decline of 10 per cent. in the population of their inner districts. This population loss is the result both of the expansion of non-residential land uses and of the redevelopment of slum property at lower population densities. Those people remaining close to the centre often have relatively low spending power and hence the population in the immediate catchment area of central shops provides little attraction for new retail investment.

The traffic congestion of present-day central areas and their lack of car parking space are probably the most important factors in central-area decline. A survey of members of the American National Retail Merchants Association (ANRMA) suggests these two factors are of overriding importance.[11] Equally definite views are held by the consumers. In a consumer survey of Wilmington, U.S.A., 80 per cent. of respondents cited lack of parking as the most undesirable feature in city-centre shopping.[12] The results of both surveys are summarized in Table 8–1. Further related evidence is provided

Table 8–1.   Reasons given for central area decline

Reason	Percentage of respondents	
	ANRMA study	Wilmington study
Lack of parking	81	80
Traffic congestion	79	74
Antiquated buildings	38	11
Poor retail promotion	27	11
Slums around central area	16	

Source: O. Luder (1965), C. H. Brown (1963)

by a survey in Edinburgh, Scotland, which showed that 20 per cent. of the city's motorists made a conscious effort to avoid the city centre.[13] For this 20 per cent. the choice between shopping at the centre or in the suburbs is an easy one.

The age of buildings in central areas also provides an impetus for shops to move to the suburbs, since buildings in many city centres are increasingly unsuited to modern methods of retailing. The necessary rebuilding of European cities after the Second World War has helped in many cases, the Lijnbaan in Rotterdam being a prime example, but several North American city centres suffer from buildings that are unattractive and even uneconomic for modern retail enterprises. The relocation of enterprises displaced either temporarily or permanently by urban redevelopment often provides the opportunity to break the inertial locational bond to the central area and offers the shop operator a critical opportunity to move to the suburbs.[14]

4. Availability of Sites

While some economic forces within central areas push retailing away from central locations, forces concentrated within suburbs act in a positive, attractive fashion. Retail occupancy costs, in common with many other urban economic variables, decline with distance from a town centre. Cheaper land and often cheaper services coupled with the considerable space needs of modern retail premises mean that overall site costs can be significantly less in suburban locations than in the central city. Sites for shop units of over 1,500m² on a single level, and with parking close by, are either not available in a city centre or are priced out of the retail land market. Furthermore, when shops are provided after urban renewal schemes are completed, the rent differential between the centre and the suburbs is often considerably increased. This differential is apparent even with small shops. A comparison of rents in a renewal scheme in central Nottingham, England, with that of a suburban development at Beeston, six kilometres from Nottingham, shows that for comparable small shops of about 200m² the central area rents are around £24 per m² whilst in the suburbs £19 per m² is the norm. Comparisons in other English cities reveal essentially the same scale of difference between city centre and suburbs.

From the retailer's point of view, a further attraction of locations in the suburbs is the availability of labour. Modern retail enterprises require a large labour force, many of whom are employed on a part-time basis. Female labour, often relatively low-paid, is suited to many retail occupations. Reserves of part-time female labour are greatest in the suburbs and retailers have been quick to tap this potential labour supply. To the retailer, however, the overriding attraction of a suburban site remains the lower site-occupancy costs coupled with proximity to purchasers' homes.

5. *Administrative Considerations*

A final group of forces has to be considered in an attempt to determine why the decentralization of retailing is occurring and particularly to understand the speed with which it is occurring. This fifth group includes planning control and urban tax structures.

Planning considerations are particularly relevant in Britain, for until recently they have militated against mass decentralization. Investment in central areas was protected by policies of refusing permission for suburban developments. Only since the mid-1960s have major suburban schemes gone ahead and even now some disquiet is voiced over the possible decline of central shopping areas. The report on *The Future Pattern of Shopping* states that:

Discussions with a number of planning officers suggest that the programme of investment in many town centres has gone too far to be reversed and that those concerned with municipal planning would view with grave disquiet any development which would channel off a substantial proportion of the consumer spending which was reckoned on, either explicitly or implicitly, when the development programmes were started.[15]

Policies based on such views would most certainly slow down drastically the suburbanization of retail activity. This same report also suggests that the structure of the British urban tax system may also mean that planners of central cities are loathe to advocate policies which will reduce urban income. More definite information on the role of taxes in affecting retail locational decisions comes from Durr's study of Wilmington, U.S.A.[16] Although higher taxes paid by central-area retailers were not a major cost component, when added to the other diseconomies of a central location these higher taxes sometimes tilted the balance in favour of relocation in the suburbs.

Results of the Growth of Suburban Retailing

1. *Increased Retail Activity in the Suburbs*

From the inception of modern suburban life in the nineteenth century, the shops of the central area of towns have been slowly losing retail sales to shops in the suburbs. Alexander points out that between 1820 and 1850 there was a considerable growth in shop numbers in the United Kingdom and much of this was growth in what were then suburban areas, with the small general shop being particularly important.[17] Commercial directories indicate the high density of neighbourhood street-corner shops in the nineteenth-century working-class suburbs of British cities. Inevitably these shops were small, often less than 25m², and usually were general traders, grocers or beer retailers. Whilst such suburban growth did not actively steal trade from the central area, nonetheless it curbed the increase of central city sales by providing the new suburbanites with local shopping facilities. In the late nineteenth and early twentieth century, the increased availability of public transport provided a centralizing force on retail activity. This was offset considerably, however, by the development of suburban nodes with high accessibility where junctions of transport services occurred. Around these junctions shopping streets developed. British suburban retail development at that time was frequently along shopping streets radiating from such an intersection. In the United States, studies of Baltimore and Chicago have also emphasized this stimulus to development.[18]

The statistical record of the boom in suburban retailing during the last forty years has come primarily from the United States where the processes of decentralization became intense about fifteen years earlier than in Europe. One of the first cities in which major retail decentralization occurred is Los Angeles. Cassady and Bowden show that within Los Angeles County the proportion of retail trade undertaken in the central city fell from 34 per cent. in 1929 to 20 per cent. by 1939.[19] Much of the increase in sales during this decade took place in suburbs to the west of the CBD. Decentralization

continued in the postwar period: in the Los Angeles–Long Beach Standard
Metropolitan Statistical Area (SMSA) retail sales in the Los Angeles CBD
fell 16 per cent. between 1958 and 1963.[20] Over the same five years, a sales
increase of 29 per cent. was experienced in the non-central city sections of
the SMSA. By 1963, 94 per cent. of SMSA sales took place in shops located
outside a CBD.

Although Los Angeles represents an extreme position, in 1963 the average
for 102 SMSAs in the United States showed that 86 per cent. of retail sales
took place in the suburbs. A study of suburbanization based on these
SMSAs shows that the larger the city the less the penetration of the CBD
and consequently the greater the importance of suburban shopping centres.[21]
Analysis also reveals that over several periods after 1948 the rate of increase
of the suburban share of the retail market was greatest in cities with a
population between half and one million. It further emerged that the
differential between suburban and central-city growth was most pronounced
in the four highly industrialized northern and north-eastern divisions of the
United States.[22]

Somewhat similar conclusions can be drawn from the evidence of other
countries. Data on the 'central shopping areas' of English cities are available
for 1961 in the Census of Distribution.[23] Table 8–2 shows, by city size, the
percentage of retail sales accounted for by shops in non-central locations.
As in the United States, retailing is relatively less important in the central
areas of larger cities.

Table 8–2. Share of city retail sales accounted for by shops
outside the central shopping area, England and Wales, 1961

City population ('000)	Percentage
over 250	63·2
150–249	57·4
100–149	57·6
50–99	54·9
40–49	44·7

Source: Board of Trade, *Reports on the Census of Distribution
and other Services – 1961* (London, 1964)

The individual rates of decentralization of different commodity groups
may be viewed against this background. Again we must look to North
America for the majority of studies reporting decentralization of specific
types of shop. The mid-1920s mark the start of a massive move of department stores to suburban sites. Hoyt in Chicago and Cassady and Bowden in
Los Angeles indicate the intensity of this growth of suburban department

stores. In Los Angeles, for example, in 1929, 75 per cent. of all department-store sales passed through central area shops, but by 1939 the proportion had fallen to 54 per cent. This pattern is seen repeated in all the major cities of the United States[24] and the process has continued since the Second World War. General merchandise sales (consisting of departmental, variety and general stores) throughout the United States increased as shown in Table 8–3. From 1963 to 1968 the shift of department stores to the suburbs continued with the opening of 5,000 new shopping centres, many of which included at least one department or variety store. Department stores have decentralized probably the most rapidly of all shop types over the last quarter century.

Table 8–3.   Percentage change in general merchandise sales,
United States, 1953–63

	Non CBD	CBD
1953–8	+54	+3
1958–63	+89	−4

Source: Ullman, French and Meyers (1967)

Table 8–4.   Sales of shopping goods in a sample of shopping centres,
United States, 1963

Size of centre-sales ($m)	Number of centres	Percentage of sales which are shopping goods[a]
over 50	29	77
40–9	14	74
30–9	33	66
20–9	56	61
10–19	149	49

Source: Hoyt (1969)

[a] Shopping-goods sales consist of sales of general merchandise, furniture, household appliance stores

For a long time food sales constituted the major sector in suburban sales, but this is ceasing to be the case. The retail cross-section of suburban communities (particularly in the United States) is now far less weighted by convenience shops than it was in the early part of this century. Thompson has modelled this diversification of suburban retailing in the San Francisco area.[25] Results of analysis for 1939 and 1958 were projected to 1968 and showed clearly that, proportionally, food sales were declining and general-merchandise and automotive-goods sales were increasing. Hoyt shows that, in 1963, the Hillsdale planned shopping centre (San Francisco), in common with many other planned suburban centres (Table 8–4), had 76 per cent. of sales classed as shopping-goods sales.[26] Such suburban centres are now

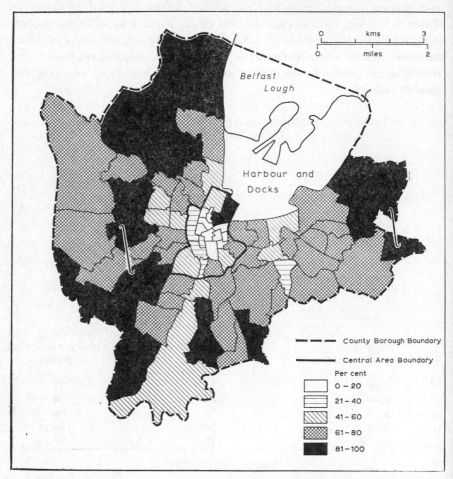

Figure 8–1   Percentage of zonal sales passing through foodshops, Belfast, Northern Ireland, 1965

major nodes of comparison-shopping facilities. The limited studies outside the United States show essentially similar results, but the diversification of suburban sales is far less marked. Beed in Sydney and Johnston and Rimmer in Melbourne report that shops selling comparison goods are beginning to move to the suburbs thus eroding the dominance of the convenience shop.[27]

In many parts of Europe, however, the convenience shop is still dominant in the suburbs. Figure 8–1 shows for 1965 the dichotomy between the Belfast, Northern Ireland, central area and suburbs in terms of sales through food and non-food shops. Several zones within the central area have less than 10 per cent. of sales through food shops and in the suburban centre of east Belfast less than half of retail sales are through food shops. This subcentre includes a wide range of non-food shops and Jones stresses its importance in the retail system of Belfast City.[28] Throughout the remainder of Belfast, food stores account for over 70 per cent. of zonal sales. The central area remains important in overall urban retail provision and is particularly important in the supply of comparison shopping goods, for the suburbanization process in European cities has not reached the stage currently found in North America.

2. *Forms of Suburban Development*

The most comprehensive study of intra-urban retailing is of Chicago.[29] Within the total retail structure Berry examines a five-tier hierarchy consisting of the CBD and four levels of outlying centres. Superimposed on this hierarchical framework is a basic and vital distinction between unplanned and planned centres. Most modern suburban retail development is in planned centres and the designed shopping area is a result of the retail suburbanization process. In most cities few planned centres date from before 1950, yet it has been shown above that suburban retailing was gaining momentum during the 1930s. Unplanned centres represent the results of early phases of the suburbanization process.

Unplanned developments. Whilst Berry identifies a well defined hierarchy of unplanned centres in Chicago, as well as 800 kilometres of retail ribbon, workers in other cities stress only the ribbon form of the older suburban shopping districts. Parker, in a detailed study of Liverpool for example, finds no evidence of definable suburban centres.[30] He distinguishes *shopping thoroughfares*, which are shown to contain practically every kind of shop with a mixture of traditional 'neighbourhood' and 'subcentre' activities; additionally, although the thoroughfares differ in size, they are very similar to each other in pattern, showing that there is no justification for distinguishing between them functionally. The radial character of the road layout of Liverpool is partly responsible for this form of the suburban retail development. Hoyt argues that the centre form of so much suburban development in Chicago is also a result of the street pattern, but in this instance the regular gridiron layout.[31] Accessibility thus appears to be the key to the form of the unplanned retail developments, and it may be wrong to attempt explanations of patterns in radial cities by reference to theories developed in gridiron cities.

Jones, in Belfast, found evidence for both ribbon development and centre development occurring together.[32] Outlying business centres were classified, but stress was laid on the way the centres merge together along major roads. Such retail development is the result of a slow process of suburban growth in which land uses change to retail functions as population numbers increase and housing spreads outwards from the city. Weekley distinguishes this process in Nottingham and is further able to identify some centres which were formerly small villages and are now absorbed into the continuous built-up area.[33] Thus it is quite possible for unplanned suburban retailing land use to have either a block or linear form, or in some instances a combination of the two. In general, unplanned suburban retail development has grown slowly, is frequently difficult to delimit precisely (particularly as centres), and is characterized by older buildings with some areas now suffering a similar *malaise* to the CBD, as competitive advantage is gained by newer planned centres.

Planned developments. In contrast, suburban planned retail land use is clearly defined, of recent occurrence, rapidly growing in area, of nodal form and consists of custom-built retail establishments.

The first shopping centre of appreciable size, planned with the car in mind, was opened in 1920 at Kansas City, U.S.A. In North America, the spread of suburban centres was slow until about 1950; in Europe they were virtually non-existent. In the United States, however, approximately 15,000 planned centres were in operation by the early 1970s. Figure 8–2 graphs the phenomenal rise in their numbers and shows their particularly rapid growth in the late 1960s. These figures cover the whole range of centre sizes, from the few giant regional centres with over 100,000 m² commercial area to the multitude of small neighbourhood centres with a commercial area of 5,000 m² or less.

In western-type cities outside North America, the whole suburbanization process began later and planned centres did not become a significant part of the retail system until the 1960s. In Australia, for example, the first of Melbourne's planned centres opened in 1958 and Chadstone and Northland, both large centres in suburban Melbourne, followed in the early and mid-1960s respectively. Around most of the major cities of Europe there are planned suburban shopping centres, large and small, dating from the mid-1960s.

In the United Kingdom and Mediterranean Europe, however, there are few if any centres of a scale comparable to even the middle-sized centres of the United States, Sweden or Germany. The small-neighbourhood planned centres in the United Kingdom are plentiful and date from the mid-1950s,[34] but only in the 1970s have major developments obtained planning permission; the Brent Cross development in North London was the first large centre to be given planning permission, but others seem likely to follow. A few medium-sized centres opened in the late 1960s – the Cowley centre at Oxford and the Yate centre at Bristol are examples – but the major development of planned suburban shopping centres has yet to occur.

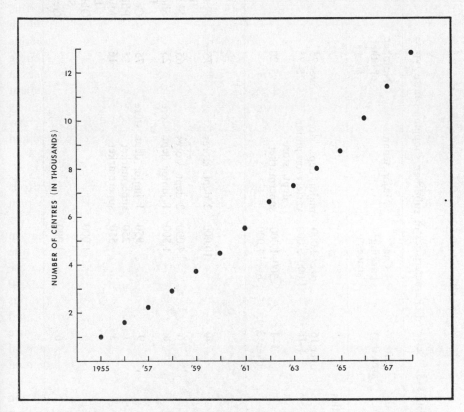

Figure 8–2   Rise in numbers of planned shopping centres, United States, 1955–68

On the basis of size and function of American centres a three-tier grouping of planned centres has been defined.[35] The largest developments are classified as *regional centres* and serve a population in excess of 100,000. *The community centres* form a second-tier and serve 20,000–100,000 people. The smallest centres, *neighbourhood centres*, serve 7,000–20,000 people. Some characteristics of the grades of centre are generalized and summarized in Table 8–5. With the addition of a fourth type, this classification has wider application to suburban retailing in both North America and Europe.

Table 8–5. Selected characteristics of suburban shopping centre types

Type of centre	Total commercial floor area (m²)	Site area (ha)	Car parking spaces	Major tenant	Number of other shops	Name of centre
I Generalized summary statistics						
Regional	over 40,000	over 16	over 3,000	major dept. store	over 75	
Community	10–40,000	4–16	1,000–3,000	variety or junior dept. store	25–75	
Neighbourhood	under 10,000	1–4	300–1,000	supermarket	5–20	
Discount Store	over 6,000	over 3	over 1,000			
II Examples						
Regional	110,000	40	10,000	2 dept. stores	75+	Peabody, North Shore Boston
Regional	56,000	16	4,000	2 dept. stores	65	Skärholm, Stockholm
Community	20,000	8	1,500	1 junior dept. store	25	Shelby Road Plaza, Louisville
Community	25,000	9	950	1 junior dept. store	75	Cowley, Oxford
Neighbourhood	3,300	1	250	supermarket	15	Phibsboro, Dublin
Neighbourhood	4,000	3	550	supermarket	16	Middleton Plaza, Louisville
Discount Store	15,000	6	1,000			Obs! Rotebro, Stockholm
Discount Store	9,400	6	1,000			Gem, Nottingham

This fourth type is the suburban superstore, or discount store, with at least 6,000 m² of selling space and plentiful car parking provision.

Taking, as a somewhat arbitrary figure, 40,000 m² commercial space as the minimum size of a regional centre, then in 1970 some four hundred existed in North America whilst it would be difficult to have found more than twenty-five in the rest of the world. These centres are characterized by containing at least one major department store, a group of speciality clothing shops, as well as supermarkets, restaurants and general convenience shops. Location is all important for the success or failure of regional centres. The Peabody North Shore Centre is located 30 kilometres from Boston's CBD at the junction of a radial route into Boston with the main ring route around Boston. Well within the metropolitan Boston area and with high accessibility, the centre has a potential catchment population of almost 1½ million people. Many regional centres are designed on a 'mall' plan, with shops facing each other along a series of intersecting pedestrian ways about 15m wide. In the United States, the earliest centres were open to the weather but many now have closed malls and air conditioning allowing all-weather shopping.

The typical community centre has about 20,000 m² commercial space with the shop units forming an I, L or U. A series of these centres is found around many cities about 15 kilometres from the CBD. Around Detroit, for example, in 1965, there were thirty-five planned community shopping centres. These, with one exception, all occur 12 kilometres and further from the CBD. Several of the planned centres supplement existing, older, un-planned centres, but the vast majority have been developed to serve the shopping needs of an extending and motorized urban population. A report on the Cowley Centre, one of the few British examples, stresses the importance of public transport accessibility, and particularly bus routing, for the success of the project.[36] This shows clearly a major distinction between Europe and North America. The community centre in North America is geared to car shopping but in Europe public transport is still important in the journey-to-shop pattern.

Public transport is also of primary importance for Japanese shopping centres, but in this case the railway network is also important.[37] Although shopping centres are new to Japanese retailing, with less than ten currently operational, most are of community-centre size. With relatively high site costs, even in the suburbs, there are pressures to build multilevel centres and to reduce car-parking to a minimum. For example in suburban Tokyo, the Tamagawa Centre has a ground floor area of 20,000 m² and a total floorspace of 40,000 m², but parking for only 1,000 cars. Despite the large commercial area the market penetration does not allow, as yet, its classification as a regional centre.

The neighbourhood centre is by far the most numerous in North America and Europe. A supermarket of about 1,000 m² is the typical major tenant in such developments. Shops in these small centres are usually in a block 100–125 m long, with parking in front of the shops in the older centres and in separate car parks in the newer centres. Provision of neighbourhood centres in the United Kingdom during the 1950s and 1960s was extraordinarily haphazard, with very different planning policies in different planning authorities. A survey of local authorities in 1967 revealed that some planning authorities provided these local shops on a basis of 6 per 1,000 of the population and others on the basis of 1 per 1,000 population.[38] Furthermore, acceptable distances between centres varied from $\frac{1}{2}$ to $1\frac{1}{2}$ kilometres. Some 7 per cent. of the local authorities had no policy at all on shop provision. Under such circumstances, the number, size and density of planned neighbourhood shopping centres varies strongly from area to area. Perhaps it is not surprising that so few major suburban developments have been given planning permission in the United Kingdom.

The final group of planned developments in the suburbs is that of the discount stores located in large, cheaply-constructed buildings, often close to a regional centre but not part of it. In 1965, in the United States, there were some 1,500 such stores with a floor space over 6,000 m² of which a very high percentage was selling space. As discount houses multiplied so supermarkets discovered that, by locating nearby, their sales increased by up to 15 per cent. The logical next step was the inclusion of supermarkets in the discount stores, thus essentially producing a shopping centre under one roof. These developments are not unique to the United States. Gem and Woolco in the United Kingdom are essentially discount stores.[39] In Sweden, Obs! stores have been developed by the Swedish Consumer Co-operative sector to the north and south of Stockholm. In Belgium there are at least twenty such discount stores, some of which are located to attract Dutch customers as well as suburbanites from, for example, Antwerp. With probably two hundred discount stores of over 6,000 m² commercial space, western Europe lags behind the United States, but development in Europe is proceeding at a rapid pace.

3. *Suburban Consumer Behaviour*

The frequency of visiting a suburban shop development is inversely related to the size of the development. Thus several visits per week are made to the small convenience shopping areas whilst visits to large centres may be as infrequent as one per month. A survey of Watford, England, showed that 77 per cent. of visitors to local centres shopped there several times per week, whilst the survey of the Cowley centre at Oxford showed that rather less than 60 per cent. of shoppers visited more than once a week.[40] From Johnston's and Rimmer's work in Melbourne two more important points about suburban consumer behaviour emerge. First, patterns are different with planned and unplanned centres and, second, a new large planned centre, within acceptable shopping distance, has considerable influence on the frequency of use of small centres close to the shoppers' home. If centres of comparable size are studied, more daily visits are made to unplanned centres than to planned centres. The latter are in effect perceived by the consumer as much larger than they really are. The development of a new accessible centre further affected Melbourne's suburban shoppers by reducing their need for trips to the CBD and increasing the frequency of their visits to local centres. Consumer demand became satisfied, for the most part, by two centres – a local one and the new large development – and therefore there was no need for search visits to centres other than the local one. Consequently there was an increase in the frequency of visits to the local centre.

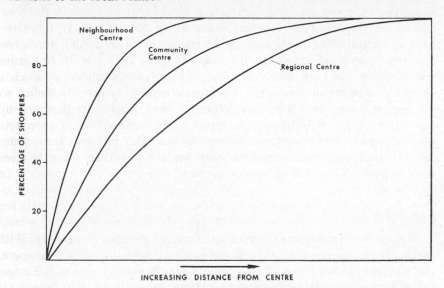

Figure 8–3 Generalized relationships of distance to number of shoppers for three types of shopping centre

Although gross figures of frequency of shopping trips can be instrumental in determining the drawing power of centres, it must be remembered that frequency of visits varies with a wide range of social and economic variables. Age, length of residence in a particular suburb, income, household size and number of children under school age all affect frequency. As household size increases, for example, shop visits become more frequent and proportionally more frequent at suburban centres in comparison with inner-city centres. Perhaps the most important single determinant of shopping frequency, however, is the distance of the consumer from shopping facilities. Most people shopping frequently travel short distances, whilst infrequent shoppers travel long distances, a general conclusion that can be drawn from surveys at many suburban shopping areas.[41] Nonetheless it must also be remembered that trip-length distributions vary by type of centre. The generalized pattern is shown in Figure 8–3; some surveys suggest that all the graphs of Figure 8–3 are moving slowly to the right as trip length to all types of centre becomes longer.[42]

The distance factor in the journey to shop is closely related to mode of transport. All studies of consumer behaviour in the suburbs show that cars dominate longer shopping trips. For middle-distance trips, cars again dominate in North America, but in Europe public transport is important, especially to 'unplanned' centres. Apart from length of journey there are a number of other variables which appear related to method of travel. Particularly important is the value of purchases per trip. The car allows large quantities of goods to be bought on a single trip and this feature is particularly important for discount stores which rely on a large turnover with a relatively low profit margin. Increases in car-ownership levels in turn create increased use of cars for shopping trips. Their use for comparison shopping has been high for some time in both North America and Europe, but in recent years there has been a notable increase in their use for grocery shopping. The distribution of trip length, frequency and expenditure may all be related to travel mode, with suburban shoppers placing considerable importance on trips by car. This in turn often means longer, fewer and more expensive trips for the suburban housewife in comparison with her inner-urban counterpart.

Conclusion

The process of suburbanization of retail activity depends to a considerable extent on the current state of both the personal technologies of consumers and the retail technologies of shop operators. Changes in personal technologies produce changes in the suburbanization process, both in its speed and its results. For example, increased personal mobility and the ability to store more food at home have resulted in fewer shopping trips, more goods purchased per trip, a need for fewer centres and a decrease in demand for the medium-sized shopping centre. Changes in retailing technology have all led to an increased scale of shop operation. More efficient stock control and retail techniques have allowed retailers to increase drastically the size of their operations, whilst advances in engineering technology enable retail outlets to grow physically with their business. The large outlet in a large suburban shopping centre seems to be the basic pattern of retailing for the immediate future. The future of retailing lies in large, widely-spaced centres serving car-borne shoppers and containing very large stores selling a wide range of goods. Experiments are already in hand with air-conditioned, tent-like structures covering over half a million square metres but enclosing a very few shop units.

The horizontal integration of retail enterprises is a second trend in evidence in suburban shopping patterns. Retail firms are increasingly taking on the functions of wholesalers, brokers and manufacturers. In some instances the production and marketing operations occur wholly within one firm. Until now the location problem of the shop operator has been one of finding a least cost transport location for a single marketing institution, namely the shop. In the late decades of the twentieth century, the problem is becoming one of simultaneously minimizing transport costs for a series of institutions, from farm to household. Tentative attempts to solve this massive transportation problem suggest that near-optimum locations for enterprises are as close as possible to final consumers. These solutions, if proved to be general, will serve to enhance the attraction of the suburbs for retail location. Suburban retailing seems likely both to gain in intensity and to operate profitably in more urban regions during the remainder of this century.

Further Reading

A wide ranging survey of the planning and design of shopping centres is provided by C. S. Jones, *Regional Shopping Centres* (London, 1969).

J. E. Vance has produced a useful background and short case study in 'Emerging patterns of commercial structure in American cities', in K. Norborg (ed.), *Proceedings of the IGU Symposium in Urban Geography* (Lund, 1962).

Various aspects of shopping behaviour in the suburbs are considered in J. Brush and H. Gauthier, 'Service centres and consumer trips: studies on the Philadelphia Metropolitan fringe', *Research Paper* 113 (University of Chicago, Department of Geography, Chicago, 1968).

Another volume in this series discusses the supply side of suburban shopping centre provision, namely Y. S. Cohen, 'Diffusion of an innovation in an urban system', *Research Paper* 140 (University of Chicago, Department of Geography, Chicago, 1972).

References

1. Examples are provided in P. Scott, *Geography and Retailing* (London, 1970) and B. J. L. Berry and A. R. Pred, *Central Place Studies – a Bibliography of Theory and Applications* (Philadelphia, 1965).
2. Important early attempts are those of M. J. Proudfoot, 'City retail structure', *Econ. Geogr.* 13 (1937), 425–8 and I. K. Rolph, *The Location Structure of Retail Trade* (Washington, D.C., 1933).
3. B. J. Garner, 'The internal structure of retail nucleations', *Northwestern University Studies in Geography* 12 (1966).
4. P. T. Kivell, 'Retailing in non-central locations', paper to *I.B.G. Urban Studies Group Meeting* (1971).

5. J. A. Giggs, 'Retail change and decentralization in the Nottingham metropolitan community', *Geog. Polonica* **24** (1972), 173–88.
6. I. K. Rolph, 'The population pattern in relation to retail buying', *Am. J. Sociol.* **38** (1932), 368–72.
7. W. William-Olsson, *Stockholm – Structure and Development* (Stockholm, 1961).
8. D. J. Duncan, 'Responses of selected retail institutions to their changing environment', 587, in P. D. Bennett (ed.), *Marketing and Economic Development*, Proceedings of the 50th National Conference of the American Marketing Association (1965), 583–602.
9. R. J. Johnston and P. J. Rimmer, *Retailing in Melbourne* (Canberra, 1969).
10. *Ibid.*, 31.
11. Reported in O. Luder, 'Out-of-town shopping – solution or mistake?', *Estates Gazette* (20 February 1965), 651.
12. C. H. Brown, *Consumer Habits and Attitudes toward Wilmington as a Place to Live, Shop and Recreate* (Newark, 1963).
13. Automobile Association, *Parking – Who Pays?* (London, 1967), 41.
14. R. G. Bogart, 'Who quits when urban renewal hits?' *Growth and Change* **2** (1971), 3–8; and B. J. L. Berry, S. J. Parsons, and R. H. Platt, *The Impact of Urban Renewal on Small Business* (Chicago, 1968).
15. Distributive trades E.D.C., *The Future Pattern of Shopping* (London, 1971), 65.
16. F. Durr, *The Relocation of Retail Business in the Wilmington, Delaware, Area* (Wilmington, 1963).
17. D. Alexander, *Retailing in England during the Industrial Revolution* (London, 1970).
18. I. K. Rolph, *The Location Structure of Retail Trade* (Washington, D.C., 1933); and H. Hoyt, *One Hundred Years of Land Values in Chicago* (Chicago, 1933).
19. R. Cassady and W. K. Bowden, 'Shifting retail trade within the Los Angeles Metropolitan market', *J. Marketing* **8** (1944), 398–404.
20. E. L. Ullman, V. O. French and C. S. Meyers, *Trends in C.B.D. and S.M.S.A. Retail Sales, 1948 to 1963* (Washington, D.C., 1967).
21. J. D. Tarver, 'Suburbanization of retail trade in the standard metropolitan areas of the United States, 1948–54', *Am. Sociol. Rev.* **22** (1957), 427–33; and S. C. McMillan, 'Recent trends in the decentralization of retail trade', *Traff. Q.* **16** (1962), 75–94.
22. J. D. Tarver, *op. cit.*, 433.
23. Board of Trade, *Reports on the Census of Distribution and Other Services – 1961* (London, 1964).
24. R. P. Doherty, 'Decentralization of retail trade in Boston', *J. Marketing* **6** (1942), 281–6; G. J. Eberle, 'Metropolitan decentralization and the retailer', *J. Retailing* **22** (1946), 91–4; and M. Kunis 'Retail trade in the New York Metropolitan Area', *J. Retailing* **17** (1941), 85–9.
25. D. L. Thompson, *Analysis of Retailing Potential in Metropolitan Areas* (Berkeley, 1964).
26. H. Hoyt, *People, Profit, Places* (New York, 1969).
27. T. W. Beed, 'An interpretation of recent trends in the geographical distribution of retail sales in Sydney', *Geographical Society of New South Wales, Research Paper,* **1** (1961) and R. J. Johnston and P. J. Rimmer,

'Recent changes in Melbourne's commercial structure', *Erdkunde* **21** (1967), 64–7.

28. E. Jones, *A Social Geography of Belfast* (London, 1960).
29. B. J. L. Berry, Commercial structure and commercial blight', *Research Paper* **85** (University of Chicago, Department of Geography, 1963).
30. H. R. Parker, 'Suburban shopping facilities in Liverpool' *Tn. Plann. Rev.* **33** (1962), 197–223.
31. H. Hoyt, *op. cit.* (1933).
32. E. Jones, *A Social Geography of Belfast* (London, 1960).
33. I. G. Weekley, 'Service centres in Nottingham, a concept in urban analysis', *E. Midld. Geog.* **6** (1956), 41–6.
34. W. Burns, *British Shopping Centres* (London, 1959); see also M. Villaneura, *Planning Neighbourhood Shopping Centres* (Washington, D.C., 1945).
35. J. W. Simmons, 'The changing pattern of retail location', *Research Paper* **92** (University of Chicago, Department of Geography, 1964); W. L. Waide 'Changing shopping habits and their impact on town planning', *J. Tn. Plann. Inst.* **49** (1963), 254–64; R. N. Percival, 'Assessment of shopping needs', *Report of Summer School of the Town Planning Institute* (1965), 107–9; and Urban Land Institute, 'Shopping centres restudied', *Technical Bulletin* **30** (1957).
36. Distributive Trades E.D.C. *The Cowley Shopping Centre* (London, 1968).
37. M. Y. Yoshino, *The Japanese Marketing System* (Cambridge, Mass., 1971).
38. Union of Shop, Distributive and Allied Workers, *Report on the Planning and Control Exercised by Local Authorities over the Number and Location of Retail Shops* (London, 1967).
39. 'Gem store Nottingham', *Self Service Supermarket Journal* (December, 1964), 30–2; and D. Thorpe and P. T. Kivell, 'Woolco Thornaby', *Research Report* **3** (Manchester Business School, Retail Outlets Research Unit, 1971).
40. L. F. Daws and A. J. Bruce, *Shopping in Watford* (Watford, 1971); and Distributive Trades E.D.C., *The Cowley Shopping Centre* (London, 1968).
41. J. E. Vance, 'Emerging patterns of commercial structure in American cities' in K. Norborg (ed.), *Proceedings of the IGU Symposium in Urban Geography* (Lund, 1962), 485–518; C. T. Jonassen, *Downtown versus Suburban Shopping* (Columbus, 1953); and E. Douglas, 'Buying practices of out-of-town customers', *J. Bus. Univ. Chicago* **23** (1950), 239–72.
42. L. P. Bucklin, *Shopping Patterns in an Urban Area* (Berkeley, 1967); D. L. Huff, 'A probabilistic analysis of shopping centre trade areas', *Land Econ.* **39** (1963), 81–90.

CHAPTER 9

New Offices in the Suburbs

P. W. DANIELS

The Growth of Office Employment

Office buildings are peculiar to the modern urban scene. The birth of free-standing, purpose-built office structures dates from the middle of the nineteenth century when the first skyscraper was constructed in Chicago.[1] There were certainly office buildings before that time, but they were mostly small and mainly associated with large financial institutions seeking the prestige of possessing their own buildings; examples include the Bank of Sweden (1668), the Bank of England (1694) and the Bank of France (1800).[2] Yet the impact of office buildings on the city bears little relationship to their limited time-span; the size and concentration of offices in central Manhattan and, on a smaller and less dramatic scale, in other American and western European cities such as Chicago, London and Paris have introduced a new dimension to urban development.[3] Until the early 1960s this had been primarily expressed by the agglomeration of offices in the Central Business Districts (CBD) of our cities, arising from the external economies derived from proximity to the wide range of other activities and services that are also found in the CBD, as well as from the superior accessibility of the city centre in comparison with most parts of the suburbs and the remainder of the city region.

The traditional location of office space has therefore been in the vicinity of the peak land-value intersection. The continuing demand for new offices is the product of several interrelated factors. Perhaps the most important of these is the rapid emergence of a quaternary sector of economic activities in which transactional work between highly qualified managerial, professional and technical personnel predominates.[4] Clerical workers provide an important link in the chain of transactions and are also included in

7

this new employment sector. In Britain, between 1921 and 1961, the total number of workers in all types of employment increased by 20 per cent., but the number of office workers, who can broadly be interpreted as forming the quaternary sector, grew by 150 per cent. during the same period. Hence by 1968 some 14 per cent. of Britain's labour force was in office employment and, allowing for variations in definition, some equivalent figures are 15 per cent. in France (1968), 17·5 per cent. in Sweden (1965) and 21·8 per cent. in the United States (1967).[5] The proportion of office employment in the total labour force will continue to expand in the wake of better telecommunications, improved methods of information flow and the increasing ability to manipulate the data upon which the day-to-day operation of the quaternary sector depends.

The postwar office booms in New York, Boston, Philadelphia, London, Moscow and numerous other major cities in our technologically advanced societies have also been encouraged by business mergers, which frequently involve consolidation of separate central-area offices into one new office block which provides the opportunity for enhanced prestige and the creation of better working conditions for employees.[6] The growth of individual firms is an additional source of demand for extra office space and creates shortage of space in existing premises and, because turnover rates in the office premises already existing may be too slow to accommodate expansion, new construction is generated. A final factor in the demand equation is the trend towards an increase in the amount of office space per employee, partly as a result of legislation relating to the minimum amount of functional space suitable for each worker and partly due to the proliferation of computers and other office machines. In 1946, the average in the United States was 10 m^2 per worker and this had increased to 12 m^2 by 1965.[7] A survey in central London showed that over 42 per cent. of offices allocated more than 14 m^2 per employee and more recently the Greater London Council (GLC) has used a figure of 18·4 m^2 (gross) per employee in its calculations of future demand for new offices.[8]

Pressures at the Centre

An amalgam of these demand factors has created characteristics which are becoming increasingly detrimental to the attraction of the CBD for offices. Experience in metropolitan areas throughout the world shows that, as the central areas of cities become increasingly congested and expensive as locations, some of the less essential activities begin to move out. The competition for land is intense and the first uses to leave the CBD are normally residential and manufacturing activities, but more recently offices have also been affected. One of the principal push factors for most CBD activities is the spiralling cost of remaining there; in Manhattan, land alone costs two-thirds as much as the new office building constructed on it and consequently rents, which averaged $60 per square metre in 1969, are expected to have doubled by 1972.[9] In the West End of London, rents of between £78 and £110 per square metre have now become common and they are some 20 per cent. higher in the City.[10] Rent increases of between 300 and 400 per cent. have therefore occurred in central London between 1964 and 1970.[11] High rents are not the only push factor. Commuter congestion on roads and trains into the centre, the difficulty and cost of parking for the car-borne commuter, the large amount of obsolescent office space which cannot easily be adapted to modern office working methods and the intense competition for labour are all factors which must also be included. It is not surprising that a second phase has emerged in the office growth continuum – the flight to the suburbs.

The migration of offices to the suburbs is largely a voluntary process in most metropolitan areas. In London, however, this process has been modified by the introduction of legislation designed to control the amount of new office development in the centre and so create conditions encouraging offices to move to the suburbs and beyond. The Control of Offices and Industrial Development Act, 1965, introduced Office Development Permits (ODPs) which were required for any office development of more than 270 m² in central London and the remainder of the metropolitan region. There have since been several changes in the extent of the areas covered by the controls as well as in the amount of floorspace exempt from an ODP. As a result, there has been increasing confusion as to whether the real objective of office policy is the redistribution of offices to areas outside central London or the reduction of pressure on development in the centre. In relation to both these objectives the policy has been singularly unsuccessful and it is the London suburbs, included in the control area, that have been most affected. While the need for developers to obtain ODPs has caused shortage of new office space in the CBD and consequently astronomically high rent increases, a growing shortage of vacant office floorspace has also been created in the suburbs. This has been caused by overstringent use of ODP's in the suburbs, in the hope that offices wishing to locate there, but unable to do so, will move to the remainder of the South East or to other Economic Planning regions.

The administration of the 1965 Act has ignored the realities of demand for suburban office space. This can be demonstrated by reference to the annual figures produced by the Location of Offices Bureau (LOB) which was set up in 1963 to provide guidance and information, as well as encouragement, to offices contemplating decentralization.[12] The number of firms leaving central London has declined steadily from a peak of 191 in 1967-8 (14,002 jobs) to 109 in 1970-1 (8,040 jobs), although the number of enquiries has remained relatively constant.[13] It is significant that 58 per cent. of the offices (45 per cent. of the jobs) have moved less than 32 kilometres from central London, i.e. to the suburbs and the immediate urban periphery.[14] The figures produced by LOB also show that 77 per cent. of the firms approaching them for information in 1970-1 wanted to move either to the suburbs or to the periphery within 32 kilometres of the centre, compared with an overall figure of 62 per cent. for the period 1963-71.[15] It is therefore very clear that the demand for new office space in the suburbs is increasing while the supply continues to decrease.

Some distortion of the 'natural' movement of offices to the suburbs has also occurred in Paris where CBD congestion is very similar to that in London. Here a 'congestion tax' is levied on new office development, although the addition to costs has to be fairly large to be effective in keeping firms out.[16] Firms already located in the centre are exempt from the tax, so that the comparative costs of new and existing office users can be significantly different.

Attraction of the Suburbs for New Offices

Many of the attractions of the suburbs for new offices are related to space. There is room for the adequate provision of on-site parking, which is particularly important in suburban areas where public transport facilities are poor. It is also possible to design office buildings which fit the needs of specific types of user, for example an insurance firm requiring a large computer installation which is space consuming and therefore could not be accommodated on the restricted, high-cost sites in the CBD. Spacious office buildings aimed at a better working environment for employees are also possible in the suburbs, and this could be an important factor in the competition for labour. The availability of space in the suburbs also allows the selection of sites which can utilize existing transport facilities, while also bringing workplaces nearer to the residences of employees and improving the journey to work. The advantages of space, as will be shown later, are particularly relevant in North American cities.

The cost of land is also much less in the suburbs, so that lower rents are also an important inducement to offices contemplating a move from the CBD. In the London suburbs, rents range between £11 and £22 per square metre rising to £33 per square metre at prime locations, while, in American cities, new suburban office space fetches, on average, between $44 and $60 per square metre.[17] These figures represent a difference of at least 50 per cent. between CBD and suburban rents which, when added to the savings derived from lower staff turnover and in some cases lower wages, imply substantially lower costs for office firms prepared to leave the city centre.

LOB estimates that offices moving outside central London expect to save up to £900 per head on the employment of staff. These savings arise mainly from the sharp reductions in rent for the space occupied by each employee but, apart from broad generalizations of this kind, little is known of the real cost advantages of suburban offices for different types of office function. There is some work in progress on quantification of the benefits to be expected from the relocation of Civil Service offices, but it still remains the responsibility of individual firms to decide whether a suburban location will reduce costs.[18] Writing in 1960, Vernon argued that after taking into account the increased space required for the installation of parking facilities, open spaces, restaurants and other consumer facilities, it was doubtful whether the cost of space per employee would be much different from that in Manhattan, so that firms could not expect to benefit much from space costs.[19] Using only the space criterion, this is a powerful argument, but it does not take into account the less easily quantifiable benefits attached to improved staff punctuality, better staff productivity and the lower cost of at least some of the office staff in suburban centres. There is considerable scope for more research into this facet of suburban office development.

The attributes of suburbia for offices need to be matched against the disadvantages. Not the least of these is the frequent absence, at least in existing development, of suitable shopping facilities and of office services which often outweighs any benefits afforded by the accessibility of a particular site. Another difficulty stems from the inadequacy of public transport in most suburban areas, particularly for trips made around the periphery. This is a less important disadvantage in the United States where car-ownership levels guarantee access to suburban offices for most households, but in Britain and most other countries in western Europe car-ownership, especially by employees in the clerical occupations, is lower and this places a significant burden upon public transport. In addition to any uncertainties which might already exist in employers' minds concerning availability of staff, there may well be the feeling that poor public transport services will make staff recruitment more difficult. On the other hand, the CBD is accessible from most parts of a metropolitan area either by public or private transport. Despite these advantages the relative attractions of the CBD for certain types of office have been devalued compared with those of the suburbs perhaps because 'as the volume of communications increases and the costs of improved systems decrease the necessity of proximity, for exchanges and interaction, will decrease leading to further erosion of offices in the centre of cities'.[20] All the evidence suggests that the suburbs stand to gain most from these changes.

To straightforward comparison of the advantages and disadvantages of the suburbs for new offices, must also be added the dispersal of population in metropolitan areas. Since the end of the Second World War, the areas outside the central cities have been the major population growth points in metropolitan areas of the United States. The white workers, who dominate employment in the office sector, are in the forefront of this growth; 140,000 per annum were leaving the central cities before 1966 rising to 500,000 a year between 1966 and 1968.[21] This outward migration has been matched by the movement of industry and offices into the suburbs, and virtually all the growth in metropolitan area employment has gone outside the central cities.[22]

Similar trends are found in Britain. The preliminary results of the 1971 Census show that the population of Greater London has decreased by approximately 8 per cent. since 1961, while that of the surrounding metropolitan area has increased by more than 12 per cent.[23] These changes conceal the movements within Greater London from the inner to the outer areas. As long as employment opportunities in the CBD continue to exceed those of the suburbs, the net effect of these changes will be to increase the length of work journeys to the centre as well as to aggravate the difficulties of accommodation on some of the commuter railways. Office workers are leading the out-movement from the inner areas, so that, as well as reducing costs to employers, the establishment of suburban offices should also help to ease the journey-to-work burden of their employees.

The development of new suburban offices within Greater London is also reflected in employment figures which show that, between 1961 and 1966, office employment increased by 125,000 jobs out of a total increase in all employment of 130,000.[24] This represents a rise of nearly 20 per cent. during the five-year period. The increase in suburban office jobs is also occupationally selective. This is a product of the types of office which move there, since these are mainly offices performing routine functions which need not depend on proximity to other activities in the centre. Hence about 50 per cent. of the increase in suburban office employment between 1961 and 1966 is in clerical occupations and, although still retaining some 500,000 office workers in clerical jobs, there has been a decrease of 16,000 in central London during the same period. It seems that the specialist office activities are retaining their CBD locations but decanting superfluous, routine activities to suburban locations where the advantages of space, cost and proximity to female labour are the principal advantages.

The relocation of offices and office employment within the metropolitan fabric will continue to be a major component of intra-suburban and peripheral expansion in the coming decades. The mushroom-like growth of new offices probably represents one of the most important facets of change in the suburbs, which have always been the preserve of residential land use. Such major changes are not taking place in a vacuum; the offices already constructed, along with the projections for future development, have posed new problems and questions for the urban planner. One of the most important of these is how to distribute the new office space, with the choice between concentration in major suburban nodes or a dispersed distribution of offices throughout the suburban areas. It may be that certain types of office function are best suited to extra-CBD but intra-metropolitan locations; these need to be identified and encouraged to move to suburban locations. Suburban offices also generate public and private transport trips, especially in relation to the journey to work, but little is known of the structure of these trips and how they vary between different types of office location. There is also scope for more work on the relationship between suburban office development and the demand for retail, housing and educational facilities. The answers to these questions have been partially provided in the form of existing development, while metropolitan growth plans provide guidance to future trends, hopefully in the light of present experience. It is not proposed to discuss all these questions here but to concentrate on the approaches to suburban office location in three major metropolitan areas (London, New York and Paris), and to consider briefly the journey-to-work changes that are generated.

Location of Suburban Offices

There seem to be three alternative strategies for suburban office development. The first involves the development of large suburban office centres, which are few in number and located at strategic points. These will probably be major transport interchanges which command large catchment areas for office staff and, by virtue of their size, attract a wide range of shopping, restaurant, entertainment and other activities. The creation of an environment possessing similar, if smaller-scale, facilities to those of the CBD would be attractive to the larger offices seeking an opportunity to transfer headquarters activities from the centre. Such offices have at least five hundred employees, and the wide distribution of their residences would make the provision of adequate transport facilities absolutely vital for the successful functioning of these large centres. Because of their size the large centres would require careful co-ordination in planning and development, and care is needed to ensure that the amount of office and other employment created does not generate the conditions of congestion which are pushing offices out of the CBD.

The distribution of existing offices and suburban nodes may exert some control on the chosen strategy in that it may be more satisfactory to add to the existing infrastructure and avoid the high costs attached to the creation of large centres. Hence a second possibility involves the development of small centres. These would be easier to create since they would avoid the major reorganization involved in the construction of large centres. It would be easier to absorb the car-based work trips generated by the smaller centres, because there would be more space available around the periphery of such developments for the provision of parking facilities. The need to select locations adjacent to major transport routes would remain, but it is likely that such centres would be less successful in attracting large head-quarters offices; they would depend upon smaller offices performing routine functions. Such offices would not require large numbers of employees and therefore need not be at the centre of a large labour market.

The third alternative is simply to allow a pattern of suburban sprawl and widely-scattered office locations, often with isolated office blocks speculatively located by office developers and unwisely allowed by zoning ordinance or planning permission. This solution is most attractive to the small offices of accountants, surveyors or insurance agents which have small catchment areas and therefore need to be near their customers. The size of office centre is not particularly important to these offices, which do not create the demand for office services or restaurant facilities concomitant with large offices.

Office Parks

The three strategies so far discussed are concerned with office develop-ment in the main built-up area of the suburbs rather than around the periphery where expansion is taking place most rapidly. The intra-suburban centres involve a certain amount of urban renewal or removal of existing facilities, while it often proves difficult, as will be demonstrated later, to provide suitable facilities to cope with the large increases in car-based trips because space is not available. Consequently the concept of 'office or business parks' has received increasing support in the United States.[25] The creation of an attractive environment, with lawns, trees and landscaping, unrestricted by site size, is very different from other kinds of suburban office-space development.

The low-density business park began soon after the Second World War, when some large firms, such as IBM, General Foods and Readers Digest in New York, began looking to the suburbs for expansion and for the creation of new headquarters offices. They were soon followed by smaller firms in research, professional and related fields.[26] Land on the urban periphery was easy to assemble and was priced by the acre rather than the square foot, and the companies were therefore able to obtain ample space and provide amenities which were impossible in the CBD. From these pioneer developments there emerged the concept of the office park, where several office buildings were brought together on one site, but recognition of the need to provide easy access to shopping and other facilities has created business parks where both types of suburban development exist side by side. Most of the business and office parks are found around metropolitan cities which are becoming regional centres for distribution, finance or commerce; and these include Washington D.C., Boston, Denver, Houston and Atlanta. The development of peripheral shopping centres and 'hypermarkets' on 'green-field' sites is proceeding apace in Britain but there are no office parks as such. The nearest equivalent is the research park at Peterlee, Co. Durham.[27]

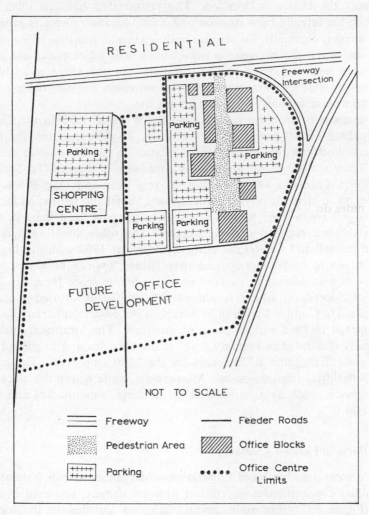

Figure 9.1   Gamble Centre, Minneapolis

In a survey of forty-one office parks, the Urban Land Institute showed that locations at the intersection of radial and cross-suburban freeways or tollways were preferred by developers as well as by the occupiers of the new offices. This allowed access to the CBD and to other office parks around the metropolitan periphery to be expressed in minutes rather than linear measure as well as reducing the time/distance between the offices and the homes of their employees. This latter factor was important in influencing market demand for space. The quality of the surroundings is also regarded to be very important, and the element of prestige arising from the location of office parks adjacent to high quality residential areas also influences the choice of location. The relationship between offices and shopping has already been stressed and a final location factor is proximity to an airport, especially for tenants with a large proportion of employees in the executive and managerial occupations. The office parks are almost completely independent of public transport, but the space available for development ensures more than adequate provision for car-parking which might take up more than 50 per cent. of any site.

An example of an office park is Oak Brook Office Park in the Chicago Metropolitan area.[28] Some 25 kilometres or 25 minutes from the Loop, this park illustrates the importance of location in suburban office development. There are two major tollways on either side of the site (Tri-State and East-West), Chicago's O'Hare airport is very near and Oak Brook itself includes an air strip for private planes. Motel, hotel and recreation facilities such as golf courses are located adjacent to the park, and there is also a well-established regional shopping centre. The office building park was opened in 1960 and was 60 per cent. developed by 1968 with five high-rise offices of six to twelve storeys and twenty-three low-rise buildings of one to three storeys. Minimum parking provision is one space for every 28 m^2 of office floorspace, which is almost the equivalent of one space per employee. The Gamble Centre in Minneapolis is a 54-acre suburban business park opened in 1965 and 60 per cent. complete. The locational attributes are clearly illustrated in Figure 9–1. Note the area devoted to ground-level parking, totalling some 1,750 spaces for the 2,000 employees. The park is ten minutes drive from downtown Minneapolis, while within the office park retail services, such as a barber's shop, cafeteria, supermarket and bank, are provided.

New Offices in London's Suburbs

The present distribution of London suburban offices reveals a number of small office concentrations intermixed with low-density, scattered development (Figure 9–2). The only obvious criterion satisfied in the location pattern is the relationship with either the major road, rail or underground routes into central London. The pattern may simply reflect a variety of location factors but in general it falls between two stools and is the result of a singular lack of cohesion in the strategies adopted by those responsible for planning London. It would be inappropriate to consider at length the interesting, detailed background to the present pattern; suffice it to say

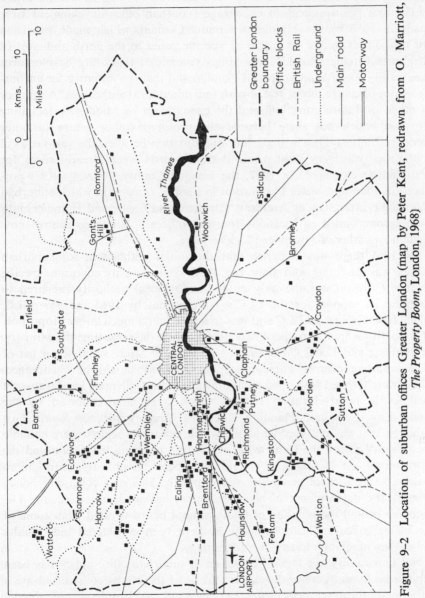

Figure 9-2 Location of suburban offices Greater London (map by Peter Kent, redrawn from O. Marriott, *The Property Boom*, London, 1968)

that, although the consensus seems to be that suburban offices should be concentrated into planned centres in association with shops and other services, there never seems to have been agreement regarding suitable areas.

The first positive steps to encourage suburban office development were made in 1956 by the Middlesex County Council, which made provision for new offices by the allocation of specific zones to the north and west of the North Circular Road.[29] This policy recognized that office development was getting out of hand in central London and that the initiative for encouraging out-of-centre offices rested with individual local authorities. A number of other local authorities followed the example set by Middlesex, including Croydon which has since become the prototype office centre in outer London. Enthusiasm was high, but co-ordination between the various local authorities was very limited, so that the seeds were already sown for scattered development. In 1957, the London County Council (LCC) produced its *Plan to Combat Congestion in Central London* in which suburban shopping centres such as Archway, Elephant and Castle and Hammersmith were recommended as locations for new offices.[30] All three centres now contain a number of new office blocks.

By 1961 there was evidence that the initial enthusiasm for suburban offices was declining and only the LCC continued to advocate specific centres. Croydon was the only outer-London local authority prepared to continue its support for the LCC's policies, but by 1964 the new GLC, which had replaced the LCC and was to administer a much larger proportion of the built-up area, introduced new proposals. At the same time the Ministry of Housing and Local Government's *South East Study* suggested a list of nine suburban centres where office development should be encouraged. These were selected with good communications and adequate local transport facilities in mind – location criteria which were later endorsed by the South East Economic Planning Council's *Strategy for the South East* although this was not specific about which suburban centres were suitable for offices.[31] Given the framework of existing planning legislation and the more recent use of ODPs, it should have been possible to control more closely the location of new office space, but the lack of a consistent policy towards the development of specific centres has made this difficult. The *rationale* behind the granting of ODPs cannot be exonerated from some of the blame, since applications seem to have been considered individually rather than in relation to any overall strategy.

Not unnaturally, the lack of direction in suburban office policy has been capitalized upon by office developers. Most of the offices constructed are a reflection of the developers' estimates of demand, and they have undoubtedly made full use of the opportunities. The interstitial office blocks which are found between the nucleated groups are often built when a suitable piece of land becomes available, following speculative applications for planning permissions and ODPs by developers. Knowing that such applications are sometimes granted, the developer is content to proceed in unsatisfactory locations and given the high level of demand, difficulty in letting the new space is only experienced in exceptional cases of bad judgement. Meanwhile the unfortunate planners strive, hopefully, to organize on some reasonable basis the rapid growth of population and employment in the suburbs. The Greater London Development Plan has forecast a 50·3 per cent. growth in suburban retail turnover between 1961 and 1981, compared with 22·6 per cent. for central London; this surely provides the ideal opportunity to create either large or small centres of combined office and shopping activities.

The most recent proposals for suburban office centres have been made in the Greater London Development Plan, which defines twenty-eight existing centres as being of 'strategic' importance.[32] These are mainly large suburban shopping centres, with a retail turnover of at least £5 million in 1961 and a population of at least 200,000 in their individual catchment areas, although factors such as accessibility, communications, position relative to other centres and potential for growth were also considered. The policy statement subsequently goes further and defines six of the twenty-eight centres as of 'major strategic' importance, so that it is possible that the end-product will be a mixture of small and large office centres. The ultimate success of these proposals rests with the individual boroughs within the GLC which are responsible for the detailed 'local' plans which utilize the overall 'structure' plan as a guideline. It is therefore too early to see whether the proposed office and shopping centres will finally materialize, but it is vital that they should do so, for they are the key to both successful containment of the outward movement of London's population and a meaningful office policy for the metropolis.

Croydon Office Centre

The detailed structure of individual office centres might resemble that of Croydon in South London (Figure 9–3). Central Croydon is the only major office centre to have emerged from the generally confused pattern of suburban offices, and it has grown steadily since it expressed support for the LCC's decentralization policies in 1956. There were over 400,000 m² completed or under construction in 1965 and the offices employed some 20,000 staff, 50 per cent. of them in offices which had moved from Central London.[33] The estimated future capacity exceeds 30,000 employees, and, with a peak hour commuter flow to and from Croydon of approximately 50,000, the potential relief for commuter transport is substantial. Some of the attributes of the location are shown in Figure 9–3 and include two suburban stations (with East Croydon just fifteen minutes by fast train

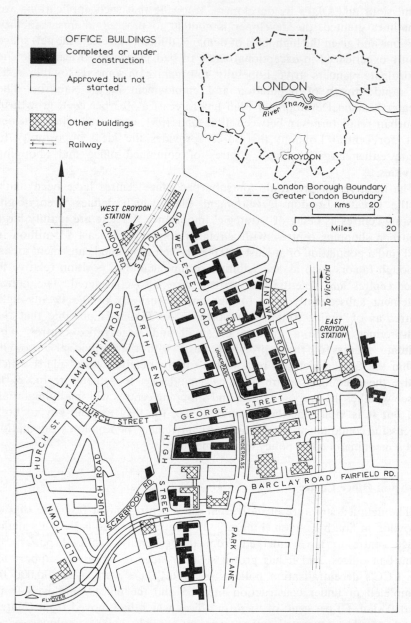

Figure 9–3   Croydon Office Centre, South London (map reproduced by
kind permission of Engineer, Surveyor and Planning Officer's Department,
London Borough of Croydon)

from central London), a conference hall complex, excellent shopping and restaurant facilities just to the west of the two main office clusters north and south of George Street, and a series of multistorey car parks strategically located around the fringes of the main office concentration. The offices are distributed along a fairly compact north-south axis about 1·6 km long and ·8 km wide. All these features make Croydon the only real suburban office centre in the London conurbation.

The undoubted success of Croydon should not be allowed to mask some of the problems which have emerged as the development has reached fruition. The concentration of so many office employees into a relatively small area has created major car-parking problems: a survey in 1968 for example, showed that there were over 7,000 vehicles both on and off the highway at any one time in the central area.[34] Not all the cars belonged to office employees, but it is reasonable to suppose that at least 60 per cent. of them did. The narrow streets, frequent intersections, the inadequacy of off-street parking and the conflict between pedestrian and vehicle movements within the office centre all make Croydon patently unsuitable for the increasing use of the private car for work, business and other trips. A similar situation exists in other large suburban office centres like Wembley or Ealing. The growing demand for office staff has also tended to inflate wage rates in Croydon, which are lower than those in central London, but higher than elsewhere in the suburbs.[35] It may well be that Croydon has too many offices which are generating transport and socio-economic problems that could have been more closely controlled, if the scale of office development had been carefully aligned with provision of adequate off-street car-parks, the construction of local highways able to accommodate the rapid growth of vehicular traffic, and progress at other office centres elsewhere in the suburbs. There are clearly some important lessons to be learned from the experience of Croydon and it can only be hoped that future development of new suburban office centres will be based on careful attention to the location problem as well as to the consequences of excessive concentration in specific centres.

Suburban Offices in New York

As suggested earlier, London is not the only metropolis where new offices are springing up in the suburbs. While London is trying to organize its office location policies, New York faces similar problems and the Regional Plan Association seems to be advancing a solution similar to that proposed for London's future.[36] Offices are regarded as one of the key metropolitan activities, and it is estimated that the region will require an increase of 87·5 per cent. in the number of office workers between 1965 and 2000, from 1·6 to 3 million. In view of the increasingly wide spread of

residences around the core area of New York, the report suggests that much
of this increase will not be accommodated in Manhattan. Suburban nuclei
in which new offices would be a major activity are therefore being promoted,
and it is argued that there is still time to focus development into a number

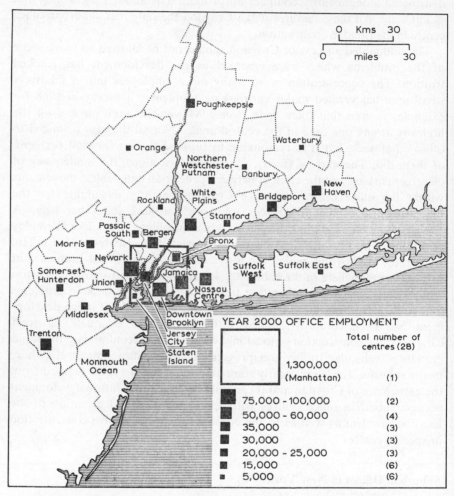

Figure 9-4   Proposed distribution of office centres and office employment
by the year 2000, New York; the assumption is made that the present
percentage of all office employment that is currently located in centres
(70 per cent.) will also be found in 2000

of centres of varying size (Figure 9-4), thereby preventing the mixture of
scattered and linear office patterns along major highways through the
suburbs. As in the case of London, most of the metropolitan centres shown
in Figure 9-4 will be located where embryo facilities already exist in the

suburban fabric, although detailed agreement with local and county officials
has still to be achieved.

A feature of interest in the New York proposals is the priority given to
the creation of three large office centres in the core area, i.e. within 32
kilometres of the CBD. The three centres are Jamaica (Queens), downtown
Newark and downtown Brooklyn, which are regarded as potential counter-
attractions to the outward movement of middle-class families and middle-
income employees. The residential areas within easy reach of the three
centres are satisfactory; but without strong and attractive centres providing

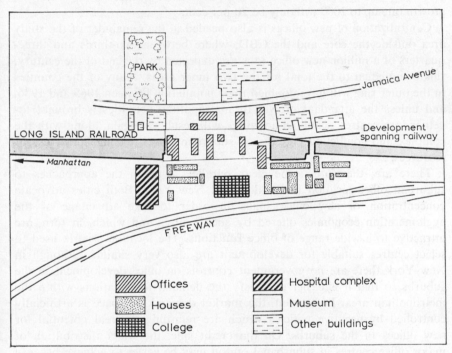

Figure 9–5   Proposed structure of the Jamaica Centre, New York

employment and other facilities it is unlikely that those who can afford
anything else will live there. The success of these three centres will rest
largely on their attraction for offices, and New York seems prepared to
accept the realities of demand and will allow large-scale development within
easy reach of Manhattan. All three centres are excellent locations for the
large offices of headquarters organizations as well as the more typical
district or regional office activities. It takes less time, for example, to get
from downtown Brooklyn to downtown Manhattan than from midtown to
downtown Manhattan, and Newark is little further in time from either part

of Manhattan. A further locational attribute of the Jamaica Centre in particular is that almost 490,000 office workers live within sixty minutes' travelling time, compared with 513,000 for Manhattan (Figure 9–5).[37] The cost of introducing office jobs in the three centres is also lower than at centres further out in the suburbs, because subway and surface railway facilities already exist and possess sufficient capacity to cope with the projected increase of 150,000 jobs between 1965 and 2000. This would more than double the 108,000 office jobs already there (59,000 in Newark, 40,000 in Brooklyn and 9,000 in Jamaica), and although it is expected that office jobs will continue to be added to the existing total in Manhattan, the growth rate up to 2000 will only be 20 per cent.

Centralization of new offices is also needed in the remainder of the study area outside the core and the CBD, where between two-thirds and three-quarters of a million new office jobs are expected by the end of the century, this being equal to the total for the two inner areas. Many of the counties in the outer ring will have doubled their population between 1965 and 1986, and unless the attendant growth of metropolitan activities is brought together into centres, scattered activities will result yet again, along with the complex and conflicting patterns of suburban travel and inefficient use of resources.

There are, therefore, some clear parallels between the approaches to suburban office location in London and New York. Both cities advocate concentration of new office space in order to take advantage of the agglomeration economies offered by such centres and which, in turn, are attractive to a wide range of office functions. The location criteria used to select centres suitable for development are also very similar, although in New York there are no government controls on office development in the suburbs so that it is easier to satisfy the demand for locations within the metropolitan area. In London, the market demand for space is artificially controlled by negative policies which are retarding the real potential for new offices in the suburbs. On the credit side, the wider distribution of major office centres in suburban London may be easier to achieve because of the ODPs and the operation of general planning controls. In New York or any other American city, the outcome of the proposals such as those for three major centres in the core will finally depend upon the closer political involvement in planning decisions which may impede adoption of the recommended strategies.

The Case of Paris

A final example of the approach to suburban office growth is provided by Paris. Planning controls have been rigidly enforced in the centre of the city and it is one of the few major cities where the mid-twentieth-century office boom has not made a dramatic visual impression.[38] But heavy traffic congestion and an inadequate public transport system, particularly the metro, plus the strong planning measures have made office expansion difficult in the CBD. As a result some suburban office centres are beginning to emerge. The Paris Regional Plan (1960) selected three major nodes as a basis for reorganizing the chaotic pattern of Parisian suburban development, and the most impressive of these is on the north-west bank of the Seine at La Défense, Neuilly.[39] The project, which is still in progress, involves an area of 690 ha about 4 kilometres west of the Arc de Triomphe and demonstrates that new suburban offices need not always be constructed on virgin sites on the outer periphery of a city. Old housing, warehousing and other remnants of the disorganized past are being completely removed and replaced by large multistorey office blocks, which have proved very attractive to large French and international companies. The provision of transportation has been given priority despite the proximity of the CBD and a new metro link, now partially completed, and urban motorways are an integral part of the scheme. As noted in the other examples, shops and other services which contribute to a successful office centre are also included in La Défense. The French city planners are creating push factors which encourage offices to leave the CBD but, as in New York, they are prepared to allow short-distance relocation, which satisfies the needs of the majority of the offices involved, provided that they are able to guide the demand for office space into a limited number of centres.

The Journey to Work

From the viewpoint of office employees, an important reason for encouraging new offices in the suburbs has been to ease the burden of the journey to work. The employees benefiting most should be those who previously travelled to offices in the CBD. Some support for this hypothesis has been provided by Wabe, who has shown that an office which moved to Epsom on the periphery of London generated considerable journey-to-work benefits.[40] These were mainly in the form of reduced journey times, especially for staff previously working in central London. His findings also underline the importance of the location variable for suburban offices. The fact that the Epsom office was 1·6 kilometres from the nearest station, or at least fifteen minutes' walk, reduced the value of the trip-time changes for some employees.

An increase in reverse commuting is often suggested as a bi-product of peripheral office growth. Office employees can travel with ease on the almost empty rolling stock leaving the city centre in the morning and *vice versa* in the evening. The same is true of travel to work by car or bus, but it has already been shown that the central city is being abandoned, especially by office employees, so that the scope for reverse commuting is limited. The only employees likely to benefit are those travelling through the central area from suburban residence to suburban workplace, but these are generally few. The reverse-commuting assumption, especially when it involves public transport, entails the location of individual offices on the appropriate radial transport routes and the location of the residences of employees in areas which are convenient for access to these routes. In fact, the limited information available on reverse commuting suggests that it is not an important component of the journey to work to suburban offices, and that cross-commuting is much more significant.[41]

In theory the increase in suburban office employment should therefore be associated with an easier journey to work but, in reality, the changes produced are complex. They reflect variations in office-occupation structures, in the ratio of male to female employees, in the proportion of employees who previously worked in the CBD and in the size of individual offices. A survey of twenty offices in suburban London has shown that approximately 25 per cent. of the employees travelled longer distances to the office than before, some of them by as much as 16 kilometres.[42] More than 26 per cent. of the respondents also recorded longer trip times, many of these also having the longer trip lengths. Wabe showed that 12 per cent. of his respondents spent more time travelling to the office, and a survey at three centres beyond the edge of the London conurbation produced an equivalent value of 20 per cent.[43]

The proportion of employees having longer journey times, therefore, seems to decrease with distance from the CBD. Suburban office nuclei near the CBD are likely to produce a smaller range of changes in the journey to work than centres further out, such as the office parks. There are undoubtedly still a large proportion of shorter journeys to work but these should not be allowed to create complacency; it is important to appreciate that suburban office expansion cannot be immediately correlated with positive improvements in the journey to work for all employees.

The reasons for this situation are not hard to find. Many employees, particularly those previously working in the CBD, will have changed place of work but not place of residence. The importance of this has been demonstrated by Burtt, who showed that the commuting times of industrial employees not changing address following relocation of their firms increased by 60 per cent.[44] In cases where residential location remains unchanged, journeys to work have often to be undertaken on routes which are transverse to the major radial routes to the centre and, because of the frequent highway intersections and less direct route to the office, longer journeys to work result. It is also possible that excessive concentration of office development in suburban centres such as Croydon will push the employment fields beyond the area which is easily accessible for employees using public or private transport, thereby creating longer journeys to work than originally anticipated. New suburban offices frequently provide the opportunities for higher wages and better working conditions, and this will also help to generate longer journeys to work. As a centre grows the competition for good-quality office staff tends to increase, wages spiral and employees are attracted from other less developed, but often more convenient, office centres.

The consequences of suburban office development for the journey to work have not been confined to trip time and length changes. There are also major changes in the travel mode used to get to the office. Public transport routes, particularly the railways, are strongly oriented towards the centre and are completely unsuited to the requirements of suburban journey-to-work patterns. Therefore, the dominant mode of travel to suburban offices is the private car, so that while 90 per cent. of the work trips to the CBD are still made by public transport almost 44 per cent. in the recent survey of suburban workers travelled by car, the majority as drivers. A further 10 per cent. walked to their offices, leaving public transport, mainly buses, for use by the remaining employees. The increasing dominance of the private car for the journey to work to London suburban offices has some way to go before it reaches the American situation where almost all the employees drive to their offices. The growth of car-based trips is likely to continue and it is as well for cities like London to be aware of the nature of these changes and to take appropriate steps to alleviate the problems of traffic congestion and longer journeys to work before they become even worse in the future.

There are a number of methods of resolving these journey-to-work problems. An increase in the traffic capacity of suburban highways might offer one solution, but the comparatively high density of housing in suburban London makes this less attractive than in the metropolitan suburbs of the United States which are already well served by freeways and tollways. The competitive position of public transport could be improved with a view to diverting the growing number of car users to travel by rail and bus, and it has been shown that, in theory, buses can be placed in an economically competitive position, in terms of time and convenience, with private transport modes.[45] With the number of office employees using private transport increasing steadily, this kind of solution could become inappropriate as time moves on and it becomes increasingly costly to implement. Ultimately then, the suburban office/journey-to-work dilemma may be solved by more careful selection of locations for future development. Journeys to offices are highly peaked, both in terms of time and volume of movement, and the starting and finishing times of most offices rarely vary by more than thirty minutes. As a result, locations with too high a concentration of offices generate journey-to-work traffic far in excess of the capacity of the local highway network and public transport facilities. It would therefore seem essential to isolate the variations in journey-to-work trips generated by suburban offices according to office size, function and employment structure, and to relate this information to parking-space availability, public transport services and access to suitable employment pools. Such information could be usefully exploited when pursuing any policy on office location in the suburbs.

Conclusion

The locational requirements of new suburban offices are now largely understood. The evidence from the examples discussed in this chapter reveal a certain uniformity in the approach of various metropolitan communities to the second phase in the growth and expansion of offices and office employment. London, New York and Paris are just a few of the major cities which have chosen to promote the development of large-scale office centres which rival the CBD in the range of facilities provided and in the linkages occurring between office activities. The concept of dispersed, unregulated office development is outmoded although still a common feature in many cities. The individual details of the solutions adopted by different metropolitan areas vary according to the extent of planning involvement and the influence of normal market forces. Suburban London has the additional problem of having to promote suburban office centres within the framework of office control policies designed to encourage offices leaving central London to move beyond the suburbs to elsewhere in Britain. Some of the questions posed by the emergence of new suburban offices have been discussed, journey-to-work changes in particular, but it has not been possible to refer to them all. Clearly, there are many questions remaining to be answered and probably just as many remaining to be asked concerning the future relationship between suburban growth and the office revolution.

Further Reading

R. B. Armstrong, *The Office Industry: Patterns of Growth and Location* (Cambridge, 1972).

P. Cowan, *The Office: A Facet of Urban Growth* (London, 1967).

R. M. Fisher, *The Boom in Office Buildings – An Economic Study of the Past Two Decades* (Washington, D.C., 1967).

E. M. Hoover and R. Vernon, *Anatomy of a Metropolis* (Harvard, 1960), especially Chapter 4.

O. Marriott, *The Property Boom* (London, 1968).

S. M. Robbins and N. E. Terleikyj, *Money Metropolis* (Cambridge, 1960).

References

1. E. Schultz and W. Simmons, *Offices in the Sky* (New York, 1959).
2. R. M. Fisher, *The Boom in Office Buildings – An Economic Study of the Past Two Decades* (Washington, D.C., 1967), 18.
3. J. Gottman, 'Why the Skyscraper?', *Geogr. Rev.* **56** (1966), 190–212.
4. J. Gottman, 'Urban centrality and the interweaving of quaternary activities', *Ekistics* **29** (1970), 325. See also J. Gottman, *Megalopolis* (New York, 1961), 516–80.
5. Gottman, *op. cit* (1970), 325; and Ministry of Labour, *Growth of Office Employment* (London, 1968).
6. Fisher, *op. cit.*, 4.
7. *Ibid.,* 25.
8. Figures can vary widely between different types of office activity. Location of Offices Bureau, *Offices in a Regional Centre* (London, 1968), Table 2H.
9. E. Carruth, 'Manhattan's office building binge', *Fortune* (1969), 176.
10. Location of Offices Bureau, *Annual Report 1970–1* (London, 1971), 11.
11. *Ibid.,* 11.
12. Location of Offices Bureau, *Annual Reports 1963–71* (London).
13. Location of Offices Bureau, *op. cit.* (1970–1), 7.
14. *Ibid.,* Table 10.
15. *Ibid.,* Table 4.
16. *The Sunday Times,* 'Should big city businesses pay more for the privilege?' (12 May 1968).
17. J. R. McKeever, *Business Parks* (Washington, D.C., 1970), 38–9.
18. Work in progress by the Operational Research Division of the Civil Service Department and the Institute for Operational Research.
19. R. Vernon, *Metropolis 1985* (Cambridge, 1960), 119–20.
20. A. Wise, 'The impact of communications in metropolitan form', *Ekistics* **32** (1971), 22–31.
21. Bureau of the Census, *Trends in Social and Economic Conditions in Metropolitan Areas* (Washington D.C., 1969).
22. A. Ganz, 'Emerging patterns of urban growth and travel', *Highw. Res. Rec.* **203** (1968), 21–37.
23. Office of Population Censuses and Surveys, *Census 1971, England and Wales Preliminary Report* (London, 1971).
24. General Register Office, *Census 1961 and 1966: Occupation Tables* (London, 1964 and 1968). Central London is defined as the area inside the mainline railway termini and contains the City and Westminster London borough, parts of the London boroughs of Camden, Islington, Tower Hamlets, Southwark and Lambeth.
25. McKeever, *op. cit.*, 7–10.
26. F. P. Clark, 'Office buildings in the suburbs', *Urban Land* **13** (1954), 3–10.
27. *Financial Times,* 'Peterlee, Durham's Science Park' (26 February, 1971).
28. McKeever, *op. cit.*, 52–4.
29. Middlesex County Council, *Development Plan* (1956).
30. London County Council, *A Plan to Combat Congestion in Central London* (London, 1957).
31. Ministry of Housing and Local Government, *The South East Study, 1961–81* (London, 1964), para 31; and South East Economic Planning Council, *A Strategy for the South East* (London, 1967), para 207.

32. Greater London Council, *Greater London Development Plan Statement* (London, 1969), 42.
33. London Borough of Croydon, *Office Development* (1968), 2.
34. *Ibid.*, 4.
35. P. Child, 'Location aspects of office development in Croydon, with special reference to earnings' (Unpublished Ph.D. Thesis, University of London, London, 1971).
36. New York Regional Plan Association, *The Second Regional Plan* (New York, 1968).
37. *Ibid.*, Table 3.
38. S. McConnell, 'Offices', *Off. Arch. Plann.* **31** (1968), 920–7.
39. P. Hall, *The World Cities* (London, 1966; second edition in preparation), 90–1.
40. J. S. Wabe, 'Dispersal of employment and the journey to work', *J. Trans. Econ. Policy* **3** (1967), 48–68.
41. P. W. Daniels, 'Office decentralization from London: the journey to work consequences' (Unpublished Ph.D Thesis, University of London, London, 1972).
42. *Ibid.*
43. P. W. Daniels, 'Employment decentralization and the journey to work', *Area* **3** (1970), 47–51.
44. E. J. Burtt, *Plant Relocation and the Core City Worker* (Washington D.C., 1969).
45. C. H. Sharp, 'The choice between cars and buses on urban roads', *J. Trans. Econ. Policy* **1** (1967), 104-11.

CHAPTER 10

Farming on the Urban Fringe

RICHARD J. C. MUNTON

The geographical literature contains many descriptive studies of agriculture on the urban fringe.[1] These frequently comment on the smaller size of farm, the higher intensity of production, the more rapid loss of agricultural labour and the greater preponderance of hobby farming[2] than is typical of rural areas distant from urban centres. In particular, the irregular, but continuous, conversion of agricultural land to urban uses is almost always a central theme. A general criticism may be levelled at this literature. Much of it is superficial, its primary objective being to record change in land use with distance from the urban periphery rather than to enquire into the actual effects on farming practice of particular forms of rural-urban inter-action. As a result, it is rarely possible to use the evidence collected to generalize about processes operating on the urban fringe. A more specific criticism surrounds the implied, but rarely tested, assumption that the farming pattern in metropolitan regions is wholly explicable in terms of direct urban influences. Investigations that embody this assumption inevit-ably underestimate the extent to which farming is responding to important technological and managerial innovations, introduced to meet changing market demands unrelated to metropolitan influences. Increasing capital investment, the relative decline of land and labour (not management) as factors of production and the development of horizontal and vertical integration are all evident within agriculture in advanced economies, and all are taking place largely independently of proximity to cities.

The overall effects of previous research have been twofold. On the one hand, it minimizes opportunities for generalization by its descriptive orienta-tion, whilst, on the other, it leaves the impression, well-founded in traditional tenets of agricultural location theory, that not only is it reasonable to expect a zoning of agricultural land use around cities but that such a zoning exists. This chapter will examine the evidence for this through an analysis of those urban-generated processes considered to be most likely to affect agricultural practice.

Three processes are of particular importance to agriculture.[3] First and most significant, is the land transfer mechanism itself.[4] Analyses of the operation of the land market reveal the competitive strengths of alternative economic activities, indicate the degree to which the market is in equilibrium and help to explain the decisions taken by farmers who anticipate the future sale of their land to urban developers. The farmer has to make two sets of linked decisions, the first relating to the timing of the sale and the price he is prepared to accept, and the second to the kind of farming activity he should pursue in the meanwhile. As urban growth is irregular in both time and space it creates uncertainty amongst landowners on the urban fringe. This is most evident amongst those in a weak financial position who feel unable to exert individual influence over the rate of land conversion. This apparent weakness of the rural landowner in the urban-fringe land market has led to the development of many urban growth models that totally ignore the land-supply situation.[5] The land-conversion process has ramifications far beyond the actual zone of land transfer. Not only are options taken out on farmland by speculators and developers well in advance of its anticipated sale, but landowners who make large financial gains from the sale of land for development are able to compete effectively in the agricultural land market away from the immediate urban fringe, so forcing up the general price of farmland. In Britain, reinvestment is encouraged by the 'roll-over' tax concession whereby landowners avoid paying capital gains tax provided they repurchase land within three years. In 1972 virgin building land sold for residential development was worth approximately £750m, three times the value of all rural land transactions although less than one-tenth of their acreage. A substantial proportion of this chapter will be spent examining the land-conversion process and its implications for farming.

Second, rising levels of car ownership and the development of public transportation facilities, as well as urban expansion itself, create new urban employment opportunities for the farmer, his family and his employees. Improved personal mobility also increases the area in which the hobby farmer may reside and yet maintain his urban place of work, although the degree to which hobby farming has resulted in a distinctive land-use pattern, as opposed to a change in farm business structure, is debatable.[6]

Finally, urban expansion and an increase in the use of the countryside for recreation provide new market opportunities for farmers, most obviously through farmgate sales. However, the effects of such sales on land-use patterns have yet to be demonstrated. The traditional transport cost advantage to farmers of market-oriented locations on the urban fringe is no longer considered to be of great commercial significance in advanced economies, both because of the relative decline in the farmer's cost structure of transport costs and because of changes in the spatial structure of agricultural marketing.[7]

Even from this brief outline it is clear that these urban-generated processes operate with varying intensities at different distances from the urban periphery. Moreover, where one of these processes is not of overriding significance, they offer a variety of opportunities and implications for farmers, and this feature is accentuated by the great variety of business structures that exist within farming. It is not surprising to find, therefore, that the available evidence, collected from many different urban-fringe situations, is conflicting.

The Rural Land Market on the Urban Fringe

Urban use almost always represents a much more intensive use of land than is made by any agricultural system of production. In consequence, the price paid by developers for agricultural land in the right location for conversion to urban uses is usually far more than the farmer making his living from agriculture can afford. Farmers offered 'development' prices for their land are usually very willing to sell. With the proceeds they often purchase new and better holdings, thus effectively raising agricultural land prices away from the urban fringe as well. Where a free market in land exists, or a revision in land-use zoning regulations is anticipated, speculators and developers are constantly seeking to buy or to place options on land they consider to have good development potential. In such speculative situations the farmer operates within a particularly uncertain farming environment and land may lie idle while the farmer awaits the right offer or the developer the right time to develop.[8] As a result, statutory authorities are encouraged to pass legislation to control the pattern of land conversion and to reduce the level of private speculative gain which, in practice, is usually passed on to the community in the form of higher house prices. Paradoxically, however, legislation may reduce the supply of building land, thus raising its price further. Moreover, under conditions of land shortage and a willingness and ability of the public to pay more for housing, developers and landowners tend to treat taxation on capital gains as an additional land-conversion cost which is simply added to the final house price.

Few detailed enquiries have been carried out using land-sales information,[9] often because data are confidential. Even where comprehensive information on land sales is available, data necessary for a behavioural analysis, relating to such questions as options and bargaining procedures, cannot be acquired. In Britain data are particularly sparse. Information relating to a proportion of public auction sales are published and many studies of the rural land market have been based on this source.[10] Until recently there has been no way of checking the representativeness of these sales. Since 1970, however, the Ministry of Agriculture has produced six-monthly reports, based on much more comprehensive but confidential information collected by the Inland Revenue, against which limited checks can be made.[11] Sales at public auction consistently record higher prices in all comparable farm-size groups, anything between 15 and 33 per cent. more than the prices published from the Inland Revenue's sources.[12] Nevertheless, despite these difficulties, the aggregated data published by the Ministry of Agriculture do indicate the importance of urban expansion on farmland prices. In England and Wales, during the period 1 October 1971 to 31 March 1972, the average price of farmland was £208 per acre (·4 ha), but with the highest regional price, in the southern mixed-farming area, being £271 per acre.[13] Land of comparable agricultural quality in the Midlands mixed-farming region recorded an average sale price of only £234 per acre, whilst the southern and northern arable areas of eastern England, with the best opportunities for intensive arable farming, only averaged £252 per acre and £199 per acre respectively. Competition for small farms suited to hobby farming is especially severe close to London, where farms of 10-100 acres (4-40 ha) are sold at an average price of £285 per acre compared with the national average of £236 per acre for this size of farm. In 1969, the average price of farmland in the United States was £80 per acre. Highest prices occurred in the Corn Belt where a considerable demand exists for family farms, but significantly the Pacific states and the north-east recorded prices of £149 and £136 per acre respectively.[14]

The evidence relating to the direct sale of farmland for urban development demonstrates the enormous difference that exists between agricultural and development land prices on the fringes of large cities. Data for the Standard Metropolitan Statistical Areas of the United States in 1964 indicate that development value varied between 892 and 1,875 per cent. of the agricultural value. In absolute terms, appreciation averaged $2,812 per acre, ranging from $313 per acre near Burlington, Vermont, to $21,129 per acre around San Mateo, California. Generally, appreciation was greatest around those cities that had experienced the largest population increases in the previous ten years. Despite this enormous appreciation over agricultural values, the price received by the farmer relative to the final value of the land is quite small, about 12 per cent.[15] In Britain, appreciation in absolute terms is even greater, particularly in south-east England. In 1968 the price of land sold in small plots (less than two acres) with planning permission for residential development and within 32 kilometres of London, ranged from £11,430 per acre to £58,000 per acre.[16] In 1972 it has been quite normal for well-sited farmland to reach prices at public auction of up to

£100,000 per acre. This has meant that the proportion of the final house price attributable to land price has gone up, from 4 per cent. in 1960 to 23 per cent. in 1970 in north-west England, and to 33 per cent. in 1970 in south-east England, without even allowing for an average increase in residential density from eight to ten houses per acre (20 to 25 per ha) over the same period.[17] Meanwhile, between 1969 and 1971 agricultural land prices stabilized at between £225 and £250 per acre, but in 1972 rose very fast, so that most land sold at public auction now makes at least £600 per acre.

The average price early in 1973 was £700 per acre with land in the southern mixed-farming area averaging £934 per acre, and small 'residential' farms making over £1,000 per acre. Prices are still rising, although at a slower rate – about that of inflation – and the most recent estimates (July–September, 1973) suggest an average price of about £775 per acre.

Land-Rent and Land-Value Models

Land-rent models assume that the land use that can command the highest rent for a particular location will effectively bid for it in the land market. Spatial variations in land use thus reflect spatial variations in the abilities of different activities to compete, and this normative, rent-maximizing approach to the understanding of land-use patterns forms the basis of a number of mathematically-derived spatial equilibrium models.[18] The value of these models lies in their presentation of a coherent, deductive framework, but their frequent oversimplification reduces their predictive value. They may be criticized, in general, for their conception of a dynamic situation in static terms and, in detail, in their underestimation of short-term rigidities in the supply of land which result in a spatially-irregular land-conversion process. They fail to account for variable amounts and types of fixed capital investments on individual farms and the differing anticipations of future demands for development by landowners.

Basic to these models is the assumption that land rent declines from the centre of a city outwards. A number of empirical studies substantiate this at the urban periphery by demonstrating a decline in land rent with distance from the urban fringe,[19] or infer it by relating land prices to population density.[20] This spatial pattern is generally explained by reference to the assumption that the users of locations close to city centres save transportation costs, and this advantage is expressed in land prices. 'From this observation the expectation has arisen that in a static economy land values decline as distance from the CBD increases, until the land is no longer used for urban purposes, and its value is determined by agricultural opportunities.'[21] The shape of the rent-bid curve in space for any use will depend on transportation facilities, the relative costs of transportation and housing and the preferences of individuals with regard to living close to the city centre.[22]

This simple pattern is breaking down as a result of the relative decline of many city centres as places of employment and because of increases in the significance of local shopping and schooling facilities for the residential location choice of many households.[23]

Spatial variations in the organization of agriculture at the urban periphery cannot be built directly into this model for two reasons. First, the rent model is based on ease of transportation into the city centre and agriculture, as has been previously explained, is now even less dependent on the city centre than many urban activities.[24] Second, because of the great differential in agricultural and urban land-use prices, the market rent for many locations beyond the urban fringe reflects urban development possibilities rather than existing agricultural-use value. The spatial rent margin between urban and agricultural uses is therefore some distance out into the countryside beyond the actual use boundary. In a free land market, without planning controls, in which everyone was perfectly informed and in which the rural land market responded immediately to demands for urban building land, the rent margin and the periphery of the built-up urban area would be spatially coexistent. Extensive urban use would phase into intensive agricultural use. In practice, the farmer's decisions often relate to the anticipated future sale of his land and not to its theoretical rent-generating capability, always assuming there is an agricultural use capable of commanding a land rent comparable to those earned by potential urban uses. It is then, by this argument, not inevitable that the farmer close to the urban fringe will farm intensively.

Despite these observations, it is technically possible both to determine the location of the rent margin between agricultural and urban uses, and for farmers to decide when to sell and at what price. Provided that future urban and agricultural land prices and future agricultural income can be estimated, that the rate and pattern of urban development can be forecasted and that a realistic discount rate can be specified, it is possible for the farmer to assess the market value of his land at any point in time.[25] Empirical evidence suggests, however, that this kind of normative framework is not a good indicator of actual land-sale behaviour. Short-term stochastic elements, such as changes in local economic prosperity and land-use planning legislation, as well as the variable behaviour of landowners when presented with an opportunity to sell, assume greater significance than those variables that can be accurately assessed.[26]

Unfortunately much of the empirical evidence collected is unrelated to explicit statements of theory, but for varying reasons geographers have traditionally sought, and in some cases found, intensive agricultural production near the urban fringe.[27] It has been observed that, although the Standard Metropolitan Statistical Areas of the United States include only 12·5 per cent. of all commercial farms, these areas contain 44 per cent. of all vegetable farms, 36 per cent. of all fruit and nut farms, 22 per cent. of all poultry units and 17 per cent. of all dairy holdings.[28] It has also been established that levels of investment per unit area per farm, an indirect measure of production intensity, fall within increasing distance from urban centres in the north-east of the United States.[29] However, as the size of farm[30] also increased with distance, these results cannot be seen as conclusive, especially as the authors were unable to explain why small farms should be more frequent close to urban centres. It has been suggested that farms located in metropolitan areas are often on good land capable of supporting intensive systems of production simply because many towns began as agricultural trade centres located close to commercially viable farming communities.[31] This notion, which would seem to be more relevant to the development of small rural centres than to large cities, is put in perspective by the fact that land taken for urban development in Britain is of above-average agricultural quality.[32] As a notion, it provides an alternative empirical explanation for the intensity of farming activity in some peri-urban locations to that embodied in the theoretical expectations of the land-rent model.

Contrary evidence of extensive systems of agricultural production on the urban fringe is also limited, although numerous researchers have commented on the extensive areas of idle land that await development around urban centres in North America. As much as 27 per cent. of all the land in one county of Delaware stands idle.[33] It would be incorrect, however, to attribute all, or even a substantial proportion, of this idle land to the decisions of farmers. When land prices are rising fast, all those associated with urban development may speculate. On the basis of a detailed study of one suburb in Philadelphia, Milgram records that:

> For the most part, land has been acquired by developers as they wished to put it to use, but almost a quarter of the acreage developed was purchased four or more years in advance, as a hedge against land prices, to permit continuous construction, or possibly unintentionally through misjudgement of its development potential. Somewhat under half of all land was acquired by the developer in the same year or year immediately preceding development, and thirty per cent. in the second and third years.[34]

Moreover, contrary to the generally-held assumption that land taxed at its market value as opposed to its current agricultural value would lead to more intensive systems of agricultural production, a majority of the evidence collected from states in the United States with such a system of land taxation demonstrates that the taxes are so high that before the land is ready for development many farmers are forced to give up farming and to sell out at low prices to developers, who can afford the higher taxes. This merely serves to increase the amount of land that stands idle.[35]

Uncertainty and Farming Response

In order to explain the lack of intensive agriculture around some cities, attention has been drawn to the extremely uncertain nature of the decision-making environment in which the urban-fringe farmer operates. One of the effects of this is for the farmer to withdraw his resources – both labour and capital – from farming. As the developer wishes to buy his land and not his buildings there is no incentive for the farmer to make long-term investments on farm improvements.[36] Thus, whilst the land retains a high market value, its value for farming actually declines close to the built-up area (Figure 10–1). Agriculture may cease altogether if the farmer chooses

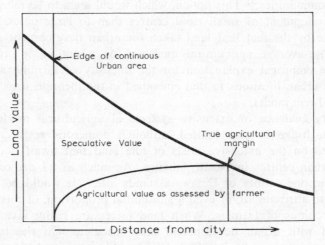

Figure 10–1   Hypothetical land-value gradient at the urban fringe with no land-use control (based on F. W. Boal [1970], 80; the relative contributions of urban potential and agricultural value to the market value of undeveloped land are not shown true to scale)

to leave farming and simply awaits a developer's offer. The most capital-intensive systems of production, such as dairying, pig and poultry production and perennial fruit farming, should, by this assumption, be most vulnerable. Unfortunately, little farming information has been provided to support this view, although a similar process has been recorded around Rome,[37] Paris[38] and within the designated area of the new city of Milton Keynes.[39] In England and Wales, the Ministry of Agriculture will not pay grants for farm improvements if sale of the farmland is anticipated before the life of the proposed investment expires. In practice, this ruling relates to land already designated for development, even if a precise date for development has not been fixed. 'Farming to quit', which can represent a short period of intense activity and use of land, may begin just prior to the sale of the land. The possibility of this kind of short-term response by farmers affecting the land-use pattern has not received much attention, although a reduction in leys and an increase in cereal acreage has been recorded on farms at Milton Keynes.[40]

A partial explanation of these different responses to loss of land may be found in the great variability in farmers' attitudes to the potential costs, benefits and expected timing of urban development, both as individuals and as a social group. As a group, attitudes and responses vary according to previous experience of development. Those groups that have previously experienced development are usually much better judges of the value of their land to the developer, and negotiate accordingly.[41] Farmers largely ignorant of the land conversion process, such as those living away from existing urban centres or those farming in regions which have experienced only modest urban growth, may show a total lack of concern as to alternative farming possibilities and do little about the loss of their land unless it is sufficiently substantial to make their existing way of life totally impossible, and even then express a general resolve to 'hang on' as long as possible.[42]

Farmers with similar experiences also vary quite considerably in their attitudes toward the sale of their land for development, despite the substantial financial gain most of them make from the sale. There is little evidence to suppose that more than an extremely small minority withhold their land for any length of time, especially as farming becomes more difficult when surrounded by residential development. Nevertheless, timing of the sale varies according to the financial position of the landowner and the amount of capital he has tied up in his business. Generally, institutional landowners have less incentive to sell than small farmers, and with their greater financial reserves can hold out longer for a better price. At least one survey suggests that the attitudes of landowners are as important as the characteristics of the land in determining whether or not a sale takes place, except where the land is located very close to the existing built-up area.[43] Non-economic motives such as the maintenance of status and privacy can affect the decision to sell. Absentee landlords, retired farmers and those who have held the rights to the land for a short time are most likely to sell. It would seem reasonable to suggest that non-economic motives would assume greatest significance where the level of appreciation on land values with development was lowest, yet the survey referred to here was carried out around Greensboro and Winston-Salem in North Carolina, where the level of appreciation, according to Schmid, was not much less than the national average for all Standard Metropolitan Statistical Areas (SMSAs) in the United States.[44] Those farmers who sell parts of their farms, but are dependent upon them for their livelihoods, have an important reinvestment decision to make. They are faced with four primary alternatives. They can invest the proceeds outside agriculture and use the money earned to supplement their reduced farming incomes. Alternatively, they can either seek

new land in the vicinity of their existing holdings, or they can sell the rest
of their businesses and buy new farms away from the urban area. Finally,
they can reinvest their proceeds in the remainder of their farms in order to
make a more intensive use of the remaining land resources. Despite the
uncertainties associated with this latter course of action and that of purchasing new land in the vicinity, farmers may be tempted to follow one of
these, as they frequently underestimate the rate of urban expansion and
are reluctant to break existing social ties.

Land Zoning and Compulsory Purchase

Planning authorities have taken steps to minimize urban sprawl and land
speculation through firmer land-use controls. Control measures can vary
from preferential taxation agreements for farmers to strict land-use controls,
and the very fact that they can differ so much in their operation, both
between states in the United States and between countries, in itself helps
to explain the conflicting agricultural land-use evidence. For example, under
one kind of agreement in the United States land is taxed on its agricultural
rather than its development value, provided the farmer agrees to maintain
his land in commercial agricultural use. Elsewhere land is taxed at its
agricultural value but annual assessments made of its market value. When
the land is developed, the farmer becomes liable for the taxes based on
previous market valuations which had been waived. The protection afforded
the farmer by these measures has frequently worked to the advantage of
the speculator who maintained land in a nominal form of extensive agricultural use, often renting out the land on very short leases and at low rents
to neighbouring farmers, in order to meet the agricultural qualification.[45]
To counter this, strict land-use zoning laws have been passed, particularly
in areas of rapid urban expansion. Typical is the California Land Conservation Act of 1965, which was drawn up with the intention of protecting
high-quality agricultural land and reducing the social and economic costs
attributable to urban sprawl.[46] The state preferentially assesses high-quality
agricultural land for a minimum period of ten years by fixing the rate of
land taxation at the level operating at the start of the period. The contract
is extended annually by one year so that the taxation due in the eleventh
year is agreed in the second year. An alternative approach has been adopted
by the residents of Dairy Valley near Los Angeles, who protected their dairy
industry from urban encroachment by creating an exclusive agricultural
'city'.[47] As part of the Los Angeles metropolitan area, Dairy Valley remains
dependent on Los Angeles for many of its public services and its farmers
have to pay high land taxes, but as a separate local government authority
it can prevent itself from being incorporated into Los Angeles or a
neighbouring urban centre without its citizens' consent. Such a move

probably provides only a short-term obstacle to development, for unless farm incomes can rise in parallel with the higher land prices offered by speculators, a majority of farmers will sooner or later be tempted to reverse the community's original decision.

In Britain, green-belt legislation has been employed to restrict urban expansion rather than to protect the farming community. It has, however, served this latter function as well. The improved security for farmers within green belts has led Boal[48] to extend Sinclair's model (Figure 10–2). The

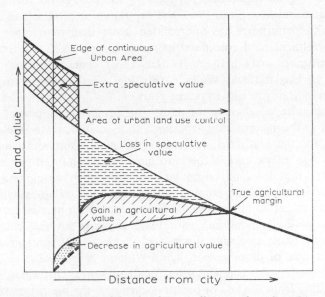

Figure 10–2 Hypothetical land-value gradient at the urban fringe with control on the spread of urban land uses (based on F. W. Boal [1970], 80; the relative contributions of urban potential and agricultural value to the market value of undeveloped land are not shown true to scale)

effect of legislation is assumed to increase the value of land for agriculture within the green belt and to eliminate its speculative value.[49] However, by reducing the supply of building land, it increases prices outside the protected zone and, ultimately, pressures on the zone itself. Land-use changes suggest that, although the amount of urban development within green belts has been small compared with that outside them, it has not ceased altogether.[50] Around London, residential and commercial land-uses, especially the extractive industries, have expanded, primarily at the expense of farmland.[51] Moreover, despite existing policy, the considerable demand for building land in south-east England at the present time has led to agricultural land being sold at much above agricultural prices and landowners being approached by speculators wishing to place options on land. Many are

8*

gambling on the possibility of a change in green-belt policy. If readjustments are made then the effect of the extra security for agriculture, as assumed in Boal's model, would be largely lost. It is important to point out, however, that the model was derived in relation to experience around Belfast, where the demand for building land is less than south-east England. The true differential between farm and development land prices is not shown on Figure 10–2 for graphical reasons. It is so great in the case of south-east England that the long-term guesswork speculation of developers in London's green belt is quite explicable, particularly as there is no real gamble in terms of financial *loss*. Since 1945, the capital value of farmland in Britain for agricultural purposes has appreciated faster than most other forms of secure investment, and considerably faster during 1972. Although a net annual return of only between 1 and 2 per cent. is normal for most farmland in England and Wales,[52] this low yield has not stopped city companies investing in land in recent years.

The compulsory purchase of land for urban development, and the associated problems created by the need to assess adequate levels of compensation for those affected, represents the most overt and controversial form of public interference in the land market. In Britain, if the farmer can demonstrate that his land could be sold for urban development in the foreseeable future, then an amount, known as 'hope' value, is added to the existing-use valuation of his land. This amount, which may be considerably in excess of its agricultural valuation, depends on the current local development value of land, discounted back to the present from the anticipated date of development. Land without 'hope' value is bought at existing-use value plus compensation for disturbance. Disturbance includes costs resulting from the loss of business earnings, the premature realization of investments and moving house. Liverpool Corporation recently set an important precedent by their dealings with farmers affected by the building of a reservoir at Tryweryn in Merionethshire. The Corporation made an additional payment to the farmers, based on the profitability of their farms and the number of years they had been farming them, explicitly recognizing the existence of the intangible social costs as well as the quantifiable economic costs that are associated with compulsory purchase.[53]

If only a small part of a farm is bought, the level of compensation paid can affect the farming system on the remainder of the holding by permitting different kinds of reinvestment opportunity. Where the farmer is dispossessed, the amount of compensation will determine his ability to compete on the agricultural land market in his search for a new farm. If a substantial number of farmers are displaced in one area their combined efforts to buy new holdings can lead to a rapid rise in land price in the local rural land market. Finally, the tenant is in a much more difficult situation than the landowner, who can usually purchase another farm if he so wishes. Under the 1948 Agricultural Holdings Act, tenants were only entitled to between one and two years' rent as compensation, and, although this was increased to four years in 1968, this low level of compensation in relation to land prices almost inevitably forces the tenant out of the industry as tenancies are almost impossible to obtain.

In summarizing the implications for agriculture of the land transfer mechanism, two points warrant emphasis. First, whilst it is possible to develop a number of agricultural land-use models for farming on the urban fringe based on the future expectations of farmers in different land-use planning contexts, there is only limited empirical evidence in support of these models' predictions. This is largely the result of the great differences in organization of agricultural production that exist at the farm level. Only where there is a lack of planning control, as well as a large land-price differential between the prices commanded by agricultural and urban uses, can a common farming response be expected. Intensive livestock farms, for example, have very different cost structures from traditional mixed farms. Long-term investments in buildings, important to the farmer, are not easily liquidated part-way through the investment cycle without financial loss, and since the investment cycle may be at least twenty years long the farmer's opportunities to sell land for urban development can change dramatically during the investment period. Indeed, some farmers may invest further in their expectation of being able to make the developer pay for their investments through a higher land-sale price.

Second, where planning controls are in force and farmers are protected from the full effects of taxation based on the market value of their land, intense urban pressures only occur on the immediate urban fringe where the sale of land is anticipated in the near future. The significance in land-use terms of these pressures is further minimized by the resolve of many farmers to 'hang on' as long as possible in their existing locations and continue to use their existing systems of farming.

New Employment Opportunities

Improved personal mobility has created new employment opportunities in urban areas for those who live in the country, and, very occasionally, for those who live in the town but prefer to work in the country.[54] One of the major reasons for the steady decline in the number of agricultural workers in advanced economies is the lower wages they receive in relation to a majority of their industrial counterparts,[55] and the decline in numbers is most evident close to the urban fringe, where industrial employment opportunities are most evident and accessible. In Britain, for example, the relatively 'urban' counties of Derbyshire, Hertfordshire and Essex lost 27, 25 and 24 per cent. respectively of their agricultural workforce between

1951 and 1961, whilst the 'rural' counties of Lincolnshire (Holland), Herefordshire and Westmorland only lost 8, 9 and 12 per cent. respectively.[56] Where farm labour is already scarce, farmers either have to increase their wage bill or go into more extensive systems of production. The replacement of dairy herds by beef rearing is a typical change in Britain, where farmers are reluctant to commit further capital in order to counter reductions in their labour forces. In parts of the south of the United States, livestock systems of production replace more labour-intensive tobacco crops.[57]

Part-time farming has long been recognized as an urban-fringe phenomenon.[58] In Britain, part-time farming is important in south-east England and in areas of small farms or marginal farming.[59] A survey carried out in Buckinghamshire in 1963-4 revealed that 41·3 per cent. of all holdings were part-time units and over 75 per cent. of these provided less than half the farmers' incomes.[60] Part-time farming is also increasing. The proportion of farmers to the south-east of London with a substantial non-agricultural source of income has risen from 30 to 50 per cent. between 1941 and 1964, with the result that by the end of 1964 part-time farmers farmed over one-third of all agricultural land.[61] The proportion of part-time to full-time farmers falls with distance from London, the proportion declining from 60 per cent. at 29–32 kilometres from London to 29 per cent. at 90–100 kilometres. Right on the urban fringe they are of lesser importance, probably because they are unable to compete with speculators for the purchase of land and because less land for agricultural purposes has come on to the market here in recent years, when the demand for part-time farms has been greatest.

Two important sub-types of part-time farming can be distinguished. First, that type which results from the farmer and the members of his family seeking non-farm employment in order to supplement their farm incomes. Second, hobby farming where the farm provides only a nominal source of income, often financially non-essential, to supplement that earned in urban employment. Distinguishing between the farming activities of these two groups is difficult, as statistical sources refer to characteristics of the holding and not of the operator. The distinction is important, however, as more part-time than hobby farmers have a rural upbringing and this, combined with their greater economic dependence on their farms, means that they tend to adopt farming systems more similar to those practised on full-time holdings.[62] The hobby farmer is of increasing importance in Britain, although this assertion is only based on the indirect evidence of the farmer's other occupation. Professional people, for example, constitute between 60 and 70 per cent. of the part-time farmers around London.[63] The most widely acknowledged motives for hobby farming include the status associated with landownership, the wish for a desirable residential location, the purchase of land as an investment and, in Britain, the desire to reduce estate duty and gain tax concessions. The limited evidence is inconclusive, but, generally, part-time farmers have smaller farms, make a less effective use of capital and land resources and have simpler, less labour-intensive farming systems than do full-time farmers. This evidence is insufficient to sustain the assumptions that hobby farmers are inefficient or that a type of hobby-farming agriculture can be clearly distinguished in land-use terms. The possibility of drawing such a distinction is reduced by the common practice of hobby farmers of leasing out their land to full-time operators. The lower priority placed by hobby farmers on income generation from their farms accounts for their effective competition with other agricultural interests in metropolitan regional land markets. The overall effect of this has been to create an increasing dualism between large, commercial units and small hobby farms, both of which have expanded at the expense of the family farm in urban-fringe zones.[64] It remains to be seen whether this dualism results in very different systems of farming.

New Business Opportunities

It has always been assumed that the low cost of transporting produce to the market has been a considerable advantage for the farmer on the urban fringe. But with the relative decline of transport costs within the total cost structure of agriculture and with the restructuring of agricultural marketing to reflect national rather than local needs, this assumption can no longer be accepted. Nevertheless, several American economists have demonstrated that urban proximity raises farming incomes,[65] although employment possibilities in the industrial sector of the economy appear to be more responsible for this than any extra earnings gained from new or better market outlets. This would imply either that these outlets are not as economically significant as has been presumed, or that farmers have not yet exploited them. Farmers have been slow to develop the income potential of farmgate sales and the retail distribution of milk, eggs and vegetables in suburban areas. This may be partly explained by the effort required to organize these outlets at a time of declining labour availability, by the extra capital required for retail deliveries and by the increasing number of part-time farmers. Nonetheless, in at least one case, that of the exclusive dairying areas around Los Angeles, farmers are only able to compete effectively with urban interests in the land market because of the additional profits they make by retailing milk.[66] With the general development of vertical integration and market consciousness in the farming industry, farmers may well make a more effective use of these market outlets in the future. At present there is little evidence to suggest that many farmers are restructuring their businesses in any substantial way to meet these opportunities. More often, those who already produce goods easily sold at the farmgate sell what they can in this way when it is convenient.

Conclusion

Despite obvious differences in detail, a common direction of change can be observed in three aspects of the urban fringe which are relevant for the future organization of agriculture. First, the considerable differential between the land prices for agricultural and urban uses is increasing in absolute terms. Second, and partly arising out of this, there is a demand for new controls to be placed on the operation of the land market. In North America there is a demand for the ending of free markets in land, where these still remain, and for a re-examination of land-taxation systems.[67] In Britain the need arises for a more positive approach to regional land-use planning, particularly where rural interests seem in conflict with urban requirements. Third, there is a continuing change in the social structure of those engaged in agriculture on the urban fringe. The number of agricultural employees is declining rapidly and the new farming entrant is a professional man with an urban background. The family farm is being squeezed out by the emergence of hobby farmers, who are not necessarily inefficient farmers, and large farming companies.

These changes, however, are not leading to the development of a clearly-defined type of 'metropolitan' agricultural land use; and a number of partial explanations can be put forward for this situation. Urban pressures are, for the most part, only of great significance to farmers' business practices on the immediate urban fringe. Hobby farming, for example, which is dispersed more widely, cannot be associated with a particular system of production. Urban pressures are also conflicting, in that they present difficulties for farming, such as uncertainty, at the same time as they offer new opportunities, such as additional retail outlets. Moreover, agriculture is also trying to adjust to rapid changes in market opportunities and technological capabilities, both largely unrelated to urban proximity. This process of adjustment is producing more capital-intensive, specialized farming, often with inflexible investment programmes which cannot be easily adjusted to meet rapid changes in urban demands. Finally, the little evidence that exists suggests that the behaviour of farmers in the face of changing urban pressures is inconsistent. This is hardly surprising when parallel changes in the social and economic structure of the industry emphasize both the need for economic efficiency and the growing importance of non-agricultural motives for landownership. This mixture of goals and the belief of many farmers that decisions affecting their interests are increasingly being taken by urban-based authorities beyond their control suggest the need for a complete reappraisal of existing notions about the effects of cities on the farming areas around them.

Further Reading

There are three basic texts which discuss in detail questions relating to the conversion of rural lands to urban uses: M. Clawson, *Suburban Land Conversion in the United States: An Economic and Government Process* (Baltimore, 1971); A. A. Schmid, *Converting Land from Urban to Rural Uses* (Baltimore, 1968); and G. P. Wibberley, *Agriculture and Urban Growth: A Study of the Competition for Rural Land* (London, 1959).

Four detailed case studies which focus on the price of land sold for purposes of urban development, are: J. McAuslan, 'Price movements for residential land: 1965–1969', *Chartered Surveyor* **102** (1969), 123–7; Grace Milgram, *The City Expands: A Study of the Conversion of Land from Rural to Urban Use, Philadelphia, 1945–62* (Philadelphia, 1967); M. T. Rancich, 'Land value changes in an area undergoing urbanization', *Land Econ.* **46** (1970), 32–40; and P. A. Stone, 'The prices of building sites in Britain', in P. Hall (ed.), *Land Values* (London, 1965). The studies by McAuslan and Stone relate to the United Kingdom and those by Milgram and Rancich to the United States.

Two attempts to extend existing rent-based land-use models for the urban fringe are contained in the papers by: F. W. Boal, Urban growth and land value patterns: government influence', *Prof. Geog.* **22** (1970), 79–82; and R. Sinclair, 'Von Thünen and urban sprawl', *Ann. Assoc. Amer. Geogr.* **57** (1967), 72–87.

Two interesting papers which discuss questions relating to land-use control and compensation are: T. F. Hady, 'Differential assessment of farmland on the rural-urban fringe', *Amer. J. Agric. Econ.* **52** (1970), 25–32; and W. D. Jones, 'The impact of public works schemes on farming: a case study relating to a reservoir and power station in North Wales', *J. Agric. Econ.* 23 (1972), 1–14.

A monograph that draws attention to social changes within the farming community in the metropolitan south-east of England is: Ruth M. Gasson, 'The influence of urbanization on farm ownership and practice', *Studies in Rural Land Use* **7** (Wye College, Ashford, Kent, 1966).

References

1. See, for example, W. Firey, 'Ecological considerations in planning for rurban fringes', *Amer. Soc. Rev.* **11** (1946), 411; G. S. Wehrwein, 'The rural-urban fringe', *Econ. Geog.* **18** (1942), 217–28; R. G. Golledge, 'Sydney's metropolitan fringe: a study in rural-urban relations', *Australian Geog.* **7** (1960), 243–55; E. Higbee, *The Squeeze: Cities without Space* (London, 1960); and R. J. Pryor, 'Defining the rural-urban fringe', *Social Forces* **47** (1968), 202–15; P. F. Mattingly, 'Intensity of agricultural land-use near cities: a case study', *Prof. Geog.* **24** (1972), 7–10; and *Planning for Agriculture in Southern Ontario*, ARDA Report No. 7 (Guelph, Ontario, 1972).
2. Not part-time farming (see p. 214).

3. Farmers would probably add a fourth, namely trespass. Trespass, for obvious reasons, is frequently discussed but little documented. It is generally accepted, however, that whilst trespass is a widespread nuisance only in a few places on the immediate edge of the built-up area is it a constraint on farming practice. Trespass is most serious near new housing estates where the population is unacquainted with farming activities. Livestock farming in general and sheep farming in particular are most affected. See G. P. Wibberley, *Agriculture and Urban Growth: A Study of the Competition for Rural Land* (London, 1959).

4. Land-market transactions are not seen as transactions in land *per se* but in rights in and over land. See D. R. Denman, 'Land on the market', *Hobart Paper* **30** (Institute of Economic Affairs, London, 1964).

5. This position is criticized in R. Drewett, 'Land values and urban growth', in M. Chisholm, A. E. Frey and P. Haggett (eds.), *Regional Forecasting, Colston Papers* **22** (1971), 335–57.

6. Hobby farmers also compete effectively on the land market, but their influence on urban-fringe agriculture will be discussed more generally in a later section (see p. 214–5).

7. Wholesale agricultural marketing is increasingly located outside urban centres and closer to the major producing areas so as to meet the marketing needs of processors and retailing groups. For a discussion with reference to horticulture see R. H. Best and Ruth M. Gasson, 'The changing location of intensive crops', *Studies in Land Use* **6** (Wye College, Ashford, Kent, 1966).

8. For detailed case studies see H. J. Gayler, 'Land speculation and urban development: contrasts in south-east Essex, 1880–1940', *Urban Studies* **7** (1970), 21–36; and M. T. Rancich, 'Land value changes in an area undergoing urbanization', *Land Econ.* **46** (1970), 32–40.

9. Exceptions include M. T. Rancich, *op. cit.*, and Grace Milgram, *The City Expands: A Study of the Conversion of Land from Rural to Urban Use, Philadelphia, 1945–62* (Institute of Environmental Studies, University of Pennsylvania, Philadelphia, 1967).

10. See P. A. Stone, 'The prices of building sites in Britain', in P. Hall (ed.), *Land Values* (London, 1965), 1–18; G. H. Peters, 'Recent trends in farm real estate values in England and Wales', *Farm Economist* **11** (1966), 45–60; J. McAuslan, 'Price movements for residential land: 1965–1969', *Chartered Surveyor* **102** (1969), 123–7; A. H. Maunder, 'Farm land values in 1969', *Estates Gazette* **213** (1970), 1157–9; P. M. P. Williams, 'Agricultural land prices in England and Wales', *Farm Management* **1** (1971), 40–55; and R. J. C. Munton, 'Recent trends in farmland prices in England and Wales', *Estates Gazette* **227** (1973), 2159–65.

11. A full check still cannot be made. The Ministry of Agriculture data do not indicate the proportion of all land sales made at public auction and there is no way of knowing what percentage of public auction sales are published. It is clear, however, that only 10 to 15 per cent. of all sales are reported in the mass media and their representativeness in terms of price, location and type of farm is a matter for debate.

12. One of the major problems with the data published by the Ministry of Agriculture is that they relate to sales notified to the Inland Revenue with a particular six-month period and there is an indefinite time-lag of up to twelve months between the agreement on price by the parties concerned and its notification to the Inland Revenue. Thus auction prices, which are

published almost immediately, will reflect a higher price if prices are generally rising.

13. Ministry of Agriculture, *Sales of Agricultural Land in England and Wales, October 1971–March 1972* (London, 1972). Prices are analysed by farming region as defined by the Ministry. The approximate areas covered by the regions referred to in the text are as follows: (1) Southern Mixed-Farming Region – Hampshire, Sussex, Surrey, Berkshire, Buckinghamshire, Oxfordshire and east Wiltshire; (2) Midlands Mixed-Farming Region – Herefordshire, Warwickshire, Worcestershire, Leicestershire, most of Northamptonshire, south Staffordshire and east Gloucestershire; (3) Southern Arable Region – Kent, Essex, Hertfordshire, Suffolk, Norfolk, Cambridgeshire, Huntingdonshire and Bedfordshire; (4) Northern Arable Region – Lincolnshire, East Riding, east Nottinghamshire, east West Riding and south North Riding.

14. P. M. P. Williams, *op. cit.*

15. A. A. Schmid, *Converting Land from Urban to Rural Uses* (Baltimore, 1968).

16. J. McAuslan, *op. cit.* A review of building land prices recorded in the *Estates Gazette* during 1972 indicated a median site price for raw building land of £25,583 per acre; see *Digest of Building Land Prices* (House Builders Federation Advisory Service, London, 1973).

17. R. Drewett, *op. cit.*

18. See, for example, R. F. Muth, 'Economic change and rural-urban land conversions', *Econometrica* **29** (1961), 1–23.

19. P. A. Stone, *op. cit.;* J. McAuslan, *op. cit.*; A. A. Schmid, *op. cit.*; and H. F. Goldsmith and J. H. Cropp, 'Metropolitan dominance and agriculture', *Rur Soc.* **29** (1964), 385–95.

20. V. W. Ruttan, 'The impact of local population pressure on farm real estate values in California', *Land Econ.* **37** (1961), 125–31; W. C. Scharlach and G. E. Schuh, 'The land market as a link between the rural and urban sectors of the economy', *J. Farm Econ.* **44** (1962), 1406–11; and L. H. Russwurm, 'Expanding urbanism and selected agricultural elements: case study, south-western Ontario area, 1941–61', *Land Econ.* **43** (1967), 101–7.

21. A. A. Schmid, *op. cit.*, 29.

22. See H. Mohring, 'Land values and measurement of highway benefits', *J. Polit. Econ.* **69** (1961), 236–49.

23. M. A. Stegman, 'Accessibility models and residential location', *J. Amer. Inst. Planners* **35** (1969), 22–9.

24. Only the substantial intervention in the land market of hobby farmers, dependent on an urban place of work, could lead to a decline in farmland values away from the urban periphery and main lines of communication in a manner compatible with the model's predictions. There is no evidence to suggest that hobby farmers intervene sufficiently in the land market around any city to create such a land-price pattern.

25. If these conditions are met then the present value of a farming location may be calculated as follows:

$$V = \frac{A}{ia} + \frac{Ce}{(1+ic)^t}$$

where V = present value
A = annual income expected from rural use
Ce = expected capital gains

ia = capitalization rate for income (A)

ic = discount rate for capital gains (Ce)

t = number of years over which income (A) is expected to continue before capital gains are received.

See H. A. Clonts, 'Influence of urbanization on land values at the urban periphery', *Land Econ.* **46** (1970), 489–97. If a period of 'ripening' occurs, when the land stands idle between urban and rural use, then the loss of rural income over this time also has to be calculated, discounted back to the present and added to the agricultural value of the location. Generally, the higher the discount rate and the slower the spread of urban development, the closer the location of the rent margin is to the actual use margin.

26. See M. Clawson, 'Urban sprawl and urban speculation', *Land Econ.* **38** (1962), 99–111; and M. Clawson, *Suburban Land Conversion in the United States: An Economic and Governmental Process* (Baltimore, 1971).

27. R. G. Golledge, *op. cit.*; and H. Gregor, 'Urban pressures on Californian land', *Land Econ.* **33** (1957), 311–25.

28. A. D. Waldo, 'Farming in the urban fringe', in *A Place to Live*, Yearbook of Agriculture (USDA, Washington, 1963), 139–45.

29. H. F. Goldsmith and R. H. Cropp, *op. cit.*

30. Small farms almost always employ more capital per unit area than large farms.

31. P. F. Griffen and R. Chatham, 'Urban impact on agriculture in Santa Clara County, California', *Ann. Assoc. Amer. Geogr.* **48** (1958), 195–208.

32. G. P. Wibberley, 'Pressures on Britain's rural land', in *Land Use or Abuse*, Report of the 22nd Oxford Farming Conference (1968), 1–13.

33. H. G. Berkman, 'Decentralization and blighted vacant land', *Land Econ.* **32** (1956), 270–80; M. Clawson, *op. cit.* (1962); and M. Kottke, 'Changes in farm density in areas of urban expansion', *J. Farm. Econ.* **48** (1966), 1290–6.

34. Grace Milgram, *op. cit.*, 5. Small builders whose assets are too limited to speculate on the land market face other problems; see H. Brodsky, 'Land development and the expanding city', *Ann. Ass. Amer. Geogr.* **63** (1973), 159–67.

35. M. G. Blase and W. J. Staub, 'Real property taxes in the rural-urban fringe', *Land. Econ.* **47** (1971), 168–74. For a general discussion of the economic and legal aspects of open-space planning decisions in the United States see R. H. Platt, *'The Open Space Decision Process'*, Research Paper No. 142 (Department of Geography, University of Chicago, 1972).

36. R. Sinclair, 'Von Thünen and urban sprawl', *Ann. Assoc. Amer. Geogr.* **57** (1967), 72–87. For a different point of view see C. R. Bryant, 'The anticipation of urban expansion: some implications for agricultural land-use practices and land-use zoning', *Geographia Polonica* **28** (1973) (forthcoming). An attempt to simulate aspects of agricultural response to urban growth processes in the Toronto region has been made by W. C. Found and C. D. Morley, *'A Conceptual Approach to Rural Land-Use Transportation Modelling in the Toronto Region'*, Research Report No. 8 (Joint Program in Transportation, York University, Toronto, 1972).

37. E. Sermonti, 'Agriculture in areas of urban expansion (Italy)', *J. Town Plan. Inst.* **54** (1968), 15–17.

38. C. R. Bryant, 'Urbanisation and agricultural change since 1945: A case study from the Paris region (Unpublished Ph.D. Thesis, University of London, London, 1970).

39. University of Reading, 'Milton Keynes revisited: 1971', *Miscellaneous Study* **51** (Department of Agricultural Economics and Management, 1972).
40. University of Reading, *op. cit.* This has occurred despite, and perhaps because of, attempts by the Development Authority to put dates on the timing of development of particular areas of land, some of which will only be developed twenty or more years hence. Unfortunately, although the agricultural situation at Milton Keynes will probably be the best documented of any in which rapid urbanization is taking place, the facts that the scheme involves large-scale compulsory purchase of land and that development 'arrived' in a more unexpected manner than most urban development mean that the results may be atypical. One particularly penetrating comment in the Report, which would seem relevant to this kind of development, stated that during the 'pre-period' of Milton Keynes, that is, before the designated area was finally agreed, 'the total uncertainty of the situation – where and when development might start, how and in what measure compensation might be paid – rendered most people incapable of thinking at all precisely about when or where or how they would seek alternative dwellings and employment. Lack of information nullified any attempt to plan . . .' (p. 12).
41. G. A. McBride and M. Clawson, 'Negotiation and land conversion', *J. Amer. Inst. Planners* **36** (1970), 22–9.
42. C. R. Bryant, *op. cit.* (1970); and University of Reading, *op. cit.*
43. E. J. Kaiser *et. al.*, 'Predicting the behaviour of predevelopment landowners on the urban fringe', *J. Amer. Inst. Planners* **34** (1968), 328–33; and E. J. Kaiser and Shirley F. Weiss, 'Public policy and the residential development process', *J. Amer. Inst. Planners* **36** (1970), 30–7.
44. A. A. Schmid, *op. cit.*
45. L. H. Russwurm, *op. cit.*; T. F. Hady, 'Differential assessment of farmland on the rural-urban fringe', *Amer. J. Agric. Econ.* **52** (1970), 25–32; and W. van Vuuren, 'Farm assessment for property taxation', *Can. J. Agric. Econ.* **18** (1970), 87–94.
46. For a description of the Act see J. H. Snyder, 'Toward land use stability by contract', *J. Nat. Resources* **6** (1966), 406–23. For more general comment see R. J. Vogel and A. J. Hahn, 'On the preservation of agricultural land', *Land Econ.* **48** (1972), 190–3.
47. G. J. Fielding, 'Dairying in cities designed to keep people out', *Prof. Geog.* **14** (1962), 12–17; W. W. Crouch and R. N. Giordano, 'The example of Dairy Valley', in *A Place to Live,* Yearbook of Agriculture, (USDA, Washington, 1963), 491–8.
48. F. W. Boal, 'Urban growth and land value patterns: government influence', *Prof. Geog.* **22** (1970), 79–82.
49. The complete elimination of speculation or urban development is rarely achieved. The price paid for land within London's green belt, for example, reflects an element of 'hope' value.
50. See D. Thomas, *London's Green Belt* (London, 1970); D. G. Gregory, 'Green belts and development control: a case study in the West Midlands', *Occasional Paper* **12** (University of Birmingham, Centre for Urban and Regional Studies, 1970).
51. D. Thomas, *op. cit.*
52. C. I. C. Bosanquet, 'Investment in agriculture', *J. Agric. Econ.* **19** (1968), 3–12; see also H. A. Thomas, 'Capital intensity in agriculture', *Agriculture* **77** (1970), 13–14.

53. W. D. Jones, 'The impact of public works schemes on farming: a case study relating to a reservoir and power station in North Wales', *J. Agric. Econ.* **23** (1972), 1–14. The trend toward a better financial deal for those affected by planning decisions in Britain is reflected in a recent White Paper, *Putting People First: Development and Compensation.* Cmnd. 5124 (HMSO, London, 1972). Methods recently employed in Britain to assess the value of agricultural land alienated under urban development planning decisions are reviewed in M. A. B. Boddington, 'The evaluation of agricultural land in planning decisions', *J. Agric. Econ.* **24** (1973), 37–51.

54. With reference to employment in agriculture in California, Higbee records that: 'The hired men live in the city or in suburban developments. They drive out into the country as though they were going to an aircraft assembly plant. They have a union, social security; the may even punch time-clocks. They receive city wages . . .' (E. Higbee, *op. cit.,* 164).

55. It is extremely difficult to be precise about real wage differentials as the costs of living vary between urban and rural areas. Farm workers may have free accommodation but often experience a poorer level of social service provision than those living in urban areas.

56. M. Boddington, 'Urban pressure', *Farm Business* **9** (1968), 6–12.

57. W. N. Parker and D. G. Davies, 'Agricultural adjustment to urban growth', in F. S. Chapin and Shirley F. Weiss (eds.), *Urban Growth Dynamics* (New York, 1962), 121–34.

58. See, for example, I. Davies, 'Urban farming: a study of agriculture of the city of Birmingham', *Geography* **38** (1953), 296–303; J. Stewart, 'Economic problems of agriculture in an industrialized area: East Lancashire', *J. Agric. Econ.* **10** (1953), 315–31; G. V. Fuguitt, 'Urban influence and the extent of part-time farming', *Rur. Soc.* **23** (1958), 392–7; and A. L. Bertrand, 'Research on part-time farming in the United States', *Sociol. Rur.* **7** (1967), 295–306. The definition as to what constitutes a part-time farm has general implications of industrial growth in rural areas are discussed in A. Harrison, 'Some features of farm business structures', *J. Agric. Econ.* **16** (1965), 330–47; and A. L. Bertrand, *op. cit.*

59. J. Ashton and B. E. Cracknell, 'Agricultural holdings and farm business structure in England and Wales', *J. Agric. Econ.* **14** (1960–1), 472–506.

60. A. Harrison, *op. cit.*

61. Ruth M. Gasson, 'The influence of urbanization on farm ownership and practice', *Studies in Rural Land Use* **7** (Wye College, Ashford, Kent, 1966).

62. G. A. Donohue, 'Socio-economic characteristics of part-time and full-time farmers in the twin-cities area', *J. Farm Econ.* **31** (1957), 984–92.

63. See Ruth M. Gasson, *op. cit.*; and A. Harrison, *op. cit.*

64. Ruth M. Gasson, *op. cit.*

65. See V. W. Ruttan, 'The impact of urban-industrial development on agriculture in the Tennessee valley and the south-east', *J. Farm Econ.* **37** (1955), 38–56; D. G. Sisler, 'Regional differences in the impact of urban-industrial development on farm and non-farm income', *J. Farm Econ.* **41** (1959), 1100–12; W. H. Nicholls, 'Industrial-urban development and agricultural adjustments, Tennessee Valley and Piedmont, 1939–54', *J. Polit. Econ.* **68** (1960), 135–49; W. N. Parker and D. G. Davies, *op. cit.*; more general implications of industrial growth in rural areas are discussed in M. J. Moseley, 'The impact of growth centres in rural regions': I – 'An analysis of spatial "patterns" in Brittany', *Reg. Studies* **7** (1973), 57–75;

II – 'An analysis of spatial "flows" in East Anglia', *Reg. Studies* **7** (1973), 77–94.

66. G. J. Fielding, *op. cit.*

67. For a general description of recent developments in the United States see F. Bosselman and D. Callies, *The Quiet Revolution in Land Use Control* (Washington, 1971). See also C. E. Browning, 'The property tax and public policy: a neglected opportunity for geographic research', *Proc. Amer. Ass. Geogr.* **5** (1973), 35–9.

CHAPTER 11

Outdoor Recreation Around Large Cities

MARTIN J. BOWEN

The use of land, money and time for recreation has received steadily increasing attention from practitioners and researchers in environmental planning and social science. The level of open-air leisure activity in a community is dependent upon, amongst other considerations, its total population and the income, mobility, education and uncommitted-time characteristics of that population. Throughout the western world, each of these factors seems to be developing in a way which, over the years, will lead to a continued expansion of participation in outdoor recreation. The forces responsible for this expansion are notably at their strongest in large cities; but, although centres of population are the principal sources of those seeking outdoor recreation, the urban milieu provides only limited facilities towards meeting these needs, mainly because of the physical and financial obstacles to increasing the area of open space in fully built-up districts. Rural-urban fringes are thus of the greatest significance in this respect, being comparatively accessible zones where resources, because they are less constrained, can more readily be brought to bear on the problem of providing adequate opportunities for townspeople to follow their leisure interests.

The Diversity of Recreation

The innate heterogeneity of the range of 'optional activities' which can be undertaken during 'discretionary time'[1] precludes development of the topic without at least some brief comments on possible methods of sub-division. First, it should be stressed that the present interest is in the geographical and planning issues associated with outdoor activities; there will be no discussion of recreation within the immediate environs of the home and associated social activities, nor of capital intensive, largely indoor provision (such as sports halls and swimming pools), nor of commercial entertainments. Thus, this chapter is concerned with the more land-hungry recreations and, in particular, will centre on the existing and future role of facilities for these activities in the fabric of the rural-urban fringe.

Outdoor recreation of one type or another is the chief pursuit for perhaps a fifth of the leisure periods available to the British.[2] Statistics for North America do not lend themselves to direct comparison, but some estimates would suggest that over 20,000 million man-hours per year are devoted to outdoor recreation in the United States.[3] In most occidental societies succeeding years have witnessed a steady expansion in this use of time.[4] These trends conceal a multitude of temporal and spatial variations in the pattern at a more detailed level, the generic term 'outdoor recreation' covering a large spread of activities ranging from participation in formal team games to motoring for pleasure.

Many classifications have been put forward in the past but none have achieved universal acceptance, since different applications require different guiding criteria. Clawson et al. have suggested a threefold distinction between those areas which are, first, user-based, that is to say located at centres of population, second, resource-based, and as such to be found in the least populated areas, and third, in intermediate locations.[5] By definition, the first and third categories predominate in the urban fringe; in the context of an attempt to identify and explain the patterns of recreational activity around cities the classification is axiomatic. Of the five 'environment types' detailed by the Outdoor Recreation Resources Review Commission two categories (High Density Recreation Areas and General Outdoor Recreation Areas) cover the relevant ground, whereas the other three types (Natural Environment Areas, Unique Natural Areas and Primitive Areas) could at best be coincidentally, and in the last case almost inconceivably, located at the edge of cities.[6] Perhaps it is worth adding a schema based essentially on the pursuits involved. These include active recreation at formal venues, active recreation at informal venues, passive recreation (spectating), and passive recreation (visiting); there is no de facto reason why representatives of each of these activity groupings should not occur within, beyond and at the edge of the city.

The Spatial Incidence of Outdoor Recreation

In so much as recreation is an attitude of mind, the fundamental criterion for assessing leisure opportunities must be the extent to which resources, whether deliberately constructed or incidentally available, are in manifestly 'recreational' use, and this in turn is basically a function of population distributions. To illustrate with an extreme example, in an urban area vacant lots, dotted with derelict buildings and awaiting development, will be sought out by local children as fortuitous adventure playgrounds, whereas physically similar 'opportunities' located in, say, deserted rural mining areas will be totally unused. Whilst this proposition is acceptable for strongly user-oriented situations, the chance distribution of resources with recreational potential must also be recognized as of importance. For example natural phenomena or outstanding scenery, which are generally accepted as interesting or pleasant to visit, exist in distinct fixed locations, unrelated to the proximity of urban areas.

In practice, there will be different catchment thresholds in different leisure situations depending on the innate attractiveness of the opportunity, the distribution of competing opportunities and the time, money and transport available to potential users. It is equally true, however, that equivalent recreation resources near centres of population will be more intensively used than those at a greater distance. Moreover, the problem still remains of defining those opportunities which should be inventoried in any review of existing provision. This becomes more difficult away from city centres, as use is less formalized and constrained; town parks and playing fields are unequivocally recreation facilities, but if certain, non-agricultural, tracts of rural land around towns are used by horse-riders, cross-country athletes, anglers or naturalists the extent to which all superficially similar areas should be classified as recreation opportunities is open to question. Perhaps in these circumstances there is no substitute for local knowledge, which permits categorization on the basis of various *ad hoc* rules as to actual use, thus this chapter proceeds by drawing heavily on evidence from metropolitan south-east England. The London region can be taken as adequately demonstrating the range of recreation phenomena associated with large city environments and, wherever possible, generally applicable principles will be isolated.

Provision for Active Recreation

The most readily available measures of non-rural recreation opportunities in Britain are public open space indices which include elements of both formal and informal provision such as tennis courts, playing fields, recreation grounds, parks and common land to which the public has full or limited access. If estimates of public open space for Greater London are broken down into five-mile (8 km) distance zones, concentric on the centre, a pattern emerges of very low allocation of open space per head in the core zone, rising sharply at five to ten miles (8–16 km) before dropping back to close on overall average values beyond (Table 11–1). This suggests that, at the intermediate distances, the high provision can partially compensate for the deprived inner areas, always assuming that the resident population is prepared and able to undertake the necessary travel. It is, however, the outer zones which contain the lowest percentage of total land

Table 11–1. Public open space (POS) in Greater London, 1971

Distance zone (miles)[a]	Population ('000)	Total area (acres)	POS (acres)	POS per thousand people (acres)	POS as percentage of total area
0–4·9	2,467·3	53,616	6,120	2·5	11·4
5–9·9	2,494·5	117,114	22,181	8·9	18·9
10 and over	2,737·5	222,440	18,780	6·8	8·4
Totals	7,699·3	393,170	47,081	6·1	11·9

Source: The Greater London Boroughs and The Municipal Year Book.

[a] Data assigned to zones on the basis of distance between borough centroids and Charing Cross; Havering is the most distant at 16·4 miles; data exclude the City of London.

Table 11–2. Public open space (POS) in London new towns, 1966

Town	Distance from Charing Cross (miles)	Population (000s)	POS per thousand population (acres)	POS as percentage of total area
Basildon	27	111·3	5·9	10·8
Bracknell	28	25·4	11·7	15·9
Crawley	28	60·7	20·3	20·4
Harlow	21	68·7	21·1	22·7
Hemel Hempstead	22	63·6	17·0	18·3
Stevenage	27	56·8	13·5	12·4
Welwyn Garden City	21	41·0	24·0	22·8
Totals	(20–30)	427·5	14·7	17·0

Sources: J. T. Coppock 'Dormitory settlements around London', Chapter 11 of J. T. Coppock and H. C. Prince (eds.), *Greater London* (London, 1964); J. A. Patmore, *Land and Leisure* (Newton Abbot, 1970)

area in use as public open space. This is because housing covers a larger proportion of these boroughs at lower residential densities, but it remains paradoxical that, despite the lower per-capita provision of public open space in central districts, in general people living there will be closer to an open space which they can use as of right than people in the outer suburbs.

Although the effective size of the London region in terms of, say, daily-journey patterns is at least 100 kilometres across, the rural-urban fringe zones do not function solely in relation to the city they surround but contain smaller independent settlements creating their own localized patterns. The situation in the new towns, between approximately 30 and 50 kilometres from the centre of London, shows considerable variation in provision around the mean public open-space provision of 14·7 acres (5·94 ha) per thousand of the population covering 17 per cent. of the designated land area (Table 11–2). The high per-capita provision in the new towns on the basis of these figures does not, however, represent current thinking as to the optimum, for planned population expansion should reduce this average to 9·9 acres per thousand of the population.

Within this broad category of land the proportion available for formal sporting use varies widely. If, by way of illustration, the inventories for two London boroughs (Harrow and Islington) and for three new towns (Hemel Hempstead, Welwyn Garden City and Basildon) are compared, it becomes apparent that the area of public open space does not necessarily parallel the amount of formal provision (Table 11–3). It would seem that

Table 11–3. Formal sports provision as a proportion of public open space (POS), selected areas in south-east England

Authority	Distance (miles)	POS (acres)	Formal provision (acres)	Formal provision as percentage of POS	Formal provision per thousand population (acres)
Islington	2·8	102	38	37·3	0·16
Harrow	11·2	1,230	268	21·8	1·29
Basildon	27·0	670	158	23·6	1·42
Hemel Hempstead	22·0	1,080	93	8·6	1·46
Welwyn Garden City	21·0	980	105	10·7	2.56

Source: Islington Open Space Schedule, Harrow Directory, Eastern Sports Council Appraisal of Facilities

areas with a smaller overall allocation of open space have a greater proportion of land laid out for field and court games than areas with a larger overall allocation. This may be partly because facilities for formal sports have a higher priority where the total amount of open space is scarce, and partly because inherently attractive land, lending itself to protection for informal recreational use, is not easily found in more densely populated districts.

The divergence in precise use within an umbrella category suggests that, when attempting a detailed appraisal, 'playing units' rather than areal

9

measures are more important indicators of the level of sports provision. Furthermore, the effective capacity of an area varies depending on the sport involved. A football pitch of 2·25 acres (·91 ha) provides the facilities for twenty-two players in a period of something less than two hours; if the surface is of grass, up to three matches a week can be played before the quality of the pitch is adversely affected. Fifteen tennis courts in the same area may provide for up to sixty players an hour, and if the surfaces are 'all-weather' there is no limit to their weekly load. At the other extreme, perhaps fifty times this area would be needed to accommodate physically the ten four-ball matches of golf which could tee-off over two hours, and from a management point of view forty hours' use a week at this rate (that is, eight hundred rounds) would be considered excessive.

Both the ability of playing units to absorb those seeking recreation and the desire of the population tributary to these units to participate will be relevant to any assessment of the adequacy of the existing distribution of facilities. A number of 'standards' are in existence by which this may be judged, the most enduring of which in Britain is that for formal sports provision suggested by the National Playing Fields Association (NPFA) of six acres (2·4 ha) per thousand of the population. It is based on the capacity assumption that such an area can accommodate up to two hundred potential players of football, hockey, cricket, bowls and tennis. Since this standard is usually applied to Local Planning Authority areas, an implicit assumption is that these areas produce the relevant tributary population. Although obviously an administrative convenience, in most cases, this may indeed be a fair compromise assumption between unrealistic parochialism and blocks of open space hopelessly distant from intended users. In the mid-1920s, each thousand of the tributary population was calculated on the basis of prevalent age structures to be generating two hundred sportsmen not otherwise catered for by school or college facilities. Since then this number may have declined, but in 1955 and 1971 the NPFA reiterated its earlier standard on the grounds that higher quality is now demanded. Open-space provision in metropolitan England, excluding the innermost area, generally exceeds six acres (2·4 ha) per thousand, but more detailed schedules show that facilities for formal sports in and around London are available at much below this rate, between one and two acres (·4 to ·8 ha) per thousand for the most part, and in the extreme case of Islington only one sixth of an acre (·07 ha) per thousand. The Sports Council has recently reassessed the standards philosophy and suggested that more specific calculations be made in individual circumstances to take account of local-population structures, recreation propensities and capacity tolerances.[7] On the basis of its purely illustrative calculation for soccer, rugby, cricket, tennis, hockey, bowls and netball facilities in a *hypothetical* new town of 60,000, 94 acres (38 ha) would be required for playing space and 47 acres (19 ha) for ancillary requirements, giving a minimum allocation of 141 acres (57 ha), or about 2·4 acres (·9 ha) per thousand. This hypothetical figure is closely matched in reality by, for example, the level of playing-field provision in Welwyn Garden City.

It would seem fair to postulate that different activities attract people greater or lesser distances depending on factors such as the actual length of time involved in participating in a particular activity. Evidence as to the relevant catchments for various sports is not conclusive, for it is rarely clear whether observed journeys to various venues reflect thresholds above which sportsmen are unwilling to travel or are simply determined by the existing distribution of opportunities in relation to places of residence. A survey on behalf of the British Government found recreation journey times by the urban population to be fifteen minutes, averaged over all forms of transport and over a representative selection of activities.[8] Times for a few examples, given in the second column of Table 11–4, indicate average

Table 11–4.   Journey data for selected sports, 1966

Sport	Average journey time (mins) (usual venue)	Approx. time for sport (hrs) (minimum)	Percentage of households within given distance of a facility			
			Inner London		London new towns	
			under 1 mile	over 2 miles	under 1 mile	over 2 miles
(1)	(2)	(3)	(4)	(5)	(6)	(7)
Rugby	16	2	18	50	49	11
Cricket	13	4	91	0	92	0
Soccer	13	2	93	0	94	0
Hockey	—	2	25	33	34	23
Bowls	9	1	82	0	59	5
Tennis	9	1	99	0	83	5

Source: Sillitoe, *Planning for Leisure* (HMSO, London, 1969)

journeys of no more than a few kilometres. Thus, all else being equal, there would seem good reason to expect formal venues for active recreation to be distributed through the city and suburbs in close proximity to the population they serve. There is variation from sport to sport, but, for the most part, columns four to seven bear out the idea that, both within and at the edge of London, sports facilities are available relatively cheaply, in terms of distance costs, although per-capita indices and intensities of use need to be taken into account when considering adequacy. Difficulties in interpretation remain; for example, it is not clear from these data alone why there should be a paucity of rugby pitches in Inner London. It may represent a true lack of facilities within a reasonable distance, thus depriving would-be participants by making the sport too expensive in travel time and cost terms. Alternatively it may show that rugby players are quite willing to travel at least the distances currently necessary to make use of the facilities which do exist. Or again, it may indicate that there is no widespread call for rugby pitches, even if close at hand. Finally, it could reflect elements of all three possibilities.

The discussion so far has centred on public sports provision although, clearly, commercial operators and other agencies can help meet the need for facilities. Between half and three-quarters of urban users in Britain are catered for by local authorities, depending on the sport; private, non-commercial clubs provide the majority of the balance, and facilities made available by employers complete the picture. It is, however, provision by the non-public sector which is most inclined to cluster at the city fringes, being the most immediately sensitive to market forces. When members of this sector require new facilities they must usually be obtained in the suburbs and beyond, as recreation activities cannot normally support the high charges that would be necessary to repay current land purchase and development costs in central districts. Even long-established recreational land within cities may find itself subject to development pressure; the value of sites often rises so that the opportunity cost of the land – that is, its most profitable alternative use – exceeds by many times that which people will pay for it to remain in recreational use. In these circumstances, clubs may sell out to housing or commercial interests and there may also be displacement for purposes of transport planning. These clubs may cease activities altogether if their catchment is localized and their members immobile or, for other reasons, unwilling to travel far. Alternatively they may remove to the fringe where more extensive facilities can be bought and will perhaps more than compensate for the longer journeys involved.

Institutional factors may also reinforce this pattern. In particular, restrictions on urban expansion, by the implementation of environmental planning controls such as green-belt policies, tend to sterilize the land for development and thus lower its price to those wishing to purchase for permitted uses, which include sports fields and golf courses. In this context, London's green belt has received some attention, particularly in an early work by Lovatt[9] and later by Thomas.[10] The latter found that, in a zone stretching approximately 25 kilometres from the inner edge of the green belt, 5·4 per cent. of all land was in recreational use,[11] compared with 62·3 per cent. in agricultural and 14·6 per cent. in residential and commercial use. Considering only that land on which green-belt control was directly applied, the proportion in recreational use rose to 6·2 per cent. This land use was particularly important close to the built-up area, where it represented more than 10 per cent. of the area, but its importance rapidly decreased at three kilometres distance (Figure 11–1). Lovatt's less precise work is in line with this interpretation, with apparently user-oriented recreation venues ousted from more central urban locations to immediately adjacent sites in the fringe zone.

The importance of land prices in determining the pattern of private provision is emphasized by comparing the distribution of public parks and informal open space with that of golf courses. The former are spread

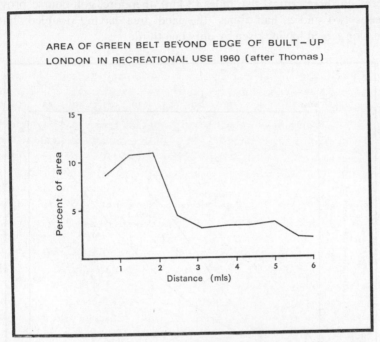

Figure 11–1   Area of green belt beyond the edge of the built-up area of London in recreational use, 1960 (simplified from D. Thomas, *London's Green Belt* (London, 1970), Figure 40)

within and beyond the urban fabric with little obvious cognizance of surrounding land-market prices but reflecting historical accidents and decisions protected and extended by contemporary public bodies. Golf courses, on the other hand, although comparable in area to the larger parks, are completely absent from the centre, but are concentrated in and immediately beyond the suburbs. Illustrating this for the London situation, Figure 11–2 plots the incidence of golf courses by distance zones based on Charing Cross, together with related indices of resident population and land area. The cumulative value for each of these measures at thirty miles (48 km) is assigned the index 100, and hence the ogives meet at this point. Up to about ten miles (16 km) the index of population far exceeds that for land, and golf courses are much fewer per head than further out. By ten miles (16 km) out just over 22 per cent. of the golf courses within a thirty-miles

(48 km) radius are encountered in about 11 per cent. of the land area, but this area is occupied by 45 per cent. of the population. There is a particularly marked increase in courses between ten and fifteen miles (16–25 km) from the centre, as land availability eases and population begins to level out; by 15 miles (24 km.), 55 per cent. of golf courses are available in 25 per cent. of the land area, whilst the population index has increased to 60 per cent. In these critical five miles (8 km), therefore, golf-course provision increases two and a half times, the land area having doubled, but the population served having risen by only one-third.

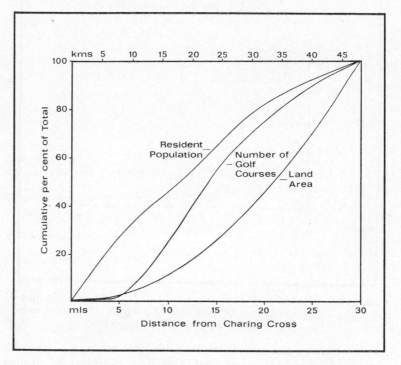

Figure 11–2   Provision of golf courses, distribution of population and total land area in relation to central London, 1970

This distinction between parks and golf courses does not necessarily reflect the ideological differences in the motives behind public and private provision alone. Local authorities do manage some of the golf courses, but, in any case, were it possible to subject both types of recreation facility to evaluations utilizing a common monetary measure, it might emerge that like is not being compared with like; the greater number of visitors received per unit area of urban parkland and the benefits accruing to each of these users *may* far exceed those relating to golf provision and so justify, economically, the use of more highly-valued land for urban parks. As an aside, it is interesting to note that, where similar types of formal provision are involved, the private sector tends to lay out its facilities to obtain more intensive use in terms of pitch units per unit of area[12] although admittedly not necessarily subjecting the land to as intensive temporal use.

The extent to which public open space can be decentralized, even were it sensitive to market pressures, depends largely on its functions, which in turn are closely related to the size of the units concerned. Table 11–5

Table 11–5. Types and accessibility of public open space

Type	Main function	Approximate size (acres)	Catchment (miles)	Characteristics
Metropolitan park	Week-end and occasional visits by car or public transport	150	2–5	Natural, heathland, downland, commons, etc., or formal parks providing for both active and passive recreation
District park	Week-end and occasional visits on foot	50	0·75	Containing playing fields but also at least 30 acres for other pursuits
Local park	For pedestrian visitors including nearby workers	5	0·25	Providing for court games, childrens' play, sitting-out areas and, if large enough, playing fields
Small local park	Pedestrian visits especially by old people, children and workers at midday	under 5	under 0·25	Gardens, sitting-out areas and/or childrens' playgrounds

Source: *Greater London Development Plan Statement* (London, 1969)

attempts to define these factors, from which it can be seen that the largest park, with a size similar to that of an eighteen-hole golf course, could perhaps function satisfactorily at up to eight kilometres from the population it is primarily intended to serve. The philosophy of providing large areas of open space, readily accessible to the urban ppopulation and capable of absorbing intensive use, but incorporating a variety of formal and informal provision, is embodied in the British 'Country Park' concept.

Since 1969, schemes of this type, whether publicly or privately sponsored, have attracted substantial central-government grants provided they appear to serve a large tributary population; thus the fringes of cities have been favoured locations. For example, 28 of the 60 parks approved or actively under consideration in south-east England by the end of 1970 were within 48 kilometres of Charing Cross, that is 47 per cent. of the schemes in 27 per cent. of the land area.

Provision for Passive Recreation

The pattern of passive recreation is not easily codified, principally because of identification problems, as pointed out earlier. The facilities involved range from ancient monuments to scenically attractive stretches of countryside, the initial distributions of which might be considered entirely gratuitous, although their subsequent management for more intensive use usually reflects proximity to urban areas. A number of indices can be selected, however, as highlighting the salient features of provision in the South East Economic Planning Region of Britain. This region, dominated by the London conurbation, occupies 18 per cent. of the land area, but contains 35 per cent. of the population of England and Wales. In general, there appear to be fewer resource-based opportunities but more facilities of the type associated with a long history of settlement, concentrated visitor demands and planning designations aimed at controlling urban morphology. Illustrating each of these points in turn, there are no National Parks and only 15 per cent. of the National Trust acreage in the region, but 23 per cent. of the 'Ancient Monuments', 34 per cent. of the 'Private Houses and Gardens open to the public' and 45 per cent. of the 'green belt' acreage.

Taking all parks, extensive grounds, commons and open land available to the public of 25 acres (10 ha) and over in south-east England, on average there are 5·3 acres (2·14 ha) per thousand of London's population within one hour's drive, but only 1·9 acres (·76 ha) within half an hour's drive. There is considerable internal variation, with values for the former index ranging between two and thirteen acres (·8 and 5·2 ha) per thousand in different geographical sectors of London, illustrating the difficulties in generalizing observations. Nonetheless, if it is assumed that the zones of greatest potential pressure are those readily reached by car and also within one and a quarter hour's travel time by public transport, the acreage per thousand available drops to 1·31 (·52 ha), or 758 people per acre, and for some sectors the value is as low as 0·10 (·04 ha).[13] Variation in provision around a city needs to be taken carefully into account as the centre usually acts as an effective barrier to travelling, especially by public transport where several interchanges may be necessary. Thus, although overall provision for informal recreation around urban concentrations may seem adequate, there may be severe deprivation in certain areas, particularly for residents without cars of their own.

This is not to say that all is well for pleasure motorists. A paper by Cracknell postulates the rural road networks necessary around cities for leisure driving, based on population, car ownership and occupancy and road-capacity factors.[14] In the context of London, the formula produces a 'living space' some 95 kilometres in radius. Much evidence suggests, however, that day-trip journeys for countryside recreation in excess of 50 or so kilometres one way are comparatively rare and it would seem probable that the prospects of congestion implied by this limit, taken in conjunction with the Cracknell formulation, may well deter potential pleasure motorists who otherwise would like to undertake this sort of trip. If a flow of over 250 cars per hour on anything but a dual carriageway is considered rather more driving than pleasure, and if it is assumed that motorway travel contains no great leisure component, it would seem that a large proportion of journeys into the countryside from conurbations will become less attractive in themselves and, in consequence, trip-end facilities will be more important if journeys are to be undertaken at all. At present the destination requirements of leisure motorists are comparatively modest, being essentially somewhere to park with a pleasant or interesting view and a small area close at hand for picnicking or walking. A number of surveys have recorded how small a space is required – perhaps only one-thirtieth of an acre (·01 ha) per car.[15] In these cases the physical resources needed are not so much large tracts of country to which there is unfettered access as localized nodes providing car parks, picnic areas and short walks in visually pleasing surroundings. In Britain, traditionally preserved open space (such as large commons) and newer protected areas (such as Areas of Outstanding Natural Beauty) can be made to satisfy these basic requirements provided they are located not much beyond 50 kilometres from the population they are intended to benefit.

In this brief review of recreation resources, little or nothing has been said of, for example, excursions to stately homes, zoos and botanical gardens, or to spectating events, which range from horse-racing to air shows. In all these cases, the resulting pattern represents an equilibrium between acceptable journey lengths, the space requirements of the particular activity and the distribution of suitable sites. Water has also received scant attention, although demands on this resource for recreation are rising fast, resulting, for example, in mounting pressure for the development of leisure facilities on otherwise disused canals or worked-out gravel pits in or near urban areas. Rather than extend these points, however, some space has been reserved to examine ways in which the importance of the rural-urban fringe for recreation provision can be quantified more precisely.

Quantifying the Influence of Relative Location: The Case of Angling

Exercises attempting to isolate the costs and benefits associated with recreation resources can throw light on the pattern of use and provision in a variety of urban, rural and fringe situations. The problems, techniques and findings of recreational cost-benefit analysis are diverse, but close consideration will be given here to one or two examples, since the general principles involved can be best illustrated by detailed evidence.

In the summer of 1970, information was collected by questionnaire from anglers fishing waters administered by the British Waterways Board.[16] Thirty-six stretches of water, distributed over eight canals and navigation systems mainly to the north and west of London, were identified as within the scope of metropolitan anglers. On the day of survey (Sunday 21 June) over five thousand anglers were enumerated as fishing these 130 miles (209 km) of water, the average number of anglers per mile (APM) being 39. The national APM index for the same day was 18. The data relating to London reflected more than this obvious link with density of resident population: water up to ten miles (16 km) from Charing Cross had an APM index of 35, and beyond thirty miles (48 km) an APM index of 30, whilst between these distances, the metropolitan rural-urban fringe zone, the APM index was 46. Intuitively it may be supposed that the extremes met different needs, with the closest sites providing easily reached fishing, but of low quality because of an urban environment, and the furthest sites providing inaccessible, but higher quality, rural fishing; the fringe-zone figures reflected a popular compromise between the two situations. Analysis of travel distances and times confirmed this impression. For example 80 per cent. of fishermen at inner-zone sites travelled less than five miles (8 km) one way, compared with 32 per cent. at fringe sites and 17 per cent. at outer sites; the modal category for one-way journey times in the furthest zone was over ninety minutes; 51 per cent. of the fishermen in the fringe zone arrived by car, compared with 48 per cent. in the outer zone and 33 per cent. in the inner zone. To summarize, it would appear that the closest waters provided accessible fishing sites, especially valuable for those without cars; the metropolitan fringe waters, being less urbanized, were more attractive for car-borne anglers willing to travel a little further as well as local suburban fishermen; and the most rural sites would appear to have had the least local element, attracting the keenest London anglers long distances.

It is possible to tie this differentiation into a single money index, if travel distance and time to and from the chosen site are accepted as part of the costs to the fisherman of 'buying' angling recreation.[17] Demand curves relating number of angling visits to costs of visits were calculated for the British Waterways data and are plotted in Figure 11–3.[18] A

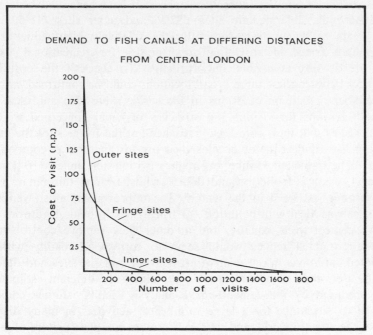

Figure 11–3   Demand to fish canals at differing distances from central
London, 1970

Table 11–6.   Differing benefits from angling in relation to central London
at a sample of British Waterways Board sites on 21 June 1970

| | Distance from central London (miles) | | |
	0–9·9	10–29·9	30 and over
Estimated bank milage	13·0	11·4	10·0
Estimated consumer surplus (£s)	62·66	435·50	129·00
Estimated site specific expenditure (£s)	71·00	161·40	36·00
Total Benefits (£s)	133·66	596·90	165·00
Benefits per mile (£s)	10·28	52·36	16·50

Source: Author's survey

value may be placed on the benefits generated by these sites, if these
are agreed to be the consumer surplus, represented by the area under each
curve, plus any actual site-specific charges, which on these waters were
found to average £0·10 per visit for licenses and fees (Table 11–6). Thus,

on this particular Sunday, inner sites appear to have generated benefits of £10·28 per mile, intermediate sites £52·36 and outer sites £16·50. This would seem to demonstrate forcefully the relatively high value of the metropolitan fringe in providing opportunities for recreational fishing which are at once accessible and attractive. To check if the postulated differences between these three broad locations could be confirmed, answers to a number of opinion questions in the survey were also analysed. The dominant reasons for visiting the stretches of canal concerned were, at the inner sites that they were 'easily reached', at the fringe sites the 'availability of fish', and at the outer sites their use for 'match (i.e. competition) fishing'. The principal dislike of anglers within ten miles (16 km) of Charing Cross was 'pollution and debris' whilst beyond this range it was the less ominous 'weed in the water'. The improvement most wanted at inner sites was 'deal with pollution', at fringe sites 'provide lavatories' and 'remove/control weed' equally, and at outer sites 'remove/control weed'. These unprompted replies would seem to correspond readily with the postulated variations in the relative attractiveness of the sites and different types of user, and go no small way in explaining the different estimates of value produced by the demand-curve analysis. Similar studies could be repeated to advantage for a large number of activities in many different parts of the western world, and thus give a more complete picture of leisure pursuits, but the type and direction of the forces at work around large cities have been sufficiently demonstrated for present purposes. This excursion into cost-benefit techniques, however, raises another important issue – the effects of the provision and use of recreational land on those not directly involved as suppliers or participants.

Quantifying the Indirect Effects of Provision for Recreation

There is a range of indirect advantages and disadvantages which make themselves felt in the local economies surrounding venues for leisure activities. This can be broadly divided into effects on tertiary trading and effects on environmental quality; the sectors via which these values are likely to be realized tangibly are the service industry, the real estate market and the local tax structure. Attention will be restricted here to the way in which recreational open space may contribute to or detract from the environmental quality of an area. At its most ephemeral, this takes the form of visual benefits, or disadvantages, for the incidental passer-by. Less elusive is the character associated with a locality because of the distribution of open space in the neighbourhood. Most tangible, and a contributory factor to the foregoing point, is the amenity value attaching to residential properties surrounding open spaces; these should express themselves in house purchase prices and local rating structures.[19] One of the patterns, amongst others, which might be expected to emerge is that, as the rural hinterland of a city is approached, formal open-space provision is of less significance in terms of absolute visual amenity benefits.

Rateable values may provide a relevant measure of this effect, since the valuation principle in England and Wales is designed to take into account 'every intrinsic quality and every intrinsic circumstance which tends to push the value [of a property] up or down'.[20] In an attempt to examine these circumstances quantitatively, data on areas of open space and ratable values have been collected on a borough scale for Greater London.[21] These show a weak direct linear relationship between the proportion of borough areas devoted to public open space and ratable values per head,[22] but increasing distance from the centre of London was also associated with many important characteristics, such as declining population densities, increasing provision of open space per head and declining ratable value per unit area. A multiple regression model was formulated to control these factors and adopted the form:

$$X_1 = 496 \cdot 54 + 176 \cdot 40 X_2 - 410 \cdot 41 X_3 - 3 \cdot 851 X_4 - 0 \cdot 0135 X_5 + 0 \cdot 00241 X_6$$

where:

X_1 = ratable value of borough per head of populations in £s

X_2 = open space as a proportion of total borough area

X_3 = $\log_{10}$ distance in miles of borough centroid from Charing Cross

X_4 = population per acre of borough area

X_5 = total acreage of borough public open space

X_6 = total acreage of borough

This expression possessed an explanatory power of just over 80 per cent. and, apart from the tendencies already mentioned, is of interest in terms of variable 5 which attempted to measure the diminishing effect of open space on ratable values at higher overall levels of provision; in the event, it did provide some indication that in the urban fringe, where open-space provision is greater, the marginal acre was less valued than towards the centre, where open space is more scarce. Perhaps these findings can be most effectively demonstrated by applying the model to three representative boroughs at varying distances and comparing the ratable values predicted on the basis of existing open-space provision with the hypothetical situation of there being no open space in the same boroughs. For a borough selected at some three miles (4·8 km) distance from Charing Cross, the apparent value per acre of open space, as reflected in the rating structure, was found to be, on the basis of the calculations outlined above, about £7,500; for another at seven miles (11 km) it was £4,500 and at 14 miles (22 km) it was £1,500. Many reservations should be made about lifting this study from context but, as with the angling exercise, the monetary values put forward here are less controversial if taken as a relative measure for different locations in the urban fabric rather than an absolute statement of worth. It would seem fair to conclude that, per unit of area, secondary amenity benefits from recreation provision (as reflected in local taxes) diminish out from the centre.

Turning now to house prices, a less generalized situation can be hypothesized in which the values of houses directly facing open spaces of various types are compared with identical houses in entirely built-up surroundings (Figure 11–4). In a study exploring this concept,[23] the consensus opinion

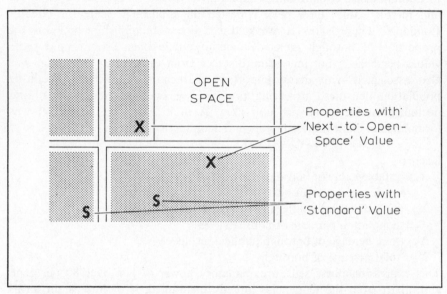

Figure 11–4 The concept of standard and next-to-open-space values; 'next-to-open-space' implies a location either immediately adjacent to or on the opposite side of the road from the open-space specified, provided no other buildings intervene; in all other respects the properties are assumed to be identical to the 'standard' value properties

of professional estate agents produced a series of 'next-to-open-space values' which differed from 'standard values' depending on type of open space, price range of property and, to some extent, proximity to a rural milieu. Table 11–7 presents the mean next-to-open-space values for nine types of open space, in three price ranges, and for areas at different distances from the centre of London. Thus, for example, in the £5,000 range of houses within ten miles(16 km) of Charing Cross the average enhancement due to a location next to heath, common or woodland was calculated to be 14·5 per cent. – that is, a £5,000 standard-value property should sell at £5,725 in these circumstances. Differences between these next-to-open-space sample values, at different distances from the centre, could not always be established statistically for the population at the 0·95 probability level, principally because of the small number of cases in certain subsets, but there was sufficient directional consistency to warrant some tentative generalizations. Value-enhancing open space had considerably more effect

Table 11–7. Value of residential properties located next to various categories of open space, expressed as a percentage of their standard value, 1971

Open space type	Standard value of property (£s)	Next-to-open-space value as percentage of standard value		
		under 10 miles from central London	10–19 miles from central London	20 miles and over from central London
Common,	5,000	114·5	110·4	112·0
heath or	10,000	113·5	110·2	112·1
woodland	20,000	110·7	109·1	110·8
Golf	5,000	114·0	107·6	110·6
courses	10,000	112·3	109·0	111·0
	20,000	111·0	108·6	110·1
Ornamental	5,000	112·8	106·9	108·5
open space	10,000	109·0	107·3	108·3
	20,000	108·6	107·5	106·5
Parks	5,000	106·6	104·2	106·1
	10,000	104·3	106·2	106·0
	20,000	106·9	106·3	103·0
Open	5,000	104·8	104·3	105·2
water	10,000	101·2	105·3	104·6
	20,000	99·0	104·8	103·5
Playing	5,000	103·1	102·7	103·0
fields	10,000	98·1	102·5	102·2
	20,000	98·5	101·6	99·0
Allotments	5,000	98·7	100·3	101·2
	10,000	94·1	98·9	97·2
	20,000	95·7	99·5	95·4
Stadia	5,000	97·3	96·6	98·3
	10,000	95·0	95·9	94·2
	20,000	88·3	95·7	92·5
Cemeteries	5,000	95·1	97·6	98·1
	10,000	88·7	94·2	94·9
	20,000	88·0	92·5	92·6

Source: Author's survey

on adjacent locations in areas less than ten miles (16 km) from Charing Cross than in areas ten to twenty miles (16–32 km) from the centre, and somewhat higher than for 20 miles (32 km) and over (although the effect in this last zone exceeded that in the ten-to-20 mile (16–32 km) range). This rise at greater distance from the centre may not at first seem in accord with the proposition that, where the countryside is more immediately at hand, open space is of less importance as a visual amenity, but the pattern can be largely explained by the fact that the sample frame of the zone furthest from the centre included urban satellite settlements, in contrast to the less urbanized zone between ten and 20 miles (16–32 km) out, dominated by the green belt. Figure 11–5 plots this pattern for ornamental open space.

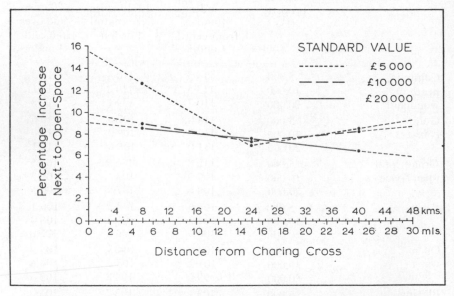

Figure 11–5   Percentage increase in value of residential properties located next to ornamental open space in relation to distance from central London, 1970 (for definition of a 'next-to-open-space' location, see Figure 11–4)

Linear regression techniques were also employed on data from this survey, and on the whole these confirmed that open space which provides residential amenity has a proportionally less marked effect as housing in the inner areas gives way to the suburbs, and the suburbs to open country.[24]

Conclusion

The urban fringe is sought after by those participating in recreation because they see it as being both accessible and attractive. Those who are responsible for providing recreational facilities also turn to this location, either because land is available there at a lower opportunity cost than closer to the city centre or because recreational land uses are compatible with policies designed to contain urban growth. It is necessary to distinguish recreational provision at the edge of the built-up area on the basis of whether it is satisfying the needs of the central city or whether it is catering for the requirements of the population of the urban fringe itself.[25] To some extent the time required to participate successfully in an activity gives a rule of thumb for making these distinctions. Provision of facilities involving comparatively short spells of use by any one individual (say tennis or bowls) will be supplying essentially local needs, and their occurrence at the periphery cannot contribute significantly to inner-area requirements. On the other hand, those involving longer stays (as with sports such as golf and many, more informal, active pursuits such as riding or fishing) make a longer journey more acceptable, in which cases fringe locations can serve both the local and central-city communities. Specialized facilities, with either exacting site constraints or a small following of devotees, will have a sparse distribution which must necessarily draw participants from both near and far. The principal characteristics of urban-fringe recreation opportunities serving central city populations can be summarized as making moderate to large demands on space, although not being dependent on the rare combination of resources that marks the spectacular or unique, and perhaps involving each participant for about three or four hours at the venue.[26]

Four major sources of non-educational recreation facilities are involved in the rural-urban fringe. They are private clubs, employees' organizations, commercial enterprises and public authorities. Although their motivations may differ, each can benefit from cognizance of the factors at work in the fringe; for example the distance people are prepared to travel for a particular type of recreation is relevant to their locational decisions. The implications of quantitatively-derived measures, such as those discussed earlier in this chapter, might particularly deserve their attention. Costed demand curves are in many cases of considerable value for comparing relative benefits at different locations; results can be combined to give useful insights into the types of investment that can be made with greatest benefit and to indicate the sections of the population that would derive the greatest advantages. Taking as an illustration the results of the angling survey, selected inner-area canals could be qualitatively upgraded to benefit the angler without a car, and by providing good fishing in easily-reached areas could create an impressively large increment in user benefits. The most distant canals could capitalize on their higher-quality fishing and inelastic-demand schedules by a direct charging policy. The undoubted value of the fringe sites for angling could be set against similar calculations for often incompatible uses like recreational boating to determine priorities and to see if mutual gains might result from spatial or temporal zoning. If the benefits measured are accepted as of relevance to resource-allocation problems in general, the associated money values can be related to the prevailing price system. In these circumstances it would then be possible to declare that the costs of providing a length of fishing waters to a reasonably high standard in the fringe zone (say, at 1970 prices, about £300 per kilometre per annum) produce benefits five times that figure. The applications to which findings on secondary benefits might be put also remain comparatively unexplored, although earlier misconceived claims about the trading gains to be made from recreation development would reinforce a counsel of caution. The enhanced value of a property built next to recreation areas may come as a fortuitous gain to the vendor or, alternatively, a developer may have specifically created the amenity space with a view to recouping some of the costs at the initial sale.[27] There would seem to be suggestions here as to how the type of housing to be built around various categories of open space might be optimized. Thus, for example, there may be net losses if housing from the higher price ranges is located on sites adjoining playing fields, but net gains if cheaper accommodation is similarly sited. Furthermore, exercises in environmental design might consider how the configuration of property-enhancing open space can be manipulated to maximize housing frontage. As regards financing public open space, there would appear to be some possibilities of taxing those properties fortuitously benefiting from amenity effects, either at the development stage, or on an annual basis.

Finally, physical expansion of the suburbs will have consequences for the continuing availability of accessible recreation facilities of regional and subregional significance. Although appropriately oriented research is still in its infancy, it would seem both economically justifiable and socially essential to preserve recreation opportunities throughout the city fringes to serve both city centre and local needs.

Further Reading

On the demands for recreational space in Britain see K. K. Sillitoe, *Planning for Leisure* (HMSO, London, 1969), and in America *Reports 19, 20, 21 and 26* of the Outdoor Recreation Resources Review Commission (Washington, 1962).

A more general exploration of British conditions is to be found in J. A. Patmore, *Land and Leisure* (Newton Abbot, 1970) and of American conditions in M. Clawson and J. L. Knetsch, *Economics of Outdoor Recreation* (Baltimore, 1966).

The Second Report from the Select Committee of the House of Lords (The Cobham Committee) on *Sport and Leisure* (HMSO, London, 1973) represents a major document on British recreational policies and discusses in particular the importance of the urban fringe.

References

1. These terms are taken from R. Maw, 'Construction of a leisure model', *Official Architecture and Planning* (August, 1969).
2. K. K. Sillitoe, *Plannng for Leisure* (HMSO, London, 1969), 17 (based on data for 1965).

3. M. Clawson and J. L. Knetsch, *Economics of Outdoor Recreation* (Baltimore, 1966) 22 and 25 (based on data for 1960).
4. In so far as a single reference might substantiate this remark, note the growth in Czechoslovakia recreation as treated by V. Gardavsky, 'Recreational hinterland of a city taking Prague as an example'. *Acta Univ. Carol. Geogr.* **1** (1969), 3–39.
5. M. Clawson, R. Burnell Held and C. H. Stoddard, *Land for the Future* (Baltimore, 1960), 136.
6. Outdoor Recreation Resources Review Commission, *Outdoor Recreation for America* (Washington, 1962).
7. The Sports Council, *Planning for Sport* (London, 1968).
8. Sillitoe, *op. cit.*, 159.
9. W. F. B. Lovatt, 'Leisure and land use in the metropolitan green belt', *Journal of the London Society* **358** (1962), 1–16 and *JTPI* **48** (1962), 150–7.
10. D. Thomas, *London's Green Belt* (London, 1970), 196–205.
11. Recreation use was principally made up of playing fields, golf courses and public open spaces; figures are for 1960.
12. M. J. Bowen, 'Outdoor recreation in the metropolitan fringe' (unpublished manuscript).
13. Greater London Council Department of Planning and Transportation, Research Memorandum **267** (London, 1971).
14. B. Cracknell, 'Accessibility to the countryside as a factor in planning for leisure', *Regional Studies* **1** (1967), 147–61.
15. J. A. Patmore, *Land and Leisure* (Newton Abbot, 1970), 131–41.
16. There is a debt to Mr P. A. Daniells of the British Waterways Board for his assistance in making available the survey data. The following discussion draws heavily on the extended analysis of these data in Bowen (*op. cit.*) but should in no way be taken as representing the views of the British Waterways Board or its staff.
17. The cost-benefit analysis approach to recreation is a controversial and, somewhat complex matter. An early paper by M. Clawson, 'Methods of measuring the demand for the value of outdoor recreation', *Resources for the Future Reprint* **10** (Washington, 1959), suggested approaches which have been variously condemned and refined. For an up-to-date review of the field see the Countryside Commission, *Seminar Report on Recreation Cost-Benefit Analysis* (London, 1971), which also abstracts some of the more important studies in the literature.
18. Details of the calculations behind these figures would be inappropriate here but include population weightings, allowances for public and private transport costs and travel-time costs at a rate related to the duration of on-site fishing.
19. For an American example of this effect see the account given by B. J. Neimann in *Better Roads* **37** (1967) no. 16 where he reports the increase in taxes derived from the development of a parkway.
20. L. J. Scott in *Robinson Bros.* v *Houghton and Chester-Le-Street Assessment Committee* (1937), 2KB, 445, 469, as quoted in the Lands Tribunal Circular LVC/1805/1964 (August, 1965).
21. Details of this work are included in Bowen, *op. cit.*
22. A simple correlation coefficient of 0·31 existed between these variables and the associated least squares regression equation explains approaching 10 per cent. of the variation in ratable value per head from borough to borough

in terms of proportion of area devoted to public open space. (As sampling is not involved significant tests appear inappropriate.)

23. See note 21.

24. Many other points arose which are, however, of marginal interest here. For example higher priced properties were proportionally less sensitive to enhancing open space, indicating perhaps that more expensive houses approach self-sufficiency in respect of visual amenity, due in part to larger gardens. On the other hand, at these higher price levels, the occupants appear to dislike more extensively the clutter concomitant with allotments, the noise accompanying the use of playing fields and the morbid associations of cemeteries.

25. R. E. Pahl, *Urbs in Rure: The Metropolitan Fringe in Hertfordshire* (London, 1965), emphasizes the need to remember that the rural-urban fringe does not exist solely in relation to the central city.

26. That is, on average, a stay two or three times longer than the duration of the return journey from home to the opportunity, motoring for pleasure being the exception.

27. There is nothing new in this. For example Birkenhead Park, Lancashire, opened in 1847, consisted of 125 acres for public use out of an initial purchase of 226 acres, the remainder being sold as private villa plots. The £70,000 cost of excavation and planting was more than recovered in the enhanced plot prices, purchased initially for one shilling a square yard in 1843 and resold between 1843 and 1847 at an average of 11s. 4d. See G. E. Chadwick, *The Park and the Town* (London, 1968), 68 ff.

Index

R